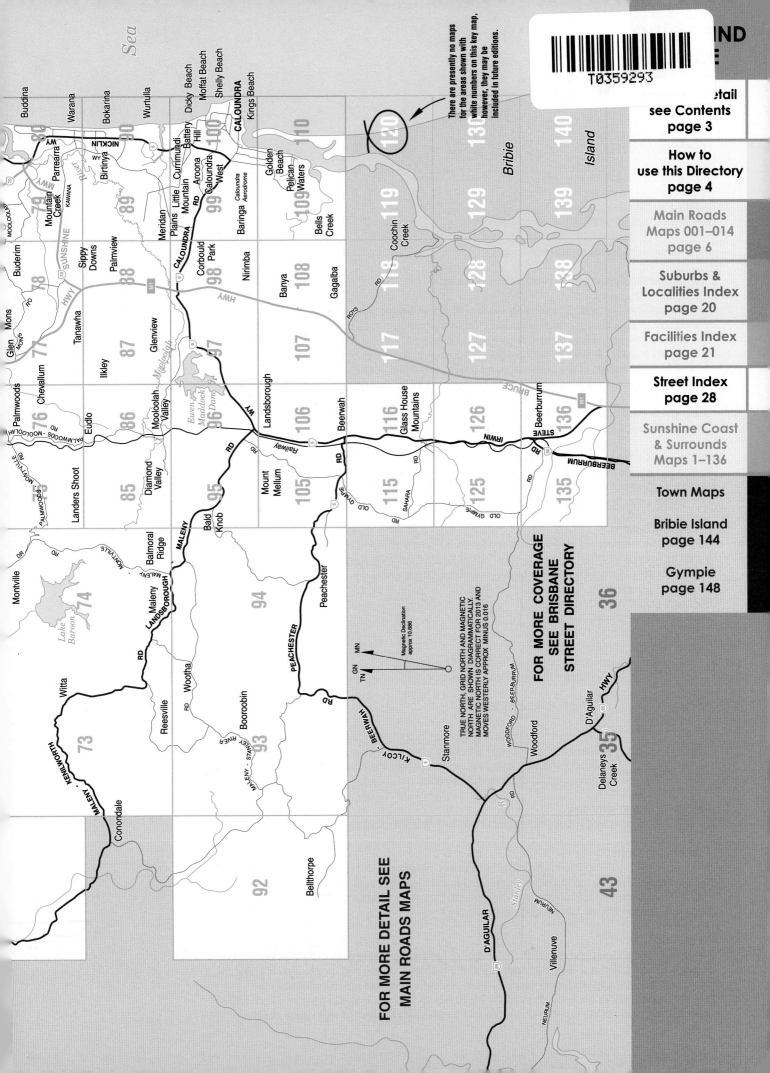

...ND
E

Sea

There are presently no maps
for the areas shown with
white numbers on this key map,
however, they may be
included in future editions.

FOR MORE COVERAGE
SEE BRISBANE
STREET DIRECTORY

FOR MORE DETAIL SEE
MAIN ROADS MAPS

TRUE NORTH, GRID NORTH AND MAGNETIC
NORTH ARE SHOWN DIAGRAMMATICALLY.
MAGNETIC NORTH IS CORRECT FOR 2013 AND
MOVES WESTERLY APPROX MINUS 0.016

Magnetic Declination
approx 10.686

Bribie

Island

Published in 2024 by Hardie Grant Explore,
an imprint of Hardie Grant Publishing

Hardie Grant Explore (Sydney)
Gadigal Country
Level 7, 45 Jones Street
Ultimo, NSW 2007

Hardie Grant Explore (Melbourne)
Wurundjeri Country
Building 1, 658 Church Street
Richmond, Victoria 3121

www.hardiegrant.com/au/explore

UBD Gregory's is an imprint of Hardie Grant Explore

Hardie Grant acknowledges the Traditional Owners of the Country on which we work, the Wurundjeri people of the Kulin Nation and the Gadigal people of the Eora Nation, and recognises their continuing connection to the land, waters and culture. We pay our respects to their Elders past, present and emerging.

Publishers note
UBD Gregory's welcomes contributions and feedback on the contents of this directory. Please e-mail us at upsales@hardiegrant.com.au. Hardie Grant Explore is Australia's largest publisher and distributor of Street Directories, Maps, Travel and Guide Books.

Sunshine Coast 12th edition
ISBN 9780 7319 3348 8

Cover: Design: pfisterer + freeman
         Caption: Noosa Heads, Sunshine Coast, Queensland
         Credit: Rowan Sims Photography/Shutterstock

Printed in China by Leo Paper Products Ltd

The paper this book is printed on is certified against the Forest Stewardship Council® Standards and other sources. FSC® promotes environmentally responsible, socially beneficial and economically viable management of the world's forests.

Custom Mapping services
For any custom mapping requirements please contact cms@hardiegrant.com.au

Acknowledgments
The revision of the information contained in this street directory could not be carried out without the assistance given by the following organisations and their representatives Nearmap; Australia Post, local government authorities, land developers, Federal and State government authorities, tourist information offices and the general public

Disclaimer
The publisher disclaims any responsibility or duty of care towards any person for loss or damage suffered from any use of this directory for whatever purpose and in whatever manner. While considerable care has been taken by the publisher in researching and compiling the directory, the publisher accepts no responsibility for errors or omissions. No person should rely upon this directory for the purpose of making any business investment or real estate decision.

CONTENTS

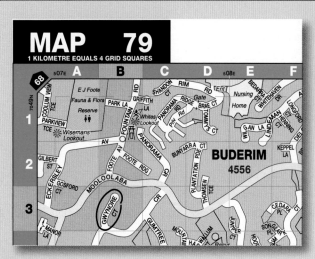

HOW TO FIND A STREET

1. Look up the street name and suburb in the Street Index (e.g. Gwynore ct, Buderim).
2. Note its map number and reference (79, B3).
3. Turn to the appropriate map (79) and locate the street by following the grid lines down from the reference letter (B) and across from the number (3) to where they meet, as shown on the diagram above.

GWENETH		
rd. Weyba Downs	28	Q6
GWYNORE		
ct. Buderim	79	B3
GYMEA		
ct. Mountain Creek	79	K8

CAN'T FIND A STREET?

If the Street Index does not list the street you are seeking under a particular suburb, check to see if the street is actually in an adjoining suburb. To do this, refer to the Suburbs and Localities Index and find on which map the suburb appears. Turn to that map and note the names of surrounding suburbs. Now return to the Street Index and look for the street in one of these suburbs.

MAP FEATURES

Direction

For all practical purposes Grid North and True North are always to the top of the maps. Each map features a directional arrow pointing to the city.

Grid Lines

The blue grid lines serve two purposes:
- they form the reference squares for locating streets and facilities etc.
- they allow easy calculation of distances (see Map Scales).

Map Symbols

Most of the map symbols are self-explanatory. However, to ensure that you gain maximum information from the street maps, we recommend that you familiarise yourself with all the map symbols used (see opposite page).

Overlap Areas & Map Borders

The street maps have an overlap area on each edge to assist in maintaining position when moving to an adjoining map. Adjoining map numbers are shown in the borders and corners.

Future Maps

Maps covering areas that may be included in future editions are indicated with white numbers on the Key Map at the beginning of this directory. They allow for future expansion of the directory without renumbering existing maps & still allow sequential map numbering.

Continuing Maps

When map numbers are not in sequential order, then a note will appear under the map number indicating the previous or following map number.

MAP SCALES

Blue Borders

Scale 1:20 000 - Grid squares measure 250m
Maps 5 - 136
Scale 1:40 000 - Grid squares measure 500m
Maps 1-4; 13-14; 31-34; 53-54; 73-74 & 92-94

Town Maps

Scale 1:20 000

AUSTRALIAN MAP GRID

The small numbers in the map borders refer to the co-ordinates of the Australian Map Grid (AMG) which are spaced at 1000 metre (1km) intervals. The co-ordinates for Sunshine Coast are derived from Zone 56 of the International Universal Transverse Mercator System and is based on the Australian Geodetic Datum of 1984 (AGD84). All of the street maps are aligned with the AMG.

✴	Ambulance Station
⚒	Barbecue
M16 ●	Beach Access Number
⛵	Boat Ramp
🎳	Bowling Club
▲	Camping Area
🚐	Caravan Park
🅿	Car Park
■ Cncl Off	Council Office
☎ 121	Emergency Telephone & Location Number
F	Fire Station
♣	Girl Guides
⛳	Golf Course
➕	Hospital
Ⓗ	Hotel
ⓘ	Information Centre
𝒊	Information Centre (accredited)
📖	Library
⛴	Lighthouse
✳	Lookout – 360° view
✳	– 180° view
⚒	Masonic Centre
▲	Memorial / Monument
⌂	Motel
⛩	Picnic Area
■ Museum	Place of Interest
✝	Place of Worship
𝌆	Playground
■ PCYC	Pol - Cmnty Youth Club
★	Police Station
✉	Post Office
🗨	Quarry
■ QT	Queensland Transport
■ RFB	Rural Fire Brigade
ⓢ	School – Private
Ⓢ	– State
✦	Scouts
⛽	Service Station
🛒	Shopping Centre
■ SES	State Emerg. Service
⚓	Swimming Pool
☎	Telephone
Ⓣ	Tertiary – Private
Ⓣ	– State
♟♙	Toilets
Ⓦ	Weighbridge
⚘	Wineries

Freeway/Motorway and Route Number	
Highway or Main Traffic Route and Footbridge	
Alternative Traffic Route	
Trafficable Road	
Untrafficable/Proposed Road	
Traffic Light, Red Light Camera, Roundabout and Level Crossing . .	
Road, Railway Bridges and Bridge Clearance Heights	
One-Way Traffic Route	
National, State & Tourist Route Numbers	
Proposed Arterial	
House or Building Number	
Railway Line with Station (distance from Central Rly Stn)	
Transmission Lines – Energex	
– Powerlink Queensland	
Suburb Name.	
Postcode Number	
Suburb Boundary.	
Unofficial Suburb Boundary	
Locality Name.	
Local Government – Name	
– Boundary	
Ferry Route.	
Cycleway, Walking Track and Equestrian Trail.	
Park, Reserve, Golf Course, etc	
School or Hospital.	
Caravan Park, Cemetery, Shopping Centre, etc	
Buildings.	
Mall, Plaza	
Swamp / Mangroves	
Land Subject to Inundation	
Pine Plantation	

BRUCE [M1] HWY
Fbr
STEVE IRWIN — WY
OBI OBI — RD
GREENHAVEN — DR
BUSHLARK — RD

5.2m — 4.7m

[M1] (70) (22)

Proposed — Arterial

20

Mooloolah 131

E — 795 / 1 — E

807

CALOUNDRA

4551

Kawana Waters

Sunshine Coast

SCALE

0 — 5 — 10 km

LIMIT OF MAPS

Kin Kin

State

Forest

Mt Mooloo +

Big Baldy +

+ Little Baldy

Long Flat

Gilldora

Woondum

Forest

Reserve

Mary

Kybong

Tandur

A1

BRUCE

Green Ridge

Traveston

Mt Pinbarren +

Cootharaba

Cooran

Pinbarren

Pomona

State Forest

Amamoor

Amamoor

Mt Cooran +

BRUCE

A1

Coles

Coles

River

Forest Reserve

Mt Cooroora +
439m

Kandanga

Nobby Glen

Federal

+ Mt Tuchekoi

Black
Mountain

HWY

A1

BRUCE

Melawondi

Bergins
Pocket

Tuchekoi

KADANGA

State

Creek

Carters
Ridge

Ridgewood

13

14

Eerwah
Vale

Imbil

Bollier

Blackfellow

State

Forest

Bella

Derrier Flat

Borumba
Dam

Brooloo

Belli
Park

Borumba
+ Mountain

Imbil

State

+ Kenilworth
Bluff

Mapleton

Cooloolabin
Dam

Coolool

Oaky

33

34

Forest

Gheerulla

National

Kiamba

Kenilworth

Kureelpa

31

53

54

Mapleton

Coolabine

Blackall

Kidaman
Creek

Obi Obi

Mapleton Falls
National Park

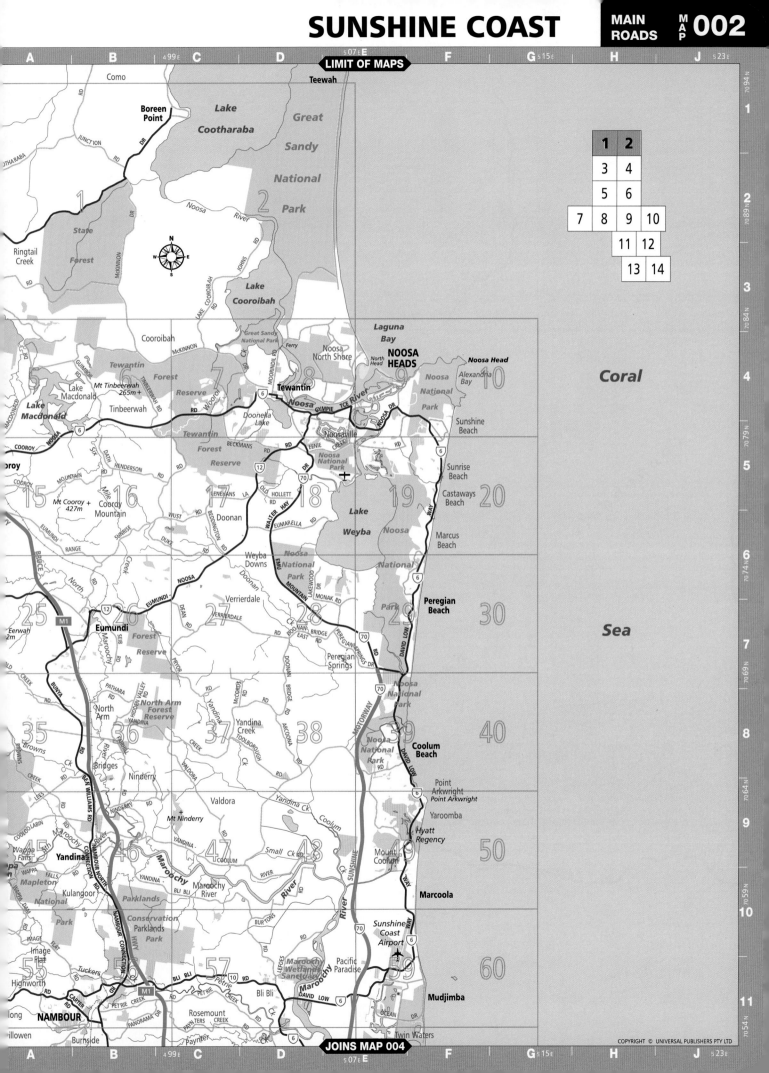

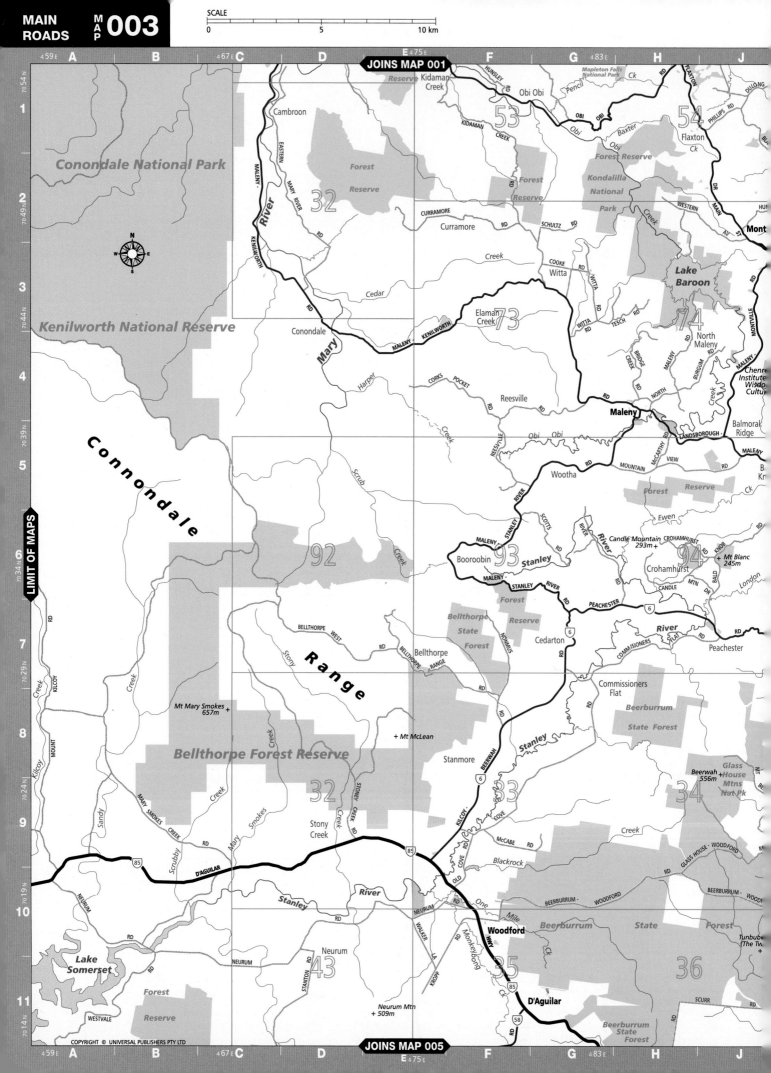

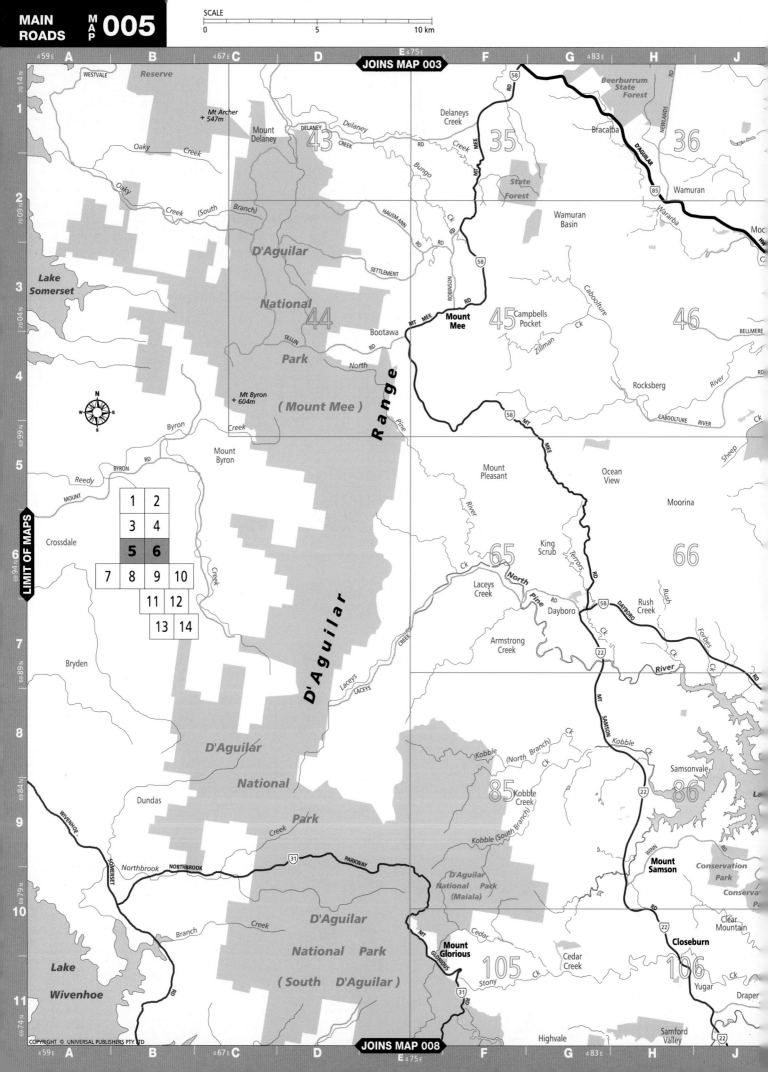

JOINS MAP 004

JOINS MAP 009

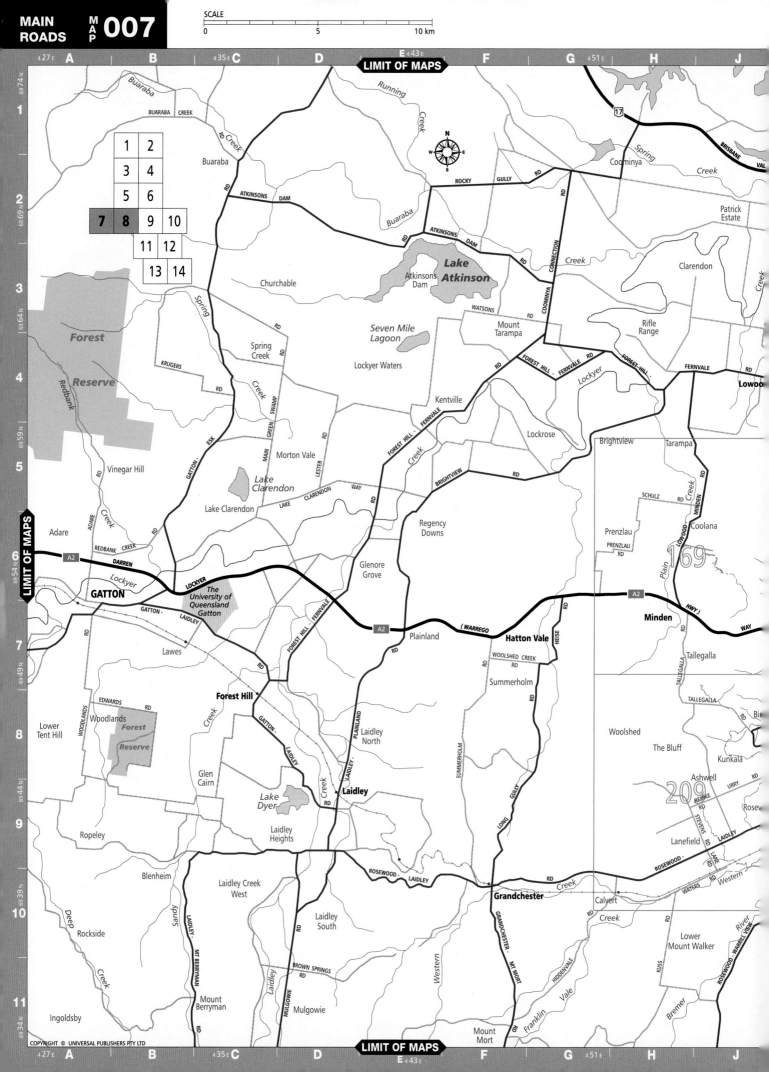

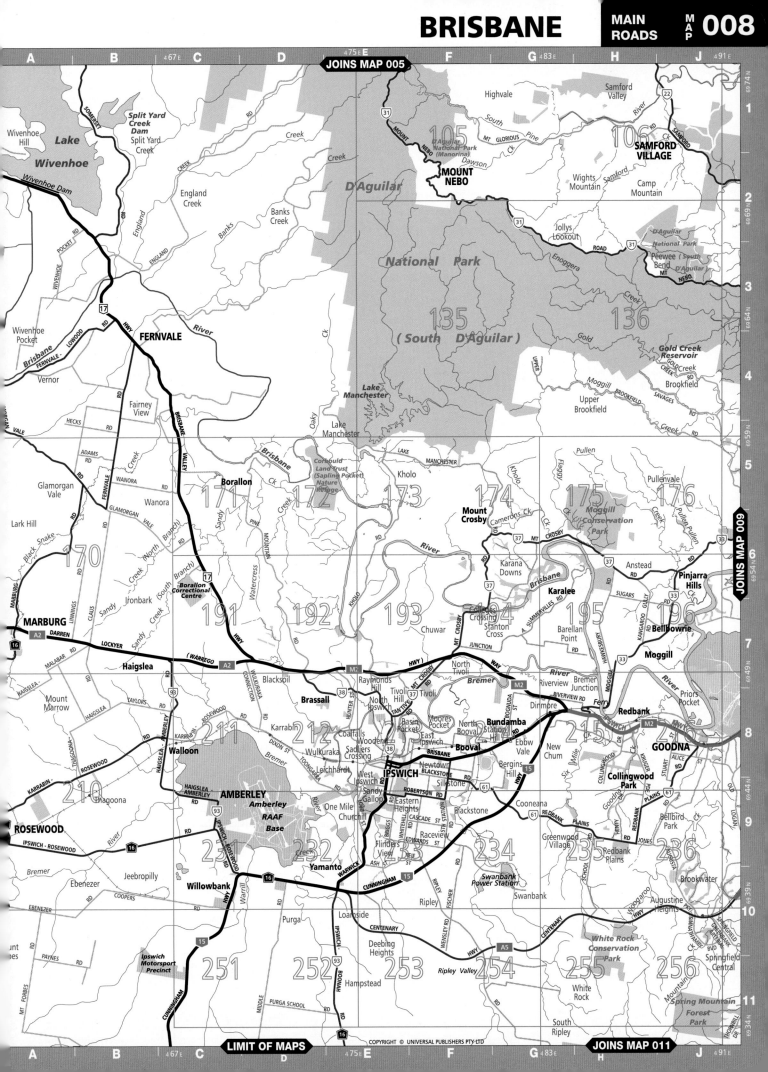

JOINS MAP 005

JOINS MAP 009

LIMIT OF MAPS

Moreton Island
Moreton Island National Park
Reeders Point

INSET A
Amity Point
Amity

Chiggil Chiggil

Weisby Lagoons

333

Arrarawai

Myora

One Mile

Dunwich

INSET B

INSET C
Point Lookout
Frenchmans Bay

334

North Stradbroke Island

Cooroon Cooroonpah Ck

Capembah Ck

Brown Lake (Bummel)

Blue Lake National Park

WildFlower Refuge

INSET A
Amity

INSET C
Point Lookout

INSET B
Dunwich

Moreton

Bay

St Helena Island
St Helena Island National Park

Green Island

Wellington Point

165   166

Geoff Skinner Wetlands

WELLINGTON POINT

Raby Bay

Cleveland Point

185   186

Ormiston

CLEVELAND

Oyster Point

205   206

Thornlands

Point Halloran
Point Halloran Conservation Area

Coochiemudlo Island

Victoria Point

VICTORIA POINT

Redland Bay

225   226   227   228

Macleay Island

Perulpa Bay

Lamb Island

REDLAND BAY

Mount Cotton

Garden Island

Point Talburpin

245   246   247   248

Pannikin Island

Karragarra Island

Krummel Passage

Oncooncoo Bay

Russell Island

Passage

Canaipa

Carbrook
Carbrook Wetlands Conservation Park 2

265   266   267   268

Logan

Alberton

Long Island

Lagoon Island

Browns Bay

Russell Island

Mosquito Islands

Cobby Cobby Island

Peel Island

North

Stradbroke

(Minjerriba)

Island

Coral

Sea

1	2
3	4
5	6
7	8	**9**	**10**
		11	12
		13	14

SCALE
0   5   10 km

JOINS MAP 008
JOINS MAP 009

South Ripley
Bundamba Lagoon
Spring Mountain
Forest Park
Crewes
England Gap
Oxley
Lyons
Tully

275 276 277 278 279 280 281 282

Stoney Camp Rd
Norris
Park Ridge South
Munruben
Carter Rd
13
Chambers Flat
Buccan
River
Tamborine
59

Flagstone
New Beith
Crowson La
North Maclean
Greenbank
Scott La
Stockleigh
Stockleigh
Logan Village
Steele
Quinzeh
Quinzeh
Miller
Reserve
School
Logan
Chambers Flat
Waterford
Kirk

Mountain Ridge Rd
South Maclean
Cusack La
Railway
Allans
95
Latimer
Rand

301 302 303

Undullah
Flagstone
Sandy
Creek
Homestead Dr
Bushman
Teviot
Jimboomba
Cedar Vale Rd
Kurrajong Rd
Cable 88
Camp
Tamborine St
Edelsten
Clutha
Yarrabilba
Waterford
95
Tamborine
Plunkett
Creek

Woolaman
Brook
Kilmoylar Rd
Kagaru
Cedar Grove
Cedar Grove Rd
Disused
Lindesay
Mount
Cedar Rd
Vale
Scrubby
Dennis
Cedar Vale
River
1 2
Tamborine
92
6

329 330 11 12

Logan
Undullah Rd
Brookland
Woodhill
13
Millstream
Creek
Collins
Mundoolin
90
16
8

Allenview
Cyrus
Veresdale
Worendo St
Veresdale Scrub Rd
Veresdale Scrub
Barnes
Veresdale Scrub School Rd
Beenleigh
Albert
Mundoolin
Connection
90
8

Teviot
90
Beaudesert
Boonah
Allan Rd
Gleneagle
Dunn Rd
Brabazon
Bromelton
House Rd
Disused
Railway
Veresdale Scrub Rd
Gould Hill Rd
Flagstone
Flagstone
Beaudesert
Birnam
21 22
Nerang
Biddaddaba

Allan
331 332
Bromelton
Beaudesert Race Club
BEAUDESERT
13
Beaudesert - Nerang
90
16
Tabragalba

1 2
3 4
5 6
7 8 9 10
11 12
13 14

Josephville
Sandy
River
Creek
Cryna
Kerry Rd
Nindooinbah
River
Kerry
Albert
Biddaddaba

Josephville
Lindesay
Mountain
13
16
Logan
Mount
Spring
Creek
Nindooinbah
Lambert Rd
Estate
Canungra
Lamington National Park
Ferny Glen

LIMIT OF MAPS

JOINS MAP 009

JOINS MAP 010

JOINS MAP 013

JOINS MAP 014

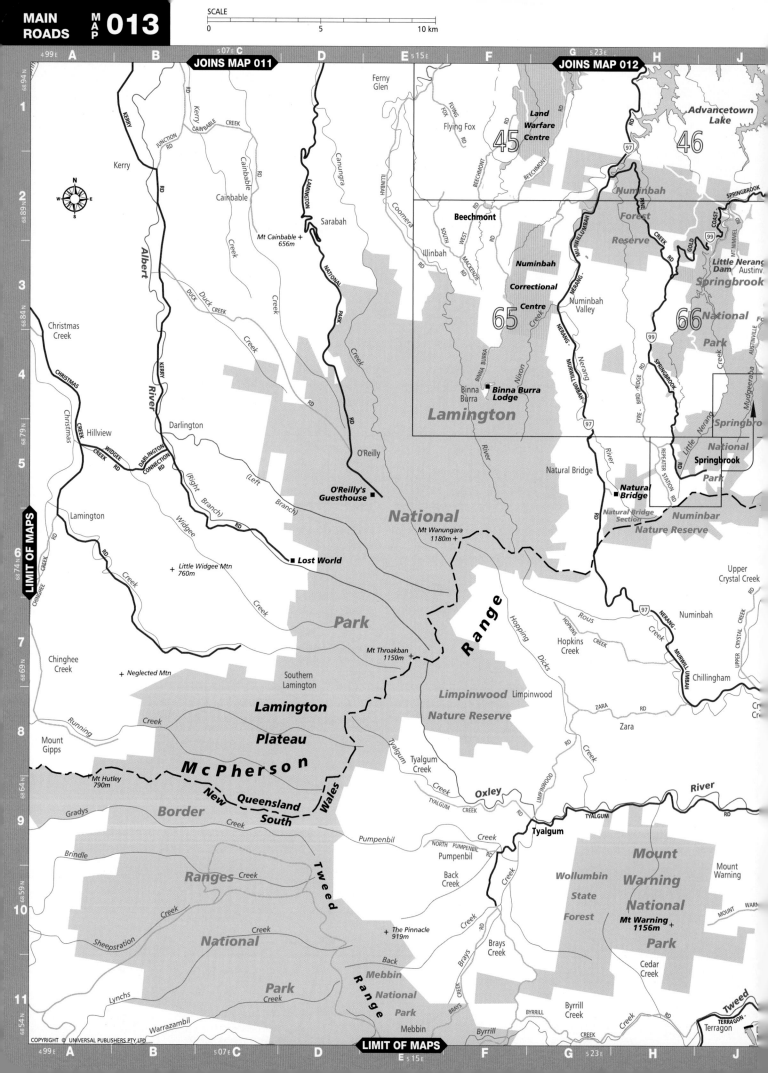

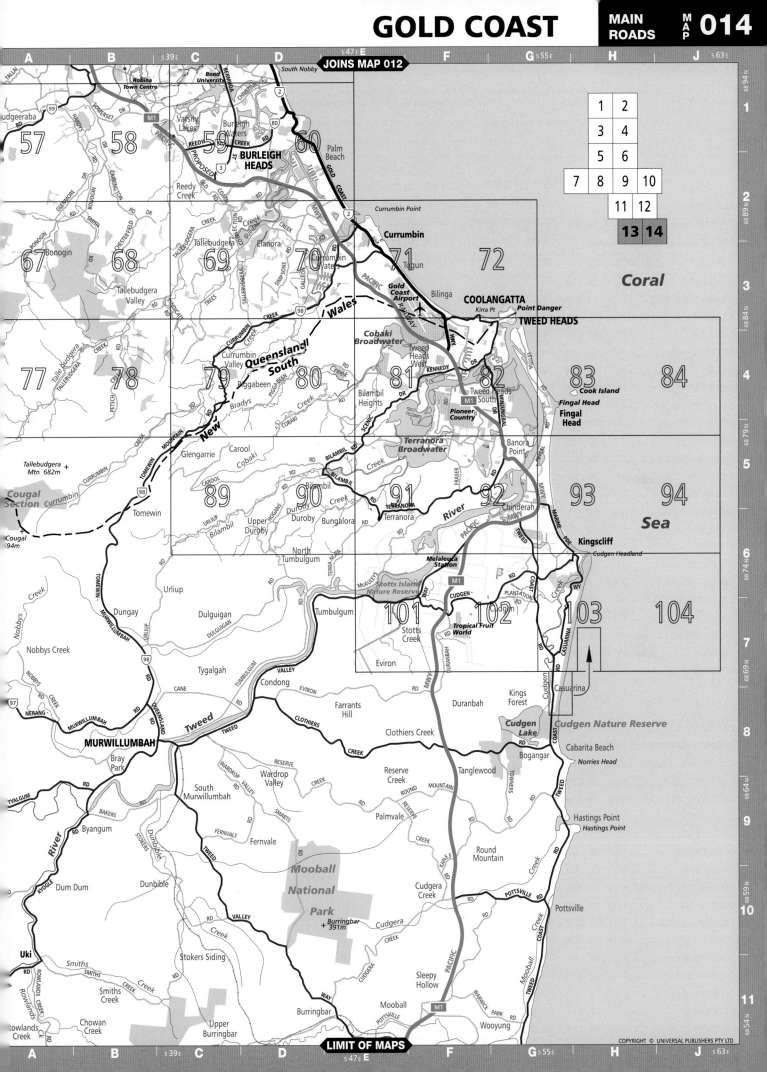

Listed below are the suburbs and localities within the area covered by the Street Maps, together with their postcodes and map references.
Many localities do not have official boundaries.

With the help of the appropriate authorities we have differentiated between suburbs and localities as follows –

CALOUNDRA ..... Suburb   **Cotton Tree** .... Locality or unofficial suburb   *Mooloolah* .... Local name or railway station

		Map	Ref

A

Suburb	Postcode	Map	Ref
ALEXANDRA HEADLAND	4572	69	N16
AROONA	4551	100	D6

B

Suburb	Postcode	Map	Ref
BALD KNOB	4552	95	B8
BALMORAL RIDGE	4552	74	N17
BANYA	4551	108	C5
BARINGA	4551	99	H19
BATTERY HILL	4551	100	H3
BEERBURRUM	4517	136	L2
BEERWAH	4519	105	P14
BELLI PARK	4562	13	J17
BELLS CREEK	4551	109	B12
BELLTHORPE	4514	92	F15
Bellthorpe West	4514	92	B12
BIRTINYA	4575	90	B7
BLACK MOUNTAIN	4563	4	E19
BLI BLI	4560	58	C8
BOKARINA	4575	90	L7
BOLLIER	4570	13	A7
BOOROOBIN	4552	93	G11
BOREEN POINT	4565	1	Q3
BRIBIE ISLAND NORTH	4507	110	E12
BRIDGES	4561	35	N18
BROOLOO	4570	31	F1
BUDDINA	4575	80	L7
BUDERIM	4556	68	P18
BURNSIDE	4560	65	N4

C

Suburb	Postcode	Map	Ref
CALOUNDRA	4551	100	E13
CALOUNDRA WEST	4551	99	N14
CAMBROON	4552	32	E6
CARTERS RIDGE	4563	13	B10
CASTAWAYS BEACH	4567	19	K10
CEDARTON	4514	93	N17
CHEVALLUM	4555	77	C7
COES CREEK	4560	65	N6
COLES CREEK	4570	3	B9
COMMISSIONERS FLAT	4514	94	B20
CONONDALE	4552	32	L17
COOCHIN CREEK	4519	109	M18
COOLABINE	4574	53	G3
COOLOOLABIN	4560	45	E6
COOLUM BEACH	4573	39	D11
COORAN	4569	3	L8
COOROIBAH	4565	2	E14
COOROY	4563	15	B14

Suburb	Postcode	Map	Ref
COOROY MOUNTAIN	4563	16	C11
COOTHARABA	4565	1	H8
CORBOULD PARK	4551	98	Q11
Cotton Tree	4558	69	N10
CROHAMHURST	4519	94	F11
CURRAMORE	4552	73	E3
CURRIMUNDI	4551	100	H1

D

Suburb	Postcode	Map	Ref
DIAMOND VALLEY	4553	85	K17
DICKY BEACH	4551	100	N6
DIDDILLIBAH	4559	67	Q5
DOONAN	4562	17	M13
DULONG	4560	54	P13

E

Suburb	Postcode	Map	Ref
EERWAH VALE	4562	25	H8
ELAMAN CREEK	4552	73	H10
ELIMBAH	4516	135	J12
EUDLO	4554	85	N3
EUMUNDI	4562	26	C12

F

Suburb	Postcode	Map	Ref
FEDERAL	4568	3	M18
FLAXTON	4560	54	H15
FOREST GLEN	4556	77	H1

G

Suburb	Postcode	Map	Ref
GAGALBA	4551	108	H14
GHEERULLA	4574	33	G13
GLASS HOUSE MOUNTAINS	4518	126	B3
GLENVIEW	4553	87	M13
GOLDEN BEACH	4551	110	E5

H

Suburb	Postcode	Map	Ref
HIGHWORTH	4560	55	G13
HUNCHY	4555	75	D3

I

Suburb	Postcode	Map	Ref
ILKLEY	4554	77	E19
IMAGE FLAT	4560	55	K9
IMBIL	4570	31	D5

K

Suburb	Postcode	Map	Ref
Kawana Waters	4575	90	G6
KENILWORTH	4574	31	E12
KIAMBA	4560	45	F17
KIDAMAN CREEK	4574	53	D15
KIELS MOUNTAIN	4559	67	L10
KINGS BEACH	4551	100	P16
KIN KIN	4571	1	A1
KULANGOOR	4560	46	B17

Suburb	Postcode	Map	Ref
KULUIN	4558	68	L10
KUNDA PARK	4556	68	D11
KUREELPA	4560	54	N5

L

Suburb	Postcode	Map	Ref
LAKE MACDONALD	4563	5	Q12
LANDERS SHOOT	4555	75	H15
LANDSBOROUGH	4550	96	B12
LITTLE MOUNTAIN	4551	99	M7

M

Suburb	Postcode	Map	Ref
MALENY	4552	74	E13
MAPLETON	4560	54	E10
MARCOOLA	4564	49	D17
MARCUS BEACH	4573	19	M17
MAROOCHYDORE	4558	69	F13
MAROOCHY RIVER	4561	47	F17
MERIDAN PLAINS	4551	98	H4
MINYAMA	4575	80	E8
MOFFAT BEACH	4551	100	J11
MONS	4556	77	M6
MONTVILLE	4560	74	L2
MOOLOOLABA	4557	80	F1
Mooloolah Railway Station	4553	86	F19
MOOLOOLAH VALLEY	4553	86	D15
MOUNTAIN CREEK	4557	79	J13
MOUNT COOLUM	4573	49	H12
MOUNT MELLUM	4550	95	K17
MOY POCKET	4574	33	C8
MUDJIMBA	4564	59	L16

N

Suburb	Postcode	Map	Ref
NAMBOUR	4560	55	Q15
Nambour Heights	4560	55	M13
NINDERRY	4561	36	J18
NIRIMBA	4551	98	F19
NOOSA HEADS	4567	9	E15
NOOSA NORTH SHORE	4565	8	N6
NOOSAVILLE	4566	8	P20
NORTH ARM	4561	36	E6
NORTH MALENY	4552	74	J11

O

Suburb	Postcode	Map	Ref
OBI OBI	4574	53	Q12

P

Suburb	Postcode	Map	Ref
PACIFIC PARADISE	4564	59	A10
PALMVIEW	4553	88	H11
PALMWOODS	4555	76	C10
PARKLANDS	4560	56	L4
PARREARRA	4575	80	F14

Suburb	Postcode	Map	Ref
PEACHESTER	4519	94	H16
PELICAN WATERS	4551	109	K12
PEREGIAN BEACH	4573	29	N9
PEREGIAN SPRINGS	4573	28	N17
PERWILLOWEN	4560	65	D2
PINBARREN	4568	4	G3
POINT ARKWRIGHT	4573	49	P1
POMONA	4568	4	K11

R

Suburb	Postcode	Map	Ref
REESVILLE	4552	73	H16
RIDGEWOOD	4563	13	P12
RINGTAIL CREEK	4565	1	Q13
ROSEMOUNT	4560	57	F18

S

Suburb	Postcode	Map	Ref
SANDY CREEK	4570	92	A9
SHELLY BEACH	4551	100	P12
SIPPY DOWNS	4556	78	N15
STANMORE	4514	93	K19
SUNRISE BEACH	4567	19	Q6
SUNSHINE BEACH	4567	10	B18

T

Suburb	Postcode	Map	Ref
TANAWHA	4556	78	E18
TEWANTIN	4565	7	Q6
The Narrows	4552	74	F2
TINBEERWAH	4563	6	J15
TOWEN MOUNTAIN	4560	65	D8
TRAVESTON	4570	3	E5
TUCHEKOI	4570	3	B17
TWIN WATERS	4564	59	F17

V

Suburb	Postcode	Map	Ref
VALDORA	4561	47	L5
VERRIERDALE	4562	27	J13

W

Suburb	Postcode	Map	Ref
WARANA	4575	80	L17
WEST WOOMBYE	4559	65	C12
WEYBA DOWNS	4562	18	D17
Whites Lookout	4556	79	C1
Wisemans Lookout	4556	78	N3
WITTA	4552	73	Q7
WOOMBYE	4559	66	L11
WOOTHA	4552	93	F4
WURTULLA	4575	90	M14

Y

Suburb	Postcode	Map	Ref
YANDINA	4561	46	F11
YANDINA CREEK	4561	37	N11
YAROOMBA	4573	49	G3

Map Ref

Aged Care, Nursing Homes & Retirement Communities

Adventist Retirement Village Caloundra 64 Sunset Dr, Little Mountain ... 99 P6
Allora Gardens Link Ct, Maroochydore ... 68 R14
Arcare Maroochydore 54 Dalton Dr ... 69 G15
Arcare Peregian Springs 33 Ridgeview Dr ... 39 C1
Aveo Lindsay Gardens 35 Lindsay Rd, Buderim ... 78 H3
Aveo Palmview 58 Harmony Bvd ... 88 P6
Aveo Peregian Springs Country Club 21 Gracemere Bvd ... 29 B18
B by Halcyon Retirement Village 2 Retreat Dr, Buderim ... 67 P18
Bellcarra Retirement Resort 17 Carree St, Caloundra West ... 99 G13
Blue Care,
Aminya Residential Aged Care 10 West Tce, Caloundra ... 100 D14
Beachwood Residential Aged Care 124 Nicklin Wy, Warana ... 80 G17
Ben Bryce Park Village 1274 Landsborough-Maleny Rd, Maleny ... 74 G19
Bli Bli Village 36 Lefoes Rd ... 58 D12
Boyanda Residential Aged Care 20 Lefoes Rd, Bli Bli ... 58 C12
Caloundra Retirement Village cnr Cooroora & Coolum Sts, Dicky Beach ... 100 J8
Elandra Village 124 Nicklin Wy, Warana ... 80 G17
Erowal Residential Aged Care 1274 Landsborough-Maleny Rd, Maleny ... 74 G20
Kirimi Village 10 West Tce, Caloundra ... 100 D13
Ninderry Residential Aged Care 20 Lefoes Rd, Bli Bli ... 58 C12
The Glebe Residential Aged Care 55 Coolum St, Dicky Beach ... 100 J8
Waroona Gardens Residential Aged Care 10 West Tce, Caloundra ... 100 D13
Buderim Gardens Retirement Village 405 Mooloolaba Rd ... 69 J19
Caloundra Gardens Retirement Village 72 Mark Rd W, Little Mountain ... 99 N10
Caroline Chisholm Hostel, Ozcare 28 Saffron Dr, Currimundi ... 100 B2
Carramar, Noosa Care 186 Cooroy-Noosa Rd, Tewantin ... 7 H16
Churches of Christ Aged Care 211 Parklands Bvd, Little Mountain ... 99 N3
Cooroy Village 1 Ferrells Rd, Cooroy ... 15 A9
Currimundi Gardens Retirement Village 28 Saffron Dr ... 100 B2
Currimundi Lake Retirement Villas Erang St, Currimundi ... 90 D20
EdenLea on Buderim cnr Burnett St & Townsend Rd ... 78 F6
Edgewater Village David Low Wy, Bli Bli ... 58 D19
Empress Relocatable Home Park 65 Caloundra Rd, Little Mountain ... 99 P11
Estia Health Amity Av, Maroochydore ... 69 D13
190 Ocean Dr, Twin Waters ... 59 G19
Estia Health Mount Coolum 15 Suncoast Beach Dr ... 49 H11
Estia Health Nambour 27 Glenbrook Dr ... 55 P13
Forest Glen Resort 25 Owen Creek Rd ... 77 J7
GemLife Maroochy Quays Retirement Village 6 Charlston Pl, Maroochydore ... 68 J11
Glenbrook Residential Aged Care Jack St, Nambour ... 55 N13
Grange Court Retirement Villas Blackwood St, Maroochydore ... 69 C11
Greenwood Forest Glen Retirenment Village 16 Grammar School Wy, Forest Glen ... 77 H5
Halcyon Lakeside Retirement Village 1 Halcyon Wy, Bli Bli ... 57 M5
Halcyon Landing Retirement Village 27 Waigani St, Bli Bli ... 58 D13
Halcyon Nirimba Retirement Community ... 108 L6
Halcyon Parks 42 Meridan Wy, Meridan Plains ... 99 N1
Harrington Court Retirement Village Townsend Rd, Buderim ... 78 E6
Hibiscus Retirement Resort 71 St Andrews Dr, Tewantin ... 7 N19
Bellflower Resort 118 Bellflower Rd, Sippy Downs ... 78 H20
Buderim Meadows Resort 183 Karawatha Dr ... 79 G9
Chancellor Park Resort 52 University Wy, Sippy Downs ... 78 J20
Nambour Resort 55 Carter Rd ... 55 R18
Immanuel Gardens Retirement Village 10 Magnetic Dr, Buderim ... 69 E19
IRT Parklands Retirement Village, Currimundi 242 Parklands Bvd, Meridan Plains ... 99 Q2
IRT The Palms Retirement Village 22 Power Rd, Buderim ... 78 P14
IRT Woodlands 22 Lacebark St, Meridan Plains ... 89 Q14
Island Point Villas Kawana Wy, Parrearra ... 80 B16
Kabara, Noosa Care 20 Topaz St, Cooroy ... 15 B7
Kensington Gardens Retirement Village 45 Glen Kyle Dr, Buderim ... 69 G20
Kookaburra Village 123 Mark Rd, Caloundra West ... 99 R10
Laguna Estate 21 Lake Weyba Dr, Noosaville ... 8 R20
Laurel Springs Retirement Village 18 Doolan St, Nambour ... 55 R16
Live Life Village Maleny Grove 9 Palm St, Maleny ... 74 C17
Living Choice Kawana Island 10 Marco Wy, Parrearra ... 80 E20
Living Choice Sunshine Cove Retirement Village Sunrise Dr, Maroochydore ... 69 C13
Living Choice Twin Waters Retirement Village 21 Baywater Dr ... 59 F19
Living Gems Pacific Paradise 596 David Low Wy ... 59 A14
McKenzie Aged Care, Buderim Views 383 Mooloolaba Rd ... 69 H20
Glasshouse Views 96 Peachester Rd, Beerwah ... 105 Q20
Maleny Hilltop Village 26 Hakea Av ... 74 C18
Mooloolah Gardens Retirement Resort King Rd, Mooloolah Valley ... 86 D19
Noosa Domain Village Eenie Creek Rd, Noosaville ... 18 J2
Noosa Nursing Centre 119 Moorindil St, Tewantin ... 8 C9
Noosa Waters Retirement Estate 39 Lake Weyba Dr, Noosaville ... 18 R1
Oak Tree Retirement Village Pelican Waters 1 Boat Shed Wy, Pelican Waters ... 109 P9
Opal Caloundra 4 Lyon St, Dicky Beach ... 100 H9
Opal Kawana Waters 1 Reflection Cr, Birtinya ... 90 B12
Opal Nambour 9 Princess Cr ... 56 A14
Ozcare Noosa Aged Care 80 Cooyar St, Noosa Heads ... 9 J20
Paddington Place Retirement Village 4 Lyon St, Dicky Beach ... 100 H8
Palm Lake Resort, Caloundra Cay 96 Village Wy, Little Mountain ... 99 D3
Cooroy-Noosa 19 Trading Post Rd, Cooroy ... 4 R19
Palm Lakes Resort 40 Mahongany Dr, Pelican Waters ... 109 H11
Palmwoods Garden Village 61 Jubilee Dr, Palmwoods ... 76 C2
Park Haven Retirement Townhouses Peregrine Dr, Wurtulla ... 90 G14
Plantation Retirement Resort 96 Petrie Creek Rd, Rosemount ... 56 N17
Regents Landing Retirement Village 252 Main Rd, Maroochydore ... 68 Q9
Regis Allora Lodge Allora Dr, Maroochydore ... 69 A13
Regis Kuluin 354 Main Rd ... 68 J11
Regis Lakeside 94 University Wy, Sippy Downs ... 78 L20
Riverlands 139 Moorindil St, Tewantin ... 8 C9
RSL Care, Centaur Memorial Retirement Community 21 West Tce, Caloundra ... 100 D13
Tantula Rise Retirement Community 96 Tantula Rd W, Alexandra Headland ... 69 L18
St Marys Aged Care Coolum Beach 17 Magenta Dr ... 39 D19
St Marys Aged Care Pelican Waters 31 Verdon St ... 110 A10
Sanctuary Park Retirement Community, Churches of Christ Care Zealey Rd, Nambour ... 56 E12
Southern Cross Care, Caloundra 57 Village Wy, Little Mountain ... 99 E4
Sundale 35 Doolan St, Nambour ... 56 B18
Sundale Retirement Resort 4 Wembley Rd, Coolum Beach ... 39 E10
Sundale Rotary Garden Village Windsor Rd, Burnside ... 65 M1
SunnyCove Maroochydore 26 Yinni St ... 68 R5
Sunrise Beach Village, UnitingCare 1 Grasstree Ct, Sunrise Beach ... 19 M3
The Menzies @ Pacific Paradise 40 Menzies Dr, Pacific Paradise ... 59 C11
The Palms Melody Ct, Warana ... 80 G17
Village Green Retirement Village 4 Caloundra Rd, Caloundra ... 100 C16
Village Green Retirement Villas North Buderim Bvd, Buderim ... 68 N14
Village Life Caloundra 30 Baldwin St, Golden Beach ... 100 C18
Waverley, EdenLea Retirement Village Townsend Rd, Buderim ... 78 E6
Woombye Care & Residences for the Elderly 26 Redmonds Rd, West Woombye ... 66 B12

Airports / Airfields

Caloundra Aerodrome ... 99 P15
Noosa Private Airstrip ... 18 P7
Sunshine Coast Airport ... 59 G8

Ambulance Stations

QAS Beerwah 23 Beerwah Pde ... 106 D19
QAS Buderim 7 Kirby Ct, Tanawha ... 78 G16
QAS Caloundra 2 West Tce ... 100 D15
QAS Coolum 48 South Coolum Rd, Coolum Beach ... 39 C20
QAS Cooroy 41 Kauri St ... 15 B4
QAS Kawana 31 Arunta St, Buddina ... 80 H12
QAS Kenilworth Margaret St ... 31 K12
QAS Maleny 8 Bean St ... 74 D18
QAS Maroochydore cnr North Buderim Bvd & Claremont St, Buderim ... 68 P14
QAS Nambour Rigby St ... 56 E14
QAS Noosa 31 Langura St, Noosa Heads ... 19 H1
QAS Pomona 17 Reserve St ... 4 E11
QAS Tewantin 4 Cooroy-Noosa Rd ... 7 Q14

Bays, Beaches, etc

Alcorn Creek ... 73 R16
Alexandra Headland Beach ... 69 Q15
Alexandria Bay ... 10 C10
Alexandria Beach ... 10 B12
Arley Creek ... 73 R18
Banana Gully ... 34 D4
Baronga Broadwater ... 80 C5
Baroona Canal ... 90 C17
Barralong Canal ... 80 G6
Baxter Creek ... 54 B15
Beerburrum Creek ... 135 Q8
Bellbird Creek ... 106 B9
Belli Creek ... 13 D18
Bells Creek ... 109 F12
Blackfellow Creek North Branch ... 13 N13
Blackfellow Creek South Branch ... 14 C14
Bluegum Creek ... 106 D16
Boggy Creek ... 47 K14
Boiling Pot ... 9 M8
Bombala Canal ... 80 G7
Brackish Lake ... 79 Q14
Bribie Island ... 110 E18
Bridge Creek ... 74 B15
Broken Bridge Creek ... 92 K10
Browns Creek ... 35 L15
Buddina Beach ... 80 L9
Bulcock Beach ... 100 G17
Bunbubah Creek ... 100 K6
Burgess Creek ... 19 K5
Caboolture Creek ... 46 L14
Cahill Brook ... 94 L16
Caloundra Head ... 100 R16
Camp Creek ... 92 K17
Caplick Creek ... 25 K17
Castaways Beach ... 19 Q14
Castaways Creek ... 19 N14
Cedar Creek ... 33 Q9
Chambers Island ... 69 D5
Channel Island ... 69 J4
Cherry Tree Creek ... 33 H7
Clark Creek ... 73 J19
Coes Creek ... 65 F1
Coles Creek ... 3 A9
Conondale Range ... 92 J16
Coochin Creek ... 116 H5
Cooloolabin Dam ... 34 L11
Coolum Creek ... 48 L6
Coondibah Creek ... 100 J1
Coonowrin Creek ... 125 K6
Cooroibah Creek ... 7 H5

Bowling Clubs

Caravan, Tourist & Mobile Home Parks

Cemeteries & Crematoria

Churches & Other Places of Worship

Other Congregations

Anglican

Apostolic Church of Queensland

Australian Christian Churches

	Map Ref

Baptist

Beerwah
Glasshouse Country,
58 Roberts Rd 116 A2
Buderim
Goodlife Community,
100 Buderim Pines Dr 79 H4
Maroochy,
186 Wises Rd 69 B17
Burnside
Nambour,
Coes Creek Rd 65 R3
Caloundra
City Life,
7 Gregson Pl 100 C14
Coolum Beach
1906 David Low Wy 39 H9
Mapleton
The Range Fellowship,
70 Obi Obi Rd....................54 G10
Noosaville
Noosa,
213 Weyba Rd 8 R19
Yandina
Low St 46 B8

Baptist Independent

Caloundra
Sonshine,
91 Queen St 100 F11

Catholic

Beerwah
Mary MacKillop,
Peachester Rd..................105 P20
Buddina
Kawana Parish Centre,
86 Undara Av....................80 J10
Buderim
St Marys,
King St 78 L3
Caloundra
Our Lady of The Rosary,
61 Edmund St..................100 N13
Coolum Beach
St Peters,
Elizabeth St 39 G14
Cooroy
Sacred Heart,
63 Maple St 14 R4
Kenilworth
St John Bosco,
Anne St............................31 L12
Landsborough
Our Lady of the Way,
Caloundra St 96 H19
Maleny
Sacred Heart,
45 Cedar St 74 C18
Maroochydore
Stella Maris,
37 Baden Powell St 69 G9
Nambour
St Josephs,
177 Currie St 56 D19
Pomona
St Patricks,
1 Church St 4 E11
Sippy Downs
St Catherine of Siena,
58 Sippy Downs Dr............78 L17
Sunshine Beach
St Thomas More,
Ben Lexcen Dr..................9 N19
Tewantin
Our Lady of Perpetual Succour,
cnr Doonella &
Moorindil Sts......................8 B14

Christadelphian

Caloundra
10 Kalinga St 100 J16

Christian Assemblies

Buderim
Glenmount Rd 78 B8

Christian Outreach Centres

Little Mountain
Caloundra City,
cnr Caloundra Rd &
Sydal St 99 N12
Maroochydore
43 Duporth Av..................69 H9
Noosaville
Noosa,
cnr Eumundi-Noosa &
Beckmans Rds 18 D2

	Map Ref

Woombye
Nambour,
Suncoast Christian,
cnr Kiel Mountain &
Schubert Rds....................66 L15

Christian Science

Nambour
First Church of
Christ Scientist,
68 Blackall Tce..................56 B15

Churches of Christ in Queensland

Buderim
Lakeshore Community,
1 Lakeshore Av..................68 N15
Dicky Beach
Caloundra,
30 Beerburrum St............100 J7
Nambour
Sanctuary Park,
22 National Park Rd 56 F13

Church of Jesus Christ of LDS

Forest Glen
Sunshine Coast Stake,
41 Stark La 67 D18
Parrearra
Buderim Ward,
cnr Sunbird Ch &
Corella Dr 80 G14
Kawana Waters Ward,
cnr Sunbird Ch &
Corella Dr 80 G14

Jehovahs Witnesses

Beerwah
24 Burys Rd......................116 H4
Cooroy
74 Mary River Rd 14 Q2
Little Mountain
Caloundra,
72 Pierce Av 99 E8
Maroochydore
Tuckwell Ct 69 A10
Mount Coolum
Mountain View Dr 49 C10
Tewantin
25 Butler St......................7 Q13
Woombye
45 Blackall Range Rd........66 C9

Lutheran

Buderim
Immanuel,
Forest Dr 69 E19
Caloundra
St Marks,
14 Bombala Tce................100 K16
Glass House Mountains
Calvery,
Reed St 116 D18
Nambour
St Lukes,
10 Sydney St 56 D18
Noosaville
Good Shepherd,
115 Eumundi Rd................18 H1
Witta
Good Shepherd,
Witta Rd............................73 R8

Lutheran (ELCR)

Woombye
Trinity Evangelical Lutheran,
Congregation of the Reformation,
Back Woombye Rd............66 E13

New Apostolic

Little Mountain
Caloundra,
Village Wy..........................99 F4

Presbyterian

Alexandra Headland
Maroochydore,
45 Okinja Rd......................69 N15
Caloundra
St Giles,
Ormuz Av 100 J16
Eumundi
123 Memorial Dr 25 Q10
Maleny
Cedar St 74 D18
Nambour
21 Solandra St 55 R16

	Map Ref

Tewantin
St Andrews,
117 St Andrews Dr..............17 M1

Salvation Army

Maroochydore
cnr Broadmeadows &
Maroochydore Rds............69 E9
Nambour
165 Currie St 56 D19
Noosaville
Noosa,
6 Bartlett Rd 18 E3

Seventh-day Adventist

Burnside
Nambour,
Coes Creek Rd 65 R4
Cooroy
Belli Creek Rd 14 Q5
Landsborough
27 Maleny St 96 F18
Little Mountain
cnr Sunset Dr &
Harker Ct 99 N6
Maroochydore
Aragorn St 68 R9
Yandina
North St 46 B8

Uniting

Beerwah
Glass House Country,
Twin Peaks Dr 116 D6
Buderim
cnr King St &
Gloucester Rd 78 K3
Caloundra
56c Queen St 100 H12
Coolum Beach
cnr Heathfield &
Elizabeth Sts 39 G14
Cooroy
51 Maple St 14 R3
Kawana Waters
cnr Dune Vista &
Thunderbird Drs 90 H6
Maleny
Lansborough-Maleny Rd 74 G20
Maroochydore
6 Millwell Rd 69 E10
Montville
Main St 74 N3
Mooloolaba
Meta St 70 B20
Nambour
Coronation Av 56 F15
Palmwoods
Church St 76 D5
Pomona
27 Factory St 4 F11
Sunrise Beach
Grasstree Ct 19 L2
Tewantin
cnr Poinciana Av &
Werin St............................8 A13
Woombye
Pine Grove Rd 66 G13

Westminster Presbyterian

Buderim
Grace Christian,
cnr Stringy Bark Rd &
Toral Dr............................78 L15

Clubs

Alex Surf Club
167 Alexandra Pde,
Alexandra Headland..........69 Q17
Beerwah RSL Club
27 Beerwah Pde..............106 D19
Caloundra Power Boat Club
Woorim Park,
Esplanade,
Golden Beach..................110 D8
Caloundra RSL Services Club
19 West Tce....................100 D14
Caloundra Surf Club
1 Spender La,
Kings Beach....................100 N16
Coolum Surf Club
David Low Wy 39 J15

	Map Ref

Cooroy RSL & Citizens
Memorial Bowls Club
25 Maple St 15 A5
Dicky Beach Surf Club
1a Coochin St..................100 L6
Glasshouse Mountains
Sports Club
Steve Irwin Wy 116 D20
Kawana Surf Club
99 Pacific Bvd,
Buddina 80 K12
Marcoola Surf Life Saving Club
64 Marcoola Esp 49 L18
Maroochydore RSL Club
Memorial Av......................69 J10
Maroochydore Surf Club
34 Alexandra Pde 69 N11
Mooloolah Valley Country Club
129 Mooloolah
Connection Rd,
Landsborough 97 H3
Mudjimba RSL Memorial Club
43 Cottonwood St............59 K14
Nambour RSL Club
Mathew St 56 E17
Noosa Croquet Club
9 Seashell Pl,
Noosaville........................18 J2
Noosa Surf Club
69 Hastings St,
Noosa Heads....................9 J11
Noosa Yacht & Rowing Club
Gympie Tce,
Noosaville........................8 K16
Sunshine Beach Surf Life
Saving Club
Belmore Tce......................10 A20
Tewantin-Noosa RSL &
Citizens Memorial Club
cnr Poinciana &
Memorial Avs,
Tewantin 8 D14
The Surf Club
Mooloolaba Esp,
Mooloolaba......................80 D2

Fire Stations

Aviation Rescue &
Fire Fighting 59 G7
Beerwah 106 D19
Buderim 78 H3
Caloundra 100 C13
Coolum 39 G14
Cooran 4 A5
Cooroy 15 A6
Kawana 80 G19
Kenilworth 31 L12
Maleny 74 B18
Maroochydore....................68 P14
Mooloolah 86 D19
Nambour 56 J13
Noosa Heads 19 H1
Pomona 4 F11
Tewantin 8 F15

Girl Guides

Buderim 78 G6
Caloundra..........................100 E14
Cooroy 15 B5
Glass House Mountains 116 D20
Kawana Waters 80 K10
Landsborough....................96 D19
Maroochydore....................69 H9
Nambour 56 F15
Noosa 8 J17
Palmwoods 75 R6
Yandina 46 A6

Golf Courses, Clubs & Driving Ranges

Beerwah & District
Memorial Golf Club..........106 F20
Caloundra Golf Club..........100 E10
Chancellor Park
Golf Driving Range 78 J17
Cooroy Golf Club 15 A8
Glenview Par 3 Golf Course ..97 K6
Headland Golf Club 79 J4
Kabi Golf Course 1 K2
Maleny Golf Club................74 H19
Maroochy River Golf Club 58 L16

	Map Ref

Mt Coolum Golf Club 49 E12
Nambour Golf Club............56 J8
Noosa Par 3 Golf Course 18 B9
Noosa Springs
Golf Resort & Spa............19 G5
Noosa Valley Country Club....17 A15
Palmer Coolum
Resort Golf Course..........49 K7
Pelican Waters Golf Club 109 H11
Peregian Springs Golf Club ...29 A18
Tanawha Valley
Golf & Tennis 77 N17
Tewantin-Noosa Golf Club....7 N15
The Oasis Golf &
Tennis Palmwoods 77 A2
Twin Waters Golf Club..........59 F18

Hospitals

Buderim Private Hospital
Elsa Wilson Dr..................79 J3
Caloundra Hospital
West Tce..........................100 D14
Eden Rehabilitation Centre
50 Maple St,
Cooroy 14 R3
Kawana Private Hospital
5 Innovation Pky,
Birtinya 90 E5
Maleny Soldiers
Memorial Hospital
Bean St............................74 C17
Nambour General Hospital
Hospital Rd......................56 A15
Nambour Selangor
Private Hospital
62 Netherton St 56 C14
Noosa Hospital
111 Goodchap St,
Noosaville........................8 F18
Ramsay Clinic Caloundra
96 Beerburrum St............100 F6
Sunshine Coast
University Hospital
Hollows La,
Birtinya 90 A10
Sunshine Coast
University Private Hospital
Birtinya Bvd ,
Birtinya 90 B9

Hotels & Motels

Abode Mooloolaba................80 C3
Alexandra on the Pacific
Alexandra Headland..........70 A19
Alex Seaside Resort
Alexandra Headland..........69 P16
Anchorage Motor Inn
Caloundra........................100 E17
Anchor Motel Noosa
Noosaville........................8 R19
Atlantis Marcoola
Beachfront Resort
Marcoola..........................59 L7
Beachside Resort-
Kawana Waters
Buddina 80 J11
Beerburrum Motel..............126 D18
Beerwah Glasshouse Motel
Glass House Mountains ...116 E12
Beerwah Motor Lodge
Landsborough..................106 E5
Bluewater Point Resort
Minyama 80 F10
BreakFree Alexandra Beach
Alexandra Headland..........69 Q17
BreakFree Grand Pacific
Caloundra........................100 H17
Buderim Fiesta Motel
Tanawha 78 B15
Caloundra Central
Apartment Hotel
Battery Hill 100 F5
Caloundra Suncoast Motel...100 G16
Central Motel Mooloolaba
Mooloolaba......................80 C3
Chateau Royale
Beach Resort
Maroochydore 69 N10
Chenrezig Institute-Tibeton
Buddhist Retreat Centre
Eudlo 74 R14
Clouds of Montville 74 P7
Coolum Budget
Accommodation
Coolum Beach..................39 H12

Places of Interest

Places of Interest

	Map Ref
Pioneer Cottage	
5 Ballinger Cr,	
Buderim	78 J4
Queensland Air Museum	
Caloundra Aerodrome,	
7 Pathfinder Dr,	
Caloundra West	99 R13
SEALIFE Sunshine Coast	
Parkyn Pde,	
Mooloolaba	80 D3
Ski N Skurf	
Cable Water Ski Park	
367 Davis Low Wy,	
Bli Bli	58 H16
Suncoast Model Aero Centre	
Quanda Rd,	
Coolum Beach	38 K8
Sunshine Castle	
292 David Low Wy,	
Bli Bli	58 D16
Tewantin Heritage &	
Tourist Information Centre	
cnr Poinciana Av &	
Diyan St	8 D13
The Australian Teamsters Hall of	
Fame & Spirit of Cobb & Co	
cnr Old Gympie &	
Mt Beerwah Rds,	
Glass House Mountains	125 D5
The Events Centre	
20 Minchinton St,	
Caloundra	100 H15
Thrill Hill Waterslides	
74 Schubert Rd,	
Woombye	66 J14
Tourism Noosa	
Parkyn Ct,	
Tewantin	8 D14
TreeTop Challenge	
76 Nambour Conection Rd,	
Woombye	67 A17
Visitor Information Centre,	
Bulcock Street Office	
77 Bulcock St	100 H16
Caloundra Office	
7 Caloundra Rd	100 B14
Coolum Office	
Tickle Park,	
David Low Wy,	
Coolum Beach	39 J15
Glasshouse Visitor &	
Interpretive Centre	
cnr Bruce Pde & Reed St,	
Glass House Mountains	116 D18
Maleny	
23 Maple St	74 E18
Maroochydore Office	
cnr Sixth Av &	
Melrose Pde	69 N13
Montville Office	
198 Main St	74 N3
Mooloolaba Office	
cnr Brisbane Rd & First Av	80 D1
Sunshine Coast Airport	
Friendship Av,	
Marcoola	59 G8
Wallace House	
7 Wallace Dr,	
Noosaville	8 H17
Wappa Falls	
Pump Station Rd,	
Kiamba	45 F12
Yandina Historic House	
3 Pioneer Rd,	
Yandina	46 D7
Yandina Information Centre	
3 Pioneer Rd	46 D7

Police Stations

	Map Ref
Beerwah	106 D18
Buderim Police Beat	78 J4
Caloundra	100 D15
Coolum	39 C19
Cooroy	15 A6
Eumundi	26 A10
Kawana Waters	90 G6
Kenilworth	31 L12
Landsborough	96 G19
Maleny	74 B17
Maleny	74 D18
Maroochydore	69 J10
Mooloolaba	
Police Shopfront	80 E2
Nambour	56 D19
Noosa Heads	19 J1
Palmwoods	76 C5
Pomona	4 E11

	Map Ref
Sippy Downs	78 R16

Police & Citizens Youth Club

Sunshine Coast
Youth Av,
Burnside 66 A1

Qld Transport Customer Service Centres

Caloundra
Customer Service Centre
54 Canberra Tce 100 K16
Maroochydore
Customer Service Centre
5 Kelly Ct 69 G17
Nambour
Customer Service Centre
cnr Stanley St &
Coronation Av 56 G13
Tewantin
Customer Service Centre
8 Sidoni St 8 C14

Racecourse & Trotting Track

Corbould Park
Pierce Av,
Meridan Plains 99 A7

RACQ Branch Offices

Cooroy Service Centre
9 Diamond St 15 A4
Maleny Autocare &
Engineering
13 Coral St 74 E19
RACQ Caloundra
104 Bulcock St 100 G17
RACQ Maroochydore
25 Cornmeal Pde 69 J10
RACQ Nambour
23 Currie St 56 D17
RACQ Noosa
Noosa Civic,
28 Eenie Creek Rd,
Noosaville 18 G4

Schools & Colleges - Private

Ananda Marga River School
Maleny 74 C13
Blackall Range
Independent School
Kureelpa 54 Q7
Caloundra Christian
College 100 D14
Caloundra City School
Pelican Waters 109 N5
Coolum Beach
Christian College
Yandina Creek 38 G17
Glasshouse
Christian College
Beerwah 116 A1
Good Samaritan
Catholic College
Bli Bli 57 M4
Good Shepherd
Lutheran College
Noosaville 18 H1
Immanuel Lutheran College
Buderim 69 D18
Matthew Flinders
Anglican College
Buderim 78 M9
Montessori International
College
Forest Glen 67 G17
Nambour Christian College
Woombye 66 D5
Noosa Christian College
Cooroy 14 Q5
Noosa Pengari Steiner School
Doonan 18 A20

	Map Ref
OneSchool Global	
Nambour	55 K15
Our Lady of The Rosary Primary	
Shelly Beach	100 N13
Pacific Lutheran College	
Meridan Plains	89 P16
Peregian Beach College	28 R12
St Andrews Anglican College	
Peregian Springs	29 B19
St Johns Secondary College	
Burnside	65 P4
St Josephs Primary	
Nambour	56 D19
St Teresas Catholic College	
Noosaville	8 A20
St Thomas More Primary	
Sunshine Beach	9 N19
Siena Catholic Primary	
Sippy Downs	78 L17
Siena Catholic Secondary	
Sippy Downs	78 L18
Stella Maris Primary	
Maroochydore	69 A9
Suncoast Christian College	
Woombye	66 L15
Sunshine Coast Grammar	
Forest Glen	77 G3
Unity College	
Caloundra West	99 H15

Schools & Colleges - State

	Map Ref
Baringa Primary	99 E18
Baringa State Secondary	
College	99 C16
Beerburrum Primary	136 C4
Beerwah High	116 B3
Beerwah Primary	105 N19
Bli Bli Primary	58 A12
Brightwater Primary	
Mountain Creek	79 R15
Buddina Primary	80 J11
Buderim Mountain Primary	
Buderim	78 J3
Burnside High	55 P20
Burnside Primary	55 R20
Caloundra High	100 F12
Caloundra Primary	100 J13
Chancellor College,	
Middle & Senior Campus	
Sippy Downs	78 Q16
Primary Campus	
Sippy Downs	78 M19
Chevallum Primary	77 D9
Coolum High	
Peregian Beach	39 H1
Coolum Primary	39 C17
Cooran Primary	3 Q6
Cooroy Primary	15 A3
Currimundi Primary	
Dicky Beach	100 K4
Currimundi Special School	100 L5
Eudlo Primary	86 C2
Eumundi Primary	26 A10
Federal State School	3 J17
Glass House	
Mountains Primary	125 R1
Glenview Primary	87 K19
Golden Beach Primary	110 B1
Kawana Waters College,	
Junior Campus	
Bokarina	90 G8
Senior Campus	
Bokarina	90 F7
Kenilworth	
Community College	31 K13
Kuluin Primary	68 M12
Landsborough Primary	96 F16
Maleny High	74 F20
Maleny Primary	74 F19
Mapleton Primary	54 H9
Maroochydore High	69 B9
Maroochydore Primary	69 F10
Meridan State College	
Meridan Plains	99 N2
Montville Primary	74 N3
Mooloolaba Primary	70 B20
Mooloolah Primary	
Mooloolah Valley	86 C20
Mountain Creek High	79 P6
Mountain Creek Primary	79 N6
Nambour Special School	
Burnside	55 Q20
Nambour State College	56 F15
Nirimba Primary	108 J4
Noosa District High	
Cooroy	14 R4
Pomona Campus	4 G8
Noosaville Primary	17 R1

	Map Ref
North Arm Primary	
Yandina	36 G12
Pacific Paradise Primary	59 D12
Palmview Primary	88 R8
Palmview Special School	89 B9
Palmwoods Primary	75 Q7
Peachester Primary	94 L17
Peregian Springs Primary	39 B2
Pomona Primary	4 G12
Sunshine Beach High	19 M1
Sunshine Beach Primary	9 M18
Talara Primary College	
Currimundi	100 C2
Tewantin Primary	8 A12
Woombye Primary	66 K16
Yandina Primary	46 D5

Scouts

	Map Ref
Buderim	78 H3
Burnside	56 B19
Caloundra	100 F14
Cooroy	14 R2
Dunethin Rock Campsite	47 H17
Eumundi	26 B14
Glass House Mountains	116 D20
Kawana	80 K10
Lake MacDonald	5 L9
Maleny	73 R7
Maroochydore	69 H8
Nambour, 2nd	56 E15
Noosa	8 H15
Palmwoods	76 A6
Rocky Creek Campsite	106 B2
Woombye	66 E13
Yandina	46 A6

Shopping Complexes - Major

	Map Ref
Bay Village On Hastings	
Noosa Heads	9 H11
Beerwah Marketplace	
Fair Shopping Centre	106 C19
Big Top Shopping Centre	
Maroochydore	69 H9
Caloundra	100 F16
Centenary Square	
Shopping Centre	
Nambour	56 C17
Centrepoint Shopping Plaza	
Caloundra	100 J17
Home Central Kawana	
Birtinya	90 D6
Kawana Shoppingworld	
Buddina	80 H12
Nambour Central	56 D17
Nambour Mill Village	56 C18
Nambour Plaza	56 E18
Noosa Civic	
Noosaville	18 H4
Noosa Fair Shopping Centre	
Noosa Heads	9 H17
Noosa Junction Plaza	
Noosa Heads	9 H16
Noosa Marina	
Tewantin	8 E15
Noosa Village	
Shopping Centre	
Noosaville	8 P18
North Shore Village	
Pacific Paradise	59 E12
Stockland Baringa	99 E19
Stockland Birtinya	90 B8
Sunshine Plaza	
Maroochydore	69 G10

Swimming Pools

	Map Ref
Aquatic Complex	79 N5
Beerwah Swimming Pool	116 B2
Buderim Community Pool	78 H3
Caloundra Aquatic	
Lifestyle Centre	100 G14
Coolum Peregian	
Aquatic Centre	39 G9
Cooroy Swimming Pool	15 A9
Cotton Tree	
Olympic Swim Centre	69 L10
Eumundi Aquatic Centre	26 A14
Kawana Aquatics &	
Leisure Centre	90 F6
Kenilworth Swimming Pool	31 L13
Kings Beach Pool	100 N16
Maleny Swimming Pool	74 F19

	Map Ref
Mooloolah Swimming Pool	86 C20
Nambour	
Olympic Swim Centre	56 C15
Noosa Aquatic Centre	9 L20
Noosa River	8 E14
Palmwoods Swimming Pool	76 A6

Tertiary Institutions

TAFE Queensland ,
Maroochydore Campus
170 Horton Pde 69 H9
Mooloolaba Campus
34 Lady Musgrave Dr,
Mountain Creek 79 P6
Nambour Campus
91 Windsor Rd,
Burnside 55 N20
University of The Sunshine Coast
90 Sippy Downs Dr,
Sippy Downs 78 M17

Theatres & Cinemas

Bigscreen Cinemas Caloundra
cnr Bulcock St &
Knox Av 100 K16
Event Cinemas,
Maroochydore Sunshine Plaza
Sunseeker Pde 69 H10
Noosa Cinemas (Noosa 5)
29 Sunshine Beach Rd,
Noosa Heads 9 J16
Majestic Nambour
(Arthouse Cinema,
Civic Centre)
Centenary Square,
Currie St 56 C17
Majestic Theatre,
Silent Movies
3 Factory St,
Pomona 4 F11
Noosa Arts Theatre
Weyba Rd,
Noosaville 9 C19
The Events Centre
20 Minchinton St,
Caloundra 100 H15

Weighbridges

North Coast Rural Supplies
57 Cordwell Rd,
Yandina 46 C14
Simsmetal
42 Hoopers Rd,
Kunda Park 68 C12
Suncoast Stockfeeds &
Equine Supplies
7173 Bruce Hwy,
Chevallum 77 E3
Woodlands Enterprises Pty Ltd
2814 Old Gympie Rd,
Beerwah 105 M18

Wineries

Flame Hill Vineyard 74 K1
Flaxton Grove Vineyard &
Cellars 54 K15

Publishing Dates

1st Edition	2000
2nd Edition	2002
3rd Edition	2004
4th Edition	2006
5th Edition	2008
6th Edition	2010
7th Edition	2013
8th Edition	2015
9th Edition	2017
10th Edition	2018
11th Edition	2022
12th Edition	2024

Street Listings

All the streets in this index are listed alphabetically and then by suburb. It is most important to have the correct name when looking for a particular street. If any difficulty is experienced with the suburb name, refer to the Suburbs and Localities Index.

Mc and **Mac:** Names beginning with 'Mc' are treated as though they are spelt 'Mac' and indexed accordingly.

Mt: Names beginning with 'Mt' are treated as though they are spelt 'Mount' and indexed accordingly.

St: Names beginning with 'St' are treated as though they are spelt 'Saint' and indexed accordingly.

The: Names beginning with 'The' are treated with 'The' first and are indexed accordingly.

Streets not Named on Maps

For reasons of clarity it is not always possible to show and name every street on the map itself. Any street or lane that is not shown on the map face is listed in italic (sloping) type and referenced to its approximate position.

Alphabet Indicators

These are the street names in capitals located on the top left and right hand corners of each page of the street index. The indicator on the left page represents the first named street in the first column on this page, while the indicator on the right page represents the last named street in the last column on this page.

ABBREVIATIONS FOR DESIGNATIONS

Alley ... al	Close ... cl	End ...end	Junction ... jnc	Pocket ... pkt	Street ... st
Approach ... app	Common ... cmn	Entrance ... ent	Key ...key	Port/Point ... pt	Tarn ... tn
Arcade ... arc	Concourse ... cnc	Esplanade ... esp	Lane ... la	Promenade ... prm	Terrace ... tce
Avenue ... av	Copse ... cps	Expressway ... exp	Link ... lk	Quadrant ... qd	Tollway ... twy
Bend ... bnd	Corner ... cnr	Fairway ...fy	Lookout...lkt	Quay/s ... qy	Top ...top
Boardwalk...bwk	Corso ... cso	Freeway ... fwy	Loop ... lp	Ramble ... ra	Tor ... tor
Boulevard ... bvd	Court ... ct	Frontage ... fr	Mall ... ml	Reach ... rch	Track ... tr
Bowl ... bl	Courtyard ... cyd	Garden/s ... gdn	Mead ... md	Reserve ... res	Trail ... trl
Brace ... br	Cove ... cov	Gate/s ... gte	Meander ... mdr	Rest ... rst	Turn ... trn
Brae ... br	Crescent ... cr	Gateway ... gwy	Mews ... mw	Retreat ... rt	Underpass ... ups
Break ... brk	Crest ... cst	Glade ... gld	Motorway ... mwy	Return ... rtn	Vale...va
Brook ... brk	Cross ... cs	Glen ... gln	Nook ... nk	Ridge ... rdg	Valley...vy
Broadway ... bwy	Crossing ... csg	Grange ... gra	North ... n	Rise ... ri	View ... vw
Brow ... brw	Curve ... cve	Green ... grn	Outlook ... out	Road ... rd	Vista ... vst
Bypass ... bps	Dale ... dle	Grove ... gr	Parade ... pde	Roadway ... rdy	Walk ... wk
Central...c	Down/s ... dn	Grovet ... gr	Park ... pk	Route ... rte	Walkway ... wky
Centre ... ctr	Drive ... dr	Haven ...hvn	Parkway ... pky	Row ...row	Way ... wy
Chase ... ch	Driveway...dwy	Heights ... hts	Pass ... ps	Serviceway ... swy	West ... w
Circle ... cir	East ... e	Highway ... hwy	Pathway ... pwy	South ... s	Wynd ... wyn
Circuit ... cct	Edge ... edg	Hike ...hk	Place ... pl	Square ... sq	
Circus ... crc	Elbow ... elb	Hill ...hill	Plaza ... plz	Strand ... sd	

ABBREVIATIONS FOR SUBURB NAMES

Airport ... Aprt	Crossing ... Csg	Harbor/our ... Hbr	Lookout ... Lkt	Plain/s ... Pl	Saint ... St
Basin ... Bsn	Down/s ... Dn	Head/s ... Hd	Lower ... Lr	Plateau ... Plat	South ... S
Bay ... B	East ... E	Headland ... Hd	Meadow/s ...Mdw	Pocket ... Pkt	Terminal ... Term
Beach ... Bch	Field/s ... Fd	Heights ... Ht	Mount ... Mt	Point/Port...Pt	University ... Uni
Bridge ... Br	Flat ... Fl	Hill/s ... Hl	Mountain/s ... Mtn	Range ... Rge	Upper ... Up
Central...Ctrl	Forest ... Frst	Island ... I	North ... N	Reach ... Rch	Valley ... Vy
Chase ... Ch	Garden/s ... Gdn	Junction ... Jctn	Paradise ... Pdse	Reserve ... Res	Vale ... Va
Corner ... Cnr	Grove ... Gr	Lagoon ...Lgn	Park ... Pk	Ridge ... Rdg	Village ... Vill
Court...Ct	Gully ... Gly	Lakes ... L	Peninsula...Pen	River ... R	Waters ... Wtr
Creek ... Ck		Lodge ... Ldg		Rocks ... Rks	West ... W

NON-STANDARD ABBREVIATIONS FOR SUBURB NAMES

Glass House Mountains ....Glass Hse Mtn   Peregian Springs...Peregian Spr

A

ABACO
st. Parrearra...... 80 E16
ABBEY
ct. Golden Bch 110 A4
ct. Pelican Wtr....... 110 A4
ABBOTTS
rd. Palmwoods 76 G1
ABELES
st. Baringa......98 R16
ABELIA
cl. Peregian Bch ...29 H3
pl. Mountain Ck ...79 K14
ABILENE
pl. Sippy Downs 78 N20
ACACIA
av. Beerburrum ...136 C6
av. Coolum Bch ...39 D15
av. Shelly Bch ...100 P14
la. Cooroy 14 N6
st. Parklands 56 H7
ACACIABARK
pl. Little Mtn 99 M5
ACADIA
rd. Palmview......88 K11
ACCENT
st. Palmview......88 L10
ACCESS
cr. Coolum Bch ...38 K11
ACHURCH
st. Palmview......88 K9
ACKERMAN
rd. Kulangoor......56 G2
ACORN
ct. Currimundi ...100 B1
la. Woombye......66 J15
ACTION
st. Noosaville 18 F4
ADA
st. Tewantin 8 D10
ADALUMA
av. Buderim......80 G5
ADAM
la. Little Mtn 99 J3
ADAMS
st. Sunshine Bch ...19 R2
ADARE
cl. Peregian Spr ...38 P1
ADDISON
la. Baringa......99 E16
ADDLINGTON
st. Landsborough ...96 F15
ADELAIDE
cct. Baringa......99 A16
ADELONG
cr. Buddina......80 H9
ADENSFIELD
ct. Cooroibah 2 A18
ADINA
ct. Buddina......80 J13
ADMIRAL
pl. Noosaville 8 H20
ADMIRALS
ct. Mooloolaba ...79 R5
ADMIRALTY
dr. Alexandra Hd ...69 N18
ADONIS
st. Sunshine Bch ...9 N20
st. Sunshine Bch ...9 P20
st. Sunshine Bch ...19 N1
ADORI
dr. Mountain Ck ...79 H8
st. Currimundi ...90 E20
ADRIAN
cct. Nirimba......108 M4
cl. Buderim......79 E10
ADRIANO
ct. Palmview......88 D15
ADSETT
pl. Baringa......99 B18
ADVANCE
pl. Sunrise Bch ...19 N1
rd. Kuluin......68 K10
AERODROME
rd. Maroochydore ...69 K12
AFFINITY
pl. Birtinya......90 D10
AFORE
pl. Bli Bli......58 D14
AGALE
st. Mooloolaba ...79 R1
AGATE
st. Cooroy......15 B3
AGATHIS
la. Cootharaba ...1 H1
pl. Noosaville 18 A1

AGILITY
pl. Birtinya......90 D12
AGINCOURT
st. Pelican Wtr......109 M7
AGNES
pl. Bli Bli......57 L7
AGNEW
ct. Baringa......99 B16
rd. Mt Mellum ...105 G2
AGRIPPA
cr. Tewantin......7 N18
AHERNS
pl. Bellthorpe......92 N6
rd. Conondale ...92 J1
AIRD
la. Woombye......67 B19
AIRLIE
cl. Mountain Ck ...79 N16
ct. Pelican Wtr......110 B1
AIRPORT
dr. Marcoola ...59 F10
AJAX
st. Verrierdale ...26 M10
AKALA
st. Flaxton ...54 H18
AKANIA
pl. Valdora......47 C3
AKERINGA
pl. Mooloolaba ...80 A6
AKOUNAH
cr. Buddina......80 K5
AKUNA
la. Cooran......3 R2
st. Birtinya......90 B14
ALAND
pl. Palmwoods ...75 R8
ALBA
ct. Currimundi ...90 F20
ALBANY
st. Sippy Downs ...88 N1
st. Sippy Downs ...89 A1
ALBATROSS
av. Aroona......100 D8
av. Nambour......55 N17
ct. Peregian Bch ...29 J7
ALBERT
st. Cooran......3 Q5
st. Eumundi......26 B11
st. Kings Beach ...100 P15
st. Noosaville 8 N17
st. Shelly Bch ...100 P15
ALBERT WOOD
rd. Eudlo......85 G1
ALBYN
pl. Glass Hse Mtn ...125 P1
ALDERLY
tce. Noosa Heads ...9 L10
ALDINGA
pl. Mooloolaba ...79 R4
ALEXANDER
st. Aroona......100 B8
ALEXANDRA
av. Nambour......56 A14
ct. Glass Hse Mtn ...116 A20
pde. Alexandra Hd ...69 P15
pde. Maroochydore ...69 N11
st. Cooran......3 R5
st. Kenilworth ...31 K12
ALEXANDRIA BAY
tr. Noosa Heads ...9 Q17
ALFORD
st. Traveston ...3 G1
ALFRED
st. Shelly Bch ...100 N13
ALFRISTON
dr. Buderim......79 F8
ALFS
rd. Bald Knob ...94 R2
ALFS PINCH
rd. Beerwah......105 D10
rd. Peachester ...105 D10
ALGARVE
ct. Dicky Beach ...100 J7
ALICE
st. Alexandra Hd ...69 Q17
st. Cooran......4 A4
st. Currimundi ...90 H20
st. Eumundi......25 R10
ALICE DIXON
dr. Flaxton ...54 J16
ALICIA
cct. Little Mtn ...99 J4
ct. Buderim......78 D3
ALISON
ct. Buderim......68 E16

ALISTAIR
cr. Nirimba......108 L5
ALKIRA
st. Buddina......80 J6
st. Maroochydore ...69 A6
ALLAMANDA
av. Buderim......78 N2
av. Little Mtn ...99 Q5
ALLAMBI
ri. Noosa Heads ...9 K11
tce. Noosa Heads ...9 F19
ALLAMBIE
ct. Buddina......80 H10
ct. Landsborough ...96 B18
st. Maroochydore ...69 K13
ALLAN
av. Glass Hse Mtn ...115 N19
rd. Yandina......45 K6
ALLANDALE
rd. North Arm ...36 P9
ALLARA
st. Flaxton ...54 H17
st. Warana......80 J14
ALLEN
st. Caloundra ...100 G11
st. Moffat Bch ...100 G11
ALLIRA
st. Pomona......4 M7
ALLONGA
st. Currimundi ...100 G2
ALLOOTA
st. Wurtulla......90 E16
ALLORA
dr. Maroochydore ...68 R13
ALLPASS
st. Baringa......99 B19
ALLUNGA
ct. Mooloolaba ...80 A2
ALLURE
st. Palmview......88 P5
ALMA
wy. Noosa Heads ...9 J13
ALMADEN
la. Maroochydore ...69 C13
ALMOND
ct. Marcus Bch ...29 L3
ALOE
pl. Currimundi ...90 B20
st. Mountain Ck ...79 R13
ALPHA
dr. Glass Hse Mtn ...115 R17
ALPINE
cr. Banya......108 E7
ALPINIA
st. Sippy Downs ...88 H2
ALSTONVILLE
wy. Currimundi ...100 D2
ALTITUDE
dr. Burnside......65 N2
ALTO
la. Palmview......88 L10
ALTONA
av. Kunda Park ...67 R15
ALYXIA
st. Noosaville 8 A19
rd. Diddillibah ...67 F6
AMANDA
av. Marcoola ...59 K7
AMANI
pl. Maroochy R......47 D10
AMARINA
av. Mooloolaba ...79 P3
AMAROO
av. Nambour......55 L15
dr. Buderim......78 G2
pl. Cooroibah 2 B16
st. Maroochydore ...69 G9
AMBAKO
pl. Golden Bch ...100 C17
AMBER
ct. Caloundra W ...99 K15
dr. Caloundra W ...99 L17
pl. Palmview......88 M7
AMBERJACK
st. Mountain Ck ...79 P15
AMBERLY
cir. Little Mtn ...99 Q8
AMBERTON
ct. Buderim......79 C8
AMBULANCE
la. Cooroy......15 B4
st. Buddina......80 J12
st. Pomona......4 G11

AMEEN
cct. Mudjimba......59 G19
cct. Twin Waters ...59 G19
AMELIA
la. Nirimba......108 M4
pl. Kureelpa......54 M4
AMETHYST
la. Cooroy......15 C5
pl. Yaroomba......49 G1
st. *Mooloolaba, off Emerald Cir*......69 M19
AMIGH
rd. Landsborough ...97 B19
AMINGA
ct. Palmwoods ...76 G3
AMINYA
la. Mooloolaba ...79 R1
AMITY
av. Maroochydore ...69 D13
av. Marcoola ...49 K16
ct. Pelican Wtr......109 P8
AMY
dr. Glass Hse Mtn ...116 E10
st. Currimundi ...100 G2
st. Battery Hl ...100 J5
ANAHEIM
st. Bli Bli......58 B14
ANCHOR
st. Noosaville 8 R19
ANCHORAGE
cct. Twin Waters ...69 F2
dr. Birtinya......90 B16
ANDANTE
cr. Palmview......88 L9
ANDERSEN
rd. Diamond Vy......85 Q17
rd. Mooloolah Vy ...85 Q17
ANDERSON
rd. Glass Hse Mtn ...126 E3
st. Battery Hl ...100 G6
ANDERSONS
rd. Eerwah Vale ...14 M19
rd. Federal......13 M1
rd. Yandina......45 K11
ANDREASENS
rd. Rosemount......56 P20
ANDREW
av. Little Mtn ...99 J3
st. Pt Arkwright ...49 M2
ANDREWS
cl. Woombye......66 G17
rd. Federal......3 Q17
ANDRIANA
dr. Buderim......78 L6
ANEMBO
pl. L Macdonald ...5 G6
ANGELOU
ct. Baringa......99 B17
ANGLER
st. Noosa Heads ...9 J15
ANGLIA
pl. Little Mtn ...99 F6
ANGUS
cr. Kureelpa......54 Q6
ANIKA
pl. Little Mtn ...99 G2
ANN
st. Coolum Bch ...39 H12
st. Cooran......4 A5
st. Dicky Beach ...100 K5
st. Nambour......56 D17
st. Noosaville 8 P17
st. Woombye......66 G13
ANNA
cl. Tanawha......77 Q14
ANNABELLE
st. Pelican Wtr......109 K14
ANNALISE
cct. Nirimba......108 M2
ANNAN
la. Nirimba......108 G3
ANNE
st. Maroochydore ...69 J14
st. Kenilworth ...31 L12
ANNIE
dr. Peregian Bch ...28 M7
la. Baringa......99 C16
la. Baringa......99 D16
st. Landsborough ...96 B15
ANNIE HEHIR
st. Peregian Bch ...29 H4
ANNING
rd. Crohamhurst ...94 A9
rd. Peachester ...94 A9
rd. Wootha......94 A9

ANN-MAREE
cl. Maroochydore ...69 E8
ANNONA
ct. Palmwoods ...75 Q1
ANNWAL
la. Hunchy......75 D5
ANSELL
rd. Witta......73 R4
ANTHONY
av. Mooloolaba ...69 N19
ANTICIPATION
cl. Nambour......55 P11
ANTIGUA
ct. Parrearra......80 G16
ANTILLES
st. Parrearra......80 E15
ANTIPODES
cl. Castaways Bch ...19 P10
ANUNA
st. Wurtulla......90 F17
ANZAC
av. Beerburrum ...136 C5
av. Maroochydore ...69 F6
rd. Eudlo......86 D2
st. Battery Hl ...100 J5
APANIE
st. Battery Hl ...100 H4
APARI
st. Warana......80 J16
APEX
ct. Kuluin......68 H12
APLIN
rd. Wootha......93 M2
APOLLO
ct. Alexandra Hd ...69 L18
APPLE
cr. Caloundra W ...99 G16
APPLEBERRY
la. Tewantin......7 F11
pl. Yandina......45 Q6
APPLEBY
ct. Glenview......87 L11
APPLEGIN
ct. Mooloolaba ...79 N1
APPLE GUM
pl. Palmview......88 D11
APPLEGUM
dr. Little Mtn ...99 P9
pl. Mountain Ck ...79 M11
st. Noosaville 18 C2
APPS
rd. Maroochy R......47 E12
APRIL
ct. Maroochydore ...69 B7
AQUA
cct. Caloundra W ...99 K15
AQUAMARINE
cct. Noosaville 18 K1
AQUARIUS
pl. Alexandra Hd ...69 P17
AQUILA
st. Bli Bli......57 E7
ARAGORN
st. Maroochydore ...68 R10
st. Maroochydore ...69 A9
ARAKOON
cr. Sunshine Bch ...10 A18
ARALUEN
ct. Mountain Ck ...79 H10
ARANA
st. Maroochydore ...68 R12
ARBOUR
pl. Doonan......17 D13
ARCADIA
dr. Beerwah......106 A17
la. Witta......73 P14
st. Noosa Heads ...9 H16
ARCHER
ct. Pelican Wtr......109 Q9
rd. Belli Park......14 H17
ARCHIBALD
cr. Nirimba......108 K6
ARCHIE
st. Nambour......56 G17
ARCOONA
rd. Coolum Bch ...38 D10
rd. Yandina Ck ...38 D10
ARDISIA
st. Peregian Bch ...29 H4
ARDMORE
cl. Moffat Bch ...100 K13
ARGUS
st. Beerwah......115 R4
st. Palmview......88 L6
st. Palmview......88 P5

ARGYLE
cr. Coes Creek ...65 R6
ct. Currimundi ...100 C4
ARIA
la. Palmview......88 H6
ARIEL
ct. Buderim......68 H15
pl. Bli Bli......57 M7
ARIES
ct. Bli Bli......57 N7
ARILLA
st. Wurtulla......90 F18
ARILPA
st. Warana......90 H1
ARINYA
st. Wurtulla......90 E16
ARISTA
ct. Bli Bli......58 C16
ARKANA
dr. Noosa Heads ...9 F19
ARLINGTON
cr. Battery Hl ...100 J4
ct. Mt Coolum ...49 H8
dr. Pelican Wtr......109 P11
ARMET
ct. Little Mtn ...99 L7
ARMITAGE
ct. Noosaville 8 J14
ARMOUR
pl. Bli Bli......58 B17
ARMSTRONG
ct. Forest Glen ...77 L9
ct. Mons......77 L9
ARNLYN
ct. Cooroy......14 L5
AROONA
av. Buddina......80 H8
ARTEMIA
ct. Palmview......88 D16
ARTHUR
ct. Cooroy......14 P5
st. Caloundra ...100 E14
st. Kings Beach ...100 J15
st. Pt Arkwright ...49 M2
ARTHYS
rd. Cooran......4 A4
ARTUNGA
pl. Pelican Wtr......109 P4
ARUMA
ct. Mooloolaba ...69 R20
pl. Currimundi ...100 H2
ARUNDELL
av. Nambour......56 C19
st. Eumundi......26 A12
ARUNTA
st. Buddina......80 J12
ARWEN
st. Maroochydore ...68 R9
ASCOT
cct. Palmview......88 M4
la. Kiels Mtn ...67 G10
wy. Little Mtn ...99 D9
ASH
la. Black Mountain ...4 J18
la. Eudlo......76 C20
rd. Diddillibah ...67 P7
st. Maleny......74 D19
ASHBURTON
cr. Sippy Downs ...88 G4
ASHBY
st. Sippy Downs ...89 B2
ASHDALE
ct. Buderim......68 K14
ASHDOWN
ct. Tinbeerwah ...17 C7
ASHFORD
st. Tewantin......8 B8
ASHGROVE
dr. Cooroy......14 Q4
ASHTONS WHARF
rd. Maroochy R......47 F13
ASHVALE
st. Coolum Bch ...39 D20
ASHWOOD
ct. Marcus Bch ...29 M1
pl. Currimundi ...90 A17
ASPECT
wy. Burnside......65 N3
ASPEN
ct. Buderim......68 P15
ct. Maleny......74 F17
ASPENNELL
rd. Bollier......13 A14

CULGOA

Map Ref

CULGOA
ct. Beerwah 105 M20
rd. Eudlo 76 A17
st. Sunshine Bch 9 P19
CULLA CULLA
st. Battery Hl 100 F3
CULLEN
dr. Little Mtn 99 P3
CULLINANE
st. Tewantin 7 R12
CUMBERLAND
cr. Meridan Pl 99 K2
wy. Buderim 69 F18
CUMNER
la. Reesville 73 N18
rd. Diamond Vy 85 G10
CUNNING
rd. Tanawha 88 B1
CUNNINGHAM
av. Landsborough 96 F13
cr. Nambour 55 Q17
ct. Golden Bch 110 B7
CUPANIA
ct. Tewantin 7 H16
st. Mudjimba 59 K13
CURBARRA
st. Buddina 80 J9
CURLEW
cr. Cooroy 15 D2
ct. Maleny 74 D16
la. Buderim 79 G3
pl. Wurtulla 90 H16
st. Aroona 100 C4
wy. Peregian Spr 29 C20
wy. Peregian Spr 39 C1
CURRAJONG
rd. Kunda Park 68 A12
CURRAMORE
rd. Curramore 32 P12
rd. Curramore 73 A2
rd. Witta 73 M5
CURRAWAN
st. Warana 80 H17
CURRAWONG
cr. Peregian Bch 29 K9
dr. Maleny 94 D3
pl. Bli Bli 57 L6
st. Mudjimba 59 L12
st. Noosa Heads 9 F20
CURRIE
st. Nambour 56 D18
CURRIMUNDI
rd. Currimundi 100 H2
CURRONG
ct. Buderim 79 C7
st. Minyama 80 E9
CURRY
ct. Cooroy 14 P4
CURTIS
ct. Little Mtn 99 M9
st. Mountain Ck 79 Q13
CUTBACK
ct. Bokarina 90 H9
CUTLER
ct. Golden Bch 110 A6
CUTMORE
rd.e,Obi Obi 53 M11
rd.w,Kidaman Creek .. 53 H10
CUTTER
st. Wurtulla 90 F11
CUTTERS
wy. Bli Bli 58 B18
CYAN
st. Caloundra W 99 J17
CYCAD
pl. Flaxton 54 J16
CYCAS
st. Marcoola 49 J17
CYCLAMEN
ct. Currimundi 89 R20
CYGNET
ct. Wurtulla 90 J15
CYGNUS
pl. Bli Bli 57 F8
CYNTHIA HUNT
dr. Flaxton 54 J19
CYPRESS
cl. Tewantin 7 E15
ct. Minyama 80 E6
pl. Peregian Spr 39 D5
st. Kuluin 68 N12
st. Nirimba 108 F2

Map Ref

D

DACMAR
rd. Coolum Bch 38 M12
DAHLIA
rd. Verrierdale 27 R17
st. Bokarina 90 H7
DAINTREE
bvd. Little Mtn 99 F3
cl. Kuluin 68 L11
dr. Palmview 88 Q10
wy. Tewantin 7 G11
DAISY
pl. Bokarina 90 H8
st. Nirimba 108 G2
DAJAMAN
ct. Maroochy R 57 N1
DAKARA
ct. Buderim 68 L15
DAKOTA
dr. Marcoola 59 G9
DALBY
st. Maroochydore 69 J13
DALES
rd. Chevallum 76 M18
DALEVIEW
la. Flaxton 54 J13
la. Mapleton 54 J13
DALMOR
ct. Coolum Bch 39 G11
DALPURA
st. Buddina 80 K7
DALTON
dr. Maroochydore 69 F14
dr. Maroochydore 69 G15
DALZELL
ct. Burnside 65 M2
DAME PATTI
dr. Sunrise Bch 19 M4
DAM WALL
wk. Landsborough 97 G4
DANA
cl. Glass Hse Mtn . 116 A18
ct. Palmwoods 76 D2
DANDALOO
dr. Cootharaba 1 H6
la. Cootharaba 1 G7
DANDELION
st. Nirimba 108 G2
DANDENONG
st. Burnside 65 Q3
DANIEL
st. Caloundra W 99 Q12
st. Nambour 56 D19
DANIELLE
pl. Buderim 78 C3
DANMARK
ct. Buderim 78 R4
DANN WK
la. Palmview 88 M8
DANUBE
ct. Bli Bli 58 C10
DARBY
cl. Buderim 69 G18
DARLING
cr. Banya 108 F5
DARLINGTON
cct. Currimundi 100 A3
DARLY
st. Buderim 68 P20
DARNLEY
st. Tewantin 8 B8
DARRUNG
st. Mooloolaba 80 A6
DARTER
tce. Maroochy R 57 N3
DATH HENDERSON
rd. Cooroy Mtn 16 G6
rd. L Macdonald 6 D19
rd. Tinbeerwah 6 D19
DAUNTLESS
av. Bli Bli 57 Q7
DAVEY
dr. Woombye 66 F16
st. Bli Bli 58 B18
DAVID
st. Nambour 55 N15
st. Noosa Heads 9 E20
st. Pacific Pdse 59 C13
DAVID CASEY
pl. Corbould Park 98 P13
DAVID LOW
wy. Bli Bli 58 C19
wy. Castaways Bch .. 19 N19
wy. Coolum Bch 39 G9
wy. Diddillibah 68 C1

Map Ref

wy. Marcoola 49 H16
wy. Marcoola 59 G11
wy. Marcus Bch 19 N19
wy. Maroochydore 69 C5
wy. Mt Coolum 49 J12
wy. Mudjimba 59 B15
wy. Pacific Pdse 59 B15
wy. Peregian Bch 29 L7
wy. Peregian Bch 39 G7
wy. Pt Arkwright 49 L1
wy. Sunrise Bch 19 Q2
wy. Sunshine Bch 19 Q2
wy. Yaroomba 49 L1
DAVIDSON
st. Nambour 56 A13
DAVIES
st. Baringa 99 B17
DAVIS
rd. Cootharaba 1 E9
st. Sippy Downs 89 A3
DAVISON
rd. Ninderry 36 J14
rd. North Arm 36 J14
DAWES
dr. Buderim 79 A9
DAWN
ct. Landsborough 96 H16
la. Palmview 88 L8
DAWSON
pde. Buderim 78 P4
st. Currimundi 99 R2
DAYBREAK
ct. Castaways Bch .. 19 P13
DAYDREAM
cr. Banya 108 H6
ct. Buderim 69 F18
st. Mountain Ck 79 P12
DAYMAN
la. Pacific Pdse 59 B12
DAYMAR
rd. Obi Obi 54 C9
DAYSPRING
st. Sunrise Bch 19 P7
DAYTONA
av. Coolum Bch 39 G16
DEAL
ct. Tewantin 7 M19
DEAN
rd. Verrierdale 27 A9
DEBORAH
cl. Mudjimba 59 J12
DEBWEND
ct. Maroochydore 69 K15
DEEFA
st. Caloundra W 99 R12
DEEJAY
st. Maroochydore 69 C6
DEEPWATER
cct. Pelican Wtr 109 Q2
cl. Bli Bli 57 R7
DEFENDER
ct. Sunrise Bch 19 N6
DE JOUNGE
ct. Boreen Point, off
Coates Dr 2 A3
DELA
ct. Cooroibah 1 R20
DELATITE
st. Nirimba 108 H4
DELAWARE
dr. Sippy Downs 88 R3
DELICIA
rd. Coolabine 53 D1
rd. Mapleton 54 B7
rd. Obi Obi 53 M3
rd. Obi Obi 54 B7
DELIGHT
st. Palmview 88 M5
DELILAH
la. Nirimba 108 M3
DELISSER
pl. Pelican Wtr 109 Q8
DELLITT
rd. North Arm 36 A8
DELORAINE
dr. Buderim 79 F1
DELORME
st. Noosa Heads 9 H17
DELTA
rd. Yandina 45 L4
DENNA
st. Maroochydore 68 R5
DENNING
rd. Reesville 93 L3
rd. Wootha 93 L3

Map Ref

DEODAR
ct. Mapleton 54 J11
DEPOT
st. Maroochydore 68 N9
DEPPER
st. Sunshine Bch 9 Q19
DERBY
ct. Buderim 68 K14
rd. Moffat Bch 100 M12
DEREE
rd. Glenview 87 F8
rd. Ilkley 87 F8
DERWENT
st. Sippy Downs 88 H4
DESIREE
cl. Buderim 79 C7
DESLEY
st. Marcoola 59 K8
DESLYNN
la. Nambour 66 C1
DEVELOPMENT
ct. Caloundra W 100 C13
DE VENE
av. Kings Beach 100 N15
DE VERE
rd. Kureelpa 54 L8
rd. Pacific Pdse 59 A16
DEVILS ELBOW
la. Curramore 73 K7
DEVLIN
ct. Tewantin 7 M16
DEVON
ct. Coolum Bch 39 F12
dr. Buderim 68 L16
DEVONSTONE
dr. Cooroibah 2 A18
DEWAR
st. Pt Arkwright 49 M2
DEWRANG
pl. Wurtulla 90 C17
DE ZEN
rd. Palmview 87 R16
DHARALEE
ct. Mt Coolum 49 G11
DIAMANTINA
dr. Beerwah 115 M4
DIAMOND
cl. Yaroomba 49 G1
la. Cooroy 15 A5
st. Cooroy 15 A5
DIAMOND VALLEY
rd. Diamond Vy 85 H14
rd. Mooloolah Vy 86 A17
DIANELLA
ct. Cooroy 15 C1
dr. Mountain Ck 79 R14
rd. Beerwah 107 G13
rd. Landsborough .. 107 G13
DIANNE
av. Mudjimba 59 F12
DICKSON
rd. Chevallum 76 Q8
DICKY BEACH
cl. Dicky Beach 100 K7
DIDDILLIBAH
rd. Diddillibah 67 A9
rd. Diddillibah 67 N7
rd. Woombye 66 H11
DIEDRICHS
ct. Palmwoods 76 F7
DIERDRE
dr. Eumundi 15 P20
DILGAR
pl. Tewantin 7 L7
DILLI
ct. Alexandra Hd 69 P19
DINGLE
av. Caloundra 100 K16
av. Kings Beach 100 K16
DINMORE
st. Woombye 66 G14
DIRUM
ct. Tewantin 7 K6
DISCOVERY
cl. Glass Hse Mtn . 116 B20
ct. Birtinya 90 A8
dr. Little Mtn 99 E6
pl. Maroochydore 69 B12
DIURA
st. Maroochydore 68 P6
DIVER
pl. Aroona 100 D9
DIVINE
st. Palmview 88 K6
DIXON
av. Maleny 74 B18
ct. Mooloolah Vy 96 B1
rd. Buderim 78 R13

Map Ref

DIYAN
st. Tewantin 8 D13
DODONAEA
cl. Noosaville 18 A2
DOGWOOD
la. Palmview 88 M8
DOHERTY
st. Birtinya 90 A10
DOLLARBIRD
dr. Pomona 4 G11
pl. Glass Hse Mtn . 115 Q16
DOLPHIN
cr. Noosaville 9 B16
dr. Nambour 55 P17
pde. Little Mtn 99 Q5
DOLPHIN BAY
dr. Noosa Heads 9 R16
dr. Sunshine Bch 9 R16
DOMATIA
pl. Meridan Pl 89 N14
DOMINICA
pl. Parrearra 80 F16
DONALDSON
rd. Nambour 56 F14
DONEGAL
ct. Little Mtn 99 L11
dr. Yaroomba 49 J2
DONNA
pl. Buderim 78 R5
DON NAPIER
rd. Eumundi 26 B16
DONNELLY
pl. Caloundra W 99 G14
DONNELLYS
rd. Ridgewood 13 J12
DONNYBROOK
rd. Elimbah 136 N17
DONOVAN
ct. Tewantin 7 N20
pl. Maroochy R 47 G9
DOOLAN
ct. Noosaville 18 C6
st. Nambour 56 A17
DOOLOOMA
st. Mountain Ck 79 N11
DOONAN BRIDGE
rd. Verrierdale 28 D20
rd.n,Doonan 27 R5
rd.n,Verrierdale 28 A10
DOONAN BRIDGE EAST
rd. Doonan 28 E14
rd. Peregian Spr 28 E14
rd. Verrierdale 28 E14
DOONDOON
st. Currimundi 90 E20
DOONELLA
st. Tewantin 8 B14
DORAL
dr. Peregian Spr 38 R2
DORANS
rd. Valdora 36 Q13
DOREEN
ct. Nambour 56 C12
DORIAN
cr. Sippy Downs 78 R20
cr. Sippy Downs 79 A20
DORMIE
pl. Tewantin 7 N16
DORNOCH
wy. Peregian Spr 28 P20
wy. Peregian Spr 38 P1
DOROTHY
st. Baringa 99 D18
DORSON
dr. Mooloolah Vy 96 D1
DOTTEREL
st. Parrearra 80 F14
DOTTERELL
dr. Bli Bli 58 C13
DOUGLAS
la. Sunshine Bch 9 R20
st. Mooloolaba 70 A20
st. Nambour 56 A14
st. Sunshine Bch 9 R20
DOVE
ct. Bokarina 90 H4
la. Noosa Heads 19 E2
DOVER
ct. Buderim 68 L16
DOVETREE
ct. Marcus Bch 29 L1
DOWNUNDER
dr. Palmview 88 F13

Map Ref

DOYLE
rd. Cedarton 93 M19
rd. Reesville 93 D3
rd. Wootha 93 D3
DRACENA
ct. Currimundi 100 A1
DRAGONFLY
la. Black Mountain .. 14 H8
DRAKE
st. Golden Bch 110 C7
DRAY
pl. Palmwoods 76 F9
DREAM
ct. Nambour 55 N11
DRESS CIRCLE
ct. Buderim 68 K18
DREW
la. Mountain Ck 79 K7
DRIERS
rd. Cooran 3 M7
DRIFTWOOD
ct. Bokarina 90 J6
dr. Castaways Bch .. 19 P10
st. Peregian Spr 29 C14
DRIVER
ct. Tewantin 7 J13
st. Palmview 88 L9
DROUGHT MASTER
cr. Kureelpa 54 R6
DROVERS
ct. Pomona 4 D16
DR PAGES
rd. Cootharaba 1 D1
DUAL
av. Warana 90 E3
DUBOIS
cl. Buderim 78 D8
DUCKETT
la. Buderim 68 K19
DUDLEY
st. Nambour 55 N15
DUHS
rd. Image Flat 55 Q10
rd. Nambour 55 Q10
rd. Nambour 56 E12
DUKE
rd. Doonan 16 N17
st. Sunshine Bch 9 Q19
st. Tewantin 7 Q7
DULARCHA
dr. Landsborough 96 J12
DULCET
wy. Palmview 88 K9
DULIN
st. Maroochydore 69 D11
DULKARA
pl. Mountain Ck 79 R11
DULONG
rd. Dulong 54 N12
rd. Dulong 54 R9
rd. Kureelpa 54 R9
rd. W Woombye 54 N13
DULONG SCHOOL
rd. Dulong 54 L11
DUMBARTON
dr. Caloundra W 99 K13
DUN
st. Tewantin 7 Q19
DUNBAR
ct. Buderim 68 N17
ct. Cooroy 14 P5
DUNBRODY
st. Caloundra W 99 J14
DUNCANS
la. Noosa N Shore 8 C2
DUNDOWRAN
la. Maroochydore 69 A15
DUNE
cl. Twin Waters 69 D2
DUNES
ct. Peregian Spr 28 N14
DUNETHIN ROCK
rd. Maroochy R 47 J16
DUNE VISTA
dr. Bokarina 90 H7
DUNGANNON
ct. Buderim 68 B16
DUNK
pl. Little Mtn 99 N8
DUNKELD
ct. Forest Glen 67 F14
DUNLOP
cr. Baringa 99 B18
la. Birtinya 90 A12
wy. Maleny 74 E20

Map Ref

DUNNART
ct. Burnside 65 P2
pl. Mt Coolum 49 E6
DUNNE
rd. Glenview 87 Q16
rd. Palmview 87 Q16
DUNNING
st. Palmwoods 76 A6
DUNNOTTAR
ct. Glass Hse Mtn 125 P1
DUNSTAN
ct. Noosaville 8 G19
DUNWICH
la. Maroochydore, off Amity Av 69 D14
DUPORTH
av. Maroochydore 69 F6
av. Maroochydore 69 H8
DURHAM
cr. Buderim 68 L16
DURRACK
pl. Buderim 78 R10
DURUNDUR
la. Peachester 94 L18
st. Pelican Wtr 109 P7
DUSK
pl. Yandina 45 P7
DWYER
st. Sunshine Bch 9 Q19
DWYERS
la. Peachester 94 J19
DYER
st. Landsborough 96 G18
DYNES
rd. Valdora 47 J5

E

EACHAM
st. Little Mtn 99 M3
EAGLE
ct. Wurtulla 90 G15
dr. Tewantin 8 D9
pl. Buderim 79 G6
EAGLE FARM
cl. Doonan 16 Q18
EAGLEFORD
ct. Peregian Spr 28 Q17
EAGLEHAWK
la. Pomona 4 C7
EAGLES
cl. Baringa 99 F20
la. Woombye 66 K17
EAGLES NEST
ct. Bald Knob 95 A4
EAGLE VIEW
dr. Caloundra W 99 Q10
la. Mooloolah Vy 86 E11
EAGLEVIEW
ct. Woombye 66 F10
EARL
cl. Landsborough 106 D3
st. Tewantin 8 E17
EARLS
ct. Buderim 79 C7
ct. Little Mtn 99 E9
EARLYBIRD
dr. Buderim 78 Q6
EARNEST
la. Sippy Downs 78 R20
EARNSHAW
st. Golden Bch 110 C1
EAST COOLABINE
rd. Coolabine 53 H5
EASTER
st. Parrearra 80 C15
EASTERN
ct. Mt Coolum 49 G11
ri. Little Mtn 99 E6
EASTERN MARY RIVER
rd. Cambroon 32 C2
rd. Cambroon 32 C3
rd. Conondale 32 F17
EASTON
st. Maroochydore 69 J14
EAST VIEW
ct. Bli Bli 57 L3
ct. Maroochy R 57 L3
EATON
rd. Elimbah 135 D9
st. Diamond Vy 85 D14
st. Sippy Downs 88 Q3
EBONY
ct. Buderim 78 K11
ct. Maleny 74 F17

Map Ref

ECCLES
bvd. Birtinya 90 B12
ECHELON
esp. Noosa N Shore 9 A5
ECHIDNA
ct. Landsborough 96 E14
la. L Macdonald 6 B20
pl. Doonan 17 J19
ECHO
ct. Buderim 79 G2
st. Pelican Wtr 110 A3
ECHUCA
ct. Warana 80 J15
ECKERSLEY
av. Buderim 78 R3
av. Buderim 79 A2
EDEN
dr. Baringa 99 E19
st. Minyama 80 D10
EDENVALE
ct. Buderim 68 P15
EDGAR BENNETT
av. Noosa Heads 9 H14
EDGEWATER
pl. Sippy Downs 88 M1
EDINBOROUGH
ct. Golden Bch 110 C4
EDINGTON
dr. Cooroibah 2 A17
EDISON
cr. Baringa 98 Q15
EDITH
la. Beerwah 115 G1
pl. Coolum Bch 39 D18
st. Caloundra 100 J14
EDLUNDH
ct. Pelican Wtr 109 H13
EDMORE
ct. Peregian Spr 38 Q2
EDMUND
st. Kings Beach 100 M15
st. Moffat Bch 100 N13
st. Shelly Bch 100 N13
EDNA
st. Currimundi 90 H20
EDRIDGE
st. Shelly Bch 100 N14
EDWARD
pl. Kenilworth 31 L11
st. Alexandra Hd 70 A19
st. Cooran 3 Q5
st. Noosaville 8 P17
st. Pt Arkwright 49 M1
EDWARDS
st. Sunshine Bch 9 N19
tce. Baringa 99 E18
EDWARDSON
dr. Pelican Wtr 109 P7
EDWIN
dr. Landsborough 106 D4
rd. Buderim 78 A7
rd. Mons 78 A7
EENIE CREEK
rd. Noosa Heads 19 B2
rd. Noosa Heads 19 K2
rd. Noosaville 18 G2
rd. Sunshine Bch 9 L20
EEWAH
ct. Pomona 4 M9
EGRET
av. Twin Waters 59 H20
av. Woombye 66 F9
av. Woombye 66 F9
ct. Caloundra 100 H13
pl. Bli Bli 57 L5
st. Peregian Bch 29 L9
EINSLEIGH
ct. Beerwah 115 N5
EIPPER
st. Pelican Wtr 109 N8
EKALA
st. Mountain Ck 79 H10
EKERT
rd. Conondale 32 Q14
rd. Conondale 73 A5
rd. Curramore 32 Q14
rd. Curramore 73 A4
ELAINE
cl. Kureelpa 54 M4
ELAMAN CREEK
rd. Elaman Creek 73 E11
ELANDA
ct. Kuluin 68 M13
st. Sunshine Bch 9 Q19

Map Ref

ELANDA POINT
rd. Boreen Point 1 Q1
ELANDRA
tce. Pomona 4 M9
ELANORA
av. Mooloolaba 80 B6
tce. Noosa Heads 9 G20
ELATION
st. Palmview 88 J6
ELDER
st. Nambour 56 C16
ELDERBERRY
ct. Twin Waters 59 B18
ELECTRA
la. Marcoola 59 G9
ELEVATE
pl. Burnside 65 N2
ELHORN
la. Palmview 88 N7
ELI
la. Maroochydore 69 B14
la. Nirimba 108 L6
ELICE
st. Nirimba 108 K3
ELIMBAH
st. Pelican Wtr 109 K8
ELINYA
st. Battery Hl 100 H3
ELISABETH VALLEY
pl. Ilkley 77 F18
ELIZA
wy. Maroochydore 69 D10
ELIZABETH
st. Buderim 78 K2
st. Coolum Bch 39 G14
st. Cooran 4 A5
st. Dicky Beach 100 L8
st. Eumundi 25 Q9
st. Kenilworth 31 L12
st. Nambour 66 C2
st. Noosaville 8 P16
wy. Nambour 56 A13
ELIZABETH DANIELS
wy. Buderim 69 K20
ELIZABETH FARM
ct. Maroochydore 68 Q12
ELIZAMAY
cl. Buderim 79 A7
ELK
rd. Cooloolabin 45 B8
ELKE
cl. Buderim 69 B19
ELKHORN
dr. Tewantin 8 D9
st. Kuluin 68 K13
ELLA-MARIE
dr. Coolum Bch 49 D1
ELLEM
ct. Kiels Mtn 67 M7
ELLENDALE
st. Maroochydore 69 B10
ELLESMERE
av. Bli Bli 58 B11
ELLINGTON
st. Sippy Downs 89 B3
ELLIOT
dr. Buderim 78 Q10
ELLIS
pl. Mountain Ck 79 P16
wy. Meridan Pl 99 M2
ELLORA
ct. Rosemount 66 M3
ELLY
cct. Coolum Bch 39 C20
ELM
ct. Yandina 46 C11
rd. Black Mountain 4 K18
rd. Cooroy 4 N18
rd. Pomona 4 K18
st. Cooroy 15 A5
st. Moffat Bch 100 L13
ELOISE
la. Nirimba 108 K1
ELONERA
st. Currimundi 100 F2
ELOUERA
cl. Landsborough 96 C18
dr. Ninderry 36 N16
ELROND
ct. Coolum Bch 39 F20
ELSA
ct. Peachester 94 L13
ELSA WILSON
dr. Buderim 79 K3

Map Ref

ELSTON
ct. Sippy Downs 88 L1
ELVENA
cct. Little Mtn 99 K3
ELY
st. Noosaville 8 H19
ELYSIUM
dr. Noosa Heads 19 C2
EMERALD
bvd. Mooloolaba 69 L19
cir. Mooloolaba 69 M19
ct. Mapleton 54 H9
la. Cooroy, off Maple La 14 R3
st. Caloundra W 99 G17
st. Cooroy 14 R3
st. Palmview 88 Q9
EMERALD VISTA
pde. Yandina 45 N6
EMERSON
st. Baringa 99 D18
EMMA
ct. Golden Bch 110 A4
pl. Beerwah 115 Q2
EMMA PARREN
dr. Nambour 56 J17
EMPEROR
av. Maroochydore 69 B11
EMPIRE
cr. Chevallum 77 F8
EMPORIO
pl. Maroochydore 69 E11
EMU
ct. Nambour 55 K16
st. Mountain Ck 79 Q12
wk. Mapleton 54 G9
EMU MOUNTAIN
rd. Doonan 17 P16
rd. Peregian Bch 28 J10
rd. Peregian Spr 28 J10
rd. Peregian Spr 29 A14
rd. Weyba Downs 18 B17
rd. Weyba Downs 28 B1
EMU MOUNTAIN
rd. Coolum Bch 29 E20
ENCHELMAIERS
rd. Pomona 4 A15
ENDEAVOUR
cr. Pelican Wtr 109 M9
dr. Kunda Park 67 R16
rd. Beerburrum 136 E6
rd. Elimbah 136 E6
ENDEAVOUR BARK
dr. Glass Hse Mtn 116 E19
ENDOTA
st. Buderim 68 P20
ENDURANCE
pl. Birtinya 90 E10
ENERGY
la. Birtinya 90 D10
ENFIELD
cr. Battery Hl 100 F6
ENGLE
rd. Reesville 73 F20
ENGLISH
rd. Kiamba 34 M16
ENSBEY
rd. Bald Knob 85 A18
rd. Bald Knob 95 A1
rd. Flaxton 54 G13
rd. Mapleton 54 E12
ENTERPRISE
st. Caloundra W 100 A12
st. Kunda Park 67 Q16
st. Noosa Heads 9 R17
st. Sunshine Bch 9 R17
ENTRANCE ISLAND
Birtinya 90 F10
ENTWOOD
av. Coolum Bch 39 E20
EPIC
la. Bokarina 90 J10
la. Bokarina 90 K10
ERANG
st. Currimundi 100 D1
ERBACHER
rd. Burnside 66 A3
rd. Nambour 66 C3
ERIC
ct. Mooloolah Vy 96 D1
st. Nambour 56 F13
ERICA
st. Currimundi 100 F1
ERLEA
st. Maroochydore 69 D11

Map Ref

ERNEST
st. Kings Beach 100 Q15
st. Tewantin 8 F16
ERNST
rd. Bli Bli 58 L11
ESCAPE
ct. Buderim 67 R19
ESCOLAR
dr. Mountain Ck 79 J12
ESMAUREL
cl. Mapleton 54 E12
ESPERANCE
dr. Twin Waters 69 C1
la. Nirimba 108 F4
ESPIN
rd. Bli Bli 58 G3
ESPLANADE
Beerwah 115 C1
Boreen Point 2 A4
Golden Bch 110 A13
Golden Bch 110 D2
Golden Bch 110 D7
Noosa N Shore 2 Q3
ESPLANADE BULCOCK BEACH
Caloundra 100 H17
ESPLANADE HEADLAND
Kings Beach 100 N16
ESPRIT
cr. Birtinya 90 D12
ESSEX
ct. Buderim 68 M16
ESTHER
pl. Nambour 56 J17
ESTUARY
ct. Twin Waters 59 F20
ETEP
ct. Nambour 55 L17
ETHERIDGE
st. Eumundi 25 R11
EUCALYPT
la. Palmview 88 L11
wy. Cootharaba 1 H5
EUCALYPTUS
cr. Ninderry 46 R1
pl. Little Mtn 99 E14
wy. Perwillowen 65 L3
EUDLO
ct. Kuluin 68 H11
rd. Eudlo 76 C19
rd. Mooloolah Vy 86 F14
rd. Palmwoods 76 E12
st. Landsborough 106 G1
EUDLO FLATS
rd. Diddillibah 67 M12
rd. Forest Glen 67 L13
EUDLO SCHOOL
rd. Eudlo 75 Q17
EUGARIE
st. Noosa Heads 9 J16
EUGENIA
rd. Forest Glen 77 K3
EULAMA
st. Ringtail Creek 1 N10
EULINGA
ct. Ninderry 36 L19
EUMARELLA
rd. Doonan 18 C16
rd. Weyba Downs 18 C16
EUMERALLA
cr. Landsborough 96 B17
EUMUNDI-KENILWORTH
rd. Belli Park 34 B3
rd. Eerwah Vale 14 L16
rd. Eerwah Vale 25 A7
rd. Gheerulla 33 A16
rd. Kenilworth 31 M11
rd. Kenilworth 33 A16
EUMUNDI-NOOSA
rd. Doonan 27 A7
rd. Eumundi 25 R15
rd. Noosaville 8 H20
rd. Noosaville 17 P11
rd. Verrierdale 26 J10
rd. Verrierdale 27 A7
EUMUNDI RANGE
rd. Eumundi 26 B9
EUNGELLA
dr. Black Mountain 14 F4
wy. Buderim 78 H11
EURUNGUNDER
la. Coolum Bch 39 J20
EVA
ct. Nambour 56 J17
st. Moffat Bch 100 H10

Map Ref

EVALMA
dr. Buderim 78 N5
EVAN
la. Parklands 56 H7
EVANS
rd. Beerburrum 126 B15
rd. Black Mountain 14 H9
rd. Black Mountain 14 K5
rd. Cooroy 14 H9
rd. Cooroy 14 K5
rd. Glass Hse Mtn 126 B15
st. Maroochydore 69 E10
EVANS GROVE
rd. Glenview 87 A16
EVAN THOMAS
rd. Federal 3 P19
EVE
la. Landers Shoot 75 F16
EVERGLADES
la. Palmview 88 M9
EVERGREEN
av. Palmwoods 76 A9
dr. Glenview 87 P18
wy. Beerwah 115 F3
EVERSLEIGH
ct. Nambour 55 Q14
EVERTON
pl. Rosemount 57 Q20
EWINGA
ct. Mountain Ck 80 A11
EXBURY
st. Minyama 80 E11
EXETER
wy. Caloundra W 99 R11
EXFORD
ct. Cooroibah 1 R17
EXHIBITION
st. Nambour 56 H15
st. Pomona 4 F10
EXPECTATION
la. Nambour 55 P12
EXPLORER
st. Sippy Downs 78 Q20
EYRE
pl. Caloundra W 99 G11
EYRIE
tce. Coolum Bch 39 K19
EYRIES
ct. Little Mtn 99 P8

F

FACTORY
st. Pomona 4 F11
FAIRFAX
st. Sippy Downs 78 N16
FAIRHILL
rd. Ninderry 36 F17
rd. North Arm 36 G12
FAIRLIE
cr. Moffat Bch 100 K12
FAIRMEADOW
rd. Nambour 56 H16
FAIRVIEW
cl. Bli Bli 57 R11
ct. Maleny 74 E15
ct. Mooloolah Vy 86 B20
FAIRWAY
cl. Mt Coolum 49 D12
dr. Maroochydore 69 H11
dr. Tewantin 7 N16
pde. Peregian Spr 28 Q20
pde. Peregian Spr 38 R1
FAIRY WREN
ct. Beerwah 116 A3
FAIRY WREN REST STOP
Landsborough 96 Q3
FAITH
ct. Meridan Pl 99 J2
FALCON
cr. Cooroy 5 D20
ct. Mapleton 54 J11
la. Peregian Spr 39 A5
FALKLAND
ct. Buderim 78 F5
FALLS CREEK
rd. Cooran 4 A2
rd. Obi Obi 53 P13
FANTAIL
cr. Cooroy 15 E2
pl. Twin Waters 59 C19
pl. Wurtulla 90 H14
sq. Peregian Spr 38 Q4
FARLEY
st. Baringa 99 F19

FARLOW

Map Ref

FARLOW
la. Caloundra 100 G16
st. Currimundi 100 G1
FARMER
rd. Baringa 98 R20
FARNE
ct. Tewantin 7 J15
FARNWYN
ct. Buderim 68 K20
FARON
la. Buderim 78 N4
FARRELL
st. Yandina 46 C8
FAUNA
tce. Coolum Bch 39 J18
FAVOUR
la. Palmview 88 K5
FEATHER
ct. Birtinya 90 D13
FEATHERTAIL
ct. Tewantin 7 F11
dr. Peregian Spr 39 B4
st. Bli Bli 57 Q7
FEATHERTOP
cr. Caloundra W 99 F12
FEATHERWOOD
cr. Beerwah 105 R17
FEELEY
st. Buderim 78 H2
FELDER
st. Palmview 88 H5
FELICIA
ct. Mountain Ck 79 L9
FELICITY
wy. Palmview 88 L5
FELLOWSHIP
dr. Doonan 17 P17
FELSTED
ct. Tewantin 7 M17
FENNER
st. Birtinya 90 A11
FERGUSON
av. Buderim 68 L20
rd. Pomona 4 B10
st. Sunshine Bch 9 Q20
FERN
cl. Little Mtn 99 Q4
ct. Buderim 79 F4
st. Nirimba 108 G2
FERN GULLY
pl. Mooloolah Vy 86 A19
FERNHAVEN
ct. Peregian Spr 29 B19
FERNHILL
pl. Diddillibah 67 K6
FERNLEA
st. Burnside 55 L20
FERNLEAF
ct. Currimundi 90 B19
FERNLEIGH
cr. Mountain Ck 79 L9
FERN TREE
rd. Glass Hse Mtn . 115 P15
FERNTREE
ct. Kuluin 68 M13
ct. Noosaville 18 D2
FERNTREE CREEK
rd. Image Flat 56 B6
rd. Kulangoor 46 D20
rd. Kulangoor 56 D3
FERNY
cl. Palmview 88 B12
cl. Peregian Bch 29 H3
FERNY GLEN
rd. Mons 77 M11
rd. Mons 77 Q9
FERRELLS
rd. Cooroy 14 Q9
rd. Cooroy 15 A10
FERRIS
la. Cedarton 93 R19
la. Commissioners Fl...93 R19
la. Peachester 93 R19
st. Sunshine Bch 9 Q18
FESTIVAL
st. Bells Creek 108 N7
FEWTRELL
st. Palmwoods 76 C4
FICUS
dr. Palmview 88 H8
FIDDLE LEAF
la. Nirimba 108 F2
FIELDING
st. Buderim 78 K1
FIETZ
la. Glass Hse Mtn . 125 L2
FIFTH
av. Marcoola 59 K10
av. Maroochydore 69 M11
FIG
ct. Buderim 78 M5
st. Maleny 74 E18
FIGBIRD
cr. Buderim 78 L13
ct. L Macdonald 5 R9
FIG TREE
dr. Beerwah 115 K1
la. L Macdonald 15 M2
la. Yandina Ck 37 B6
FIGTREE
ct. Mountain Ck 79 M10
la. Maroochydore 69 A14
FIGUREHEAD
ct. Noosaville 8 J20
FIJI
ct. Parrearra 80 C11
FINCH
ct. Bokarina 90 H6
st. Buderim 79 J2
tce. Peregian Spr 39 A3
FINGERLIME
la. Palmview 88 M9
FINLAND
rd. Bli Bli 58 P15
rd. Marcoola 59 A9
rd. Pacific Pdse 58 P15
FINLEY
rd. Eumundi 25 R6
FINNEGAN
pl. Pelican Wtr 109 Q8
st. Palmview 88 N6
FINNEY
ct. Tewantin 7 Q20
FIONA
st. Nirimba 108 L3
FIR
ct. Kulangoor 46 B20
FIREFLY
st. Pelican Wtr 109 M8
FIRESONG
ct. Nambour 55 K16
FIRESTONE
ct. Buderim 79 G7
FIRETAIL
ct. Tanawha 78 C17
ct. Wurtulla 90 K16
pl. Glenview 87 M17
FIREWHEEL
ct. Mountain Ck 79 N9
rd. Ringtail Creek 4 P4
FIRST
av. Caloundra 100 E16
av. Coolum Bch 39 H12
av. Marcoola 59 J11
av. Maroochydore 69 H12
av. Maroochydore 69 J10
av. Mooloolaba 80 C1
la. Mooloolaba 80 C1
FIRTH
ct. Landsborough .. 106 D4
FISHER
rd. Peachester 94 B11
FISHERMANS
rd. Kuluin 68 K10
rd. Maroochydore 68 K10
FITTELL
ct. Tewantin 7 P20
FITZGERALD
st. Sippy Downs 89 A3
FITZROY
ct. Pacific Pdse 59 B12
ct. Parrearra 80 C15
la. Meridan Pl 99 L2
FITZWILLIAM
dr. Sippy Downs 88 P2
dr. Sippy Downs 89 A2
FLAGSHIP
ct. Castaways Bch .. 19 N9
FLAME
st. Maleny 74 E15
FLAME TREE
av. Sippy Downs 89 B4
ct. Palmwoods 75 R9
dr. Tewantin 7 R10
FLAMETREE
pl. Currimundi 90 B16
FLAMINGO
st. Little Mtn 99 G10
FLAXTON
dr. Flaxton 54 K15
dr. Hunchy 54 K18
dr. Mapleton 54 H9
dr. Montville 54 K18
FLAXTON MILL
rd. Flaxton 54 F17
FLEETWOOD
rd. Belli Park 14 J18
st. Sippy Downs 89 B4
FLEMING
st. Yandina 46 C9
FLESSER
rd. Reesville 73 L19
FLINDERS
av. Beerwah 106 A19
av. Nambour 55 P18
la. Maroochydore 69 E13
st. Currimundi 100 J1
FLINDERSIA
dr. Traveston 3 H5
pl. Mountain Ck 79 M16
st. Marcoola 49 K17
FLINT
ct. Buderim 79 B7
FLINTWOOD
cr. Palmview 88 J6
cr. Palmview 88 J7
FLITCROFT
pl. Pelican Wtr 109 K15
FLOODED GUM
ct. Bli Bli 57 Q9
pl. Black Mountain 4 L20
pl. Black Mountain .. 14 K1
FLORENCE
st. Nambour 56 B16
FLORES
st. Parrearra 80 C15
FLOREY
bvd.Birtinya 90 B11
FLOURISH
wy. Palmview 88 L6
FLOWERS
rd. Maroochy R 46 R16
FOAMBARK
pl. Black Mountain 4 J20
FOCAL
av. Coolum Bch 38 M11
FOCUS
la. Yandina 46 G6
FOEDERA
cr. Tewantin 7 M18
FOLEY
rd. Beerwah 106 D18
rd. Woombye 66 G9
FOLEYS
rd. Ilkley 77 J16
FONTAINE
ct. Tewantin 7 F15
FOOTE
av. Buderim 79 B2
rdg.Buderim 79 B2
st. Mooloolaba 80 C3
FORD
rd. Landsborough 96 J3
rd. Mooloolah Vy 96 J3
FORESHORE
ct. Dicky Beach 100 J7
pl. Maroochydore 68 P6
FOREST
ct. Aroona 100 C6
ct. Forest Glen 77 F3
ct. Tewantin 7 D15
ct. Yandina 46 P7
dr. Buderim 69 E19
dr. Tewantin 7 C7
la. Landsborough 95 N17
la. Mt Mellum 95 N17
rd. Palmview 89 A9
FOREST ACRES
dr. L Macdonald 1 C20
dr. L Macdonald 5 F1
dr. Ringtail Creek 1 C20
FORESTDALE
rd. Landsborough .. 106 H1
FOREST GROVE
cr. Sippy Downs 88 J3
FOREST HILL
dr. Maroochy R 57 J2
FOREST OAK
cl. Cooroy 15 A1
ct. Tanawha 78 F16
FOREST PARK
st. Meridan Pl 89 N15
FOREST PINES
bvd.Forest Glen 67 L19
FOREST RIDGE
av. Palmview 88 C13
cct. Peregian Spr 29 A19
dr. Doonan 26 P4
FOREST RISE
ct. Buderim 68 H16
FORESTRY
rd. Beerwah 107 G13
rd. Landsborough 96 M17
FOREST SOUND
pl. Palmwoods 76 F10
FOREST VIEW
ct. Forest Glen 77 K5
FORESTWOOD
dr. Buderim 69 C19
FORREST VIEW
wy. Little Mtn 99 J6
FORSAYTH
la. Maroochydore 69 B13
FORSTER
pl. Pelican Wtr 109 L15
FORSYTH
pl. Mooloolah Vy 86 M16
FORT
pl. Golden Bch 110 B8
st. Buderim 78 L2
FORTE
la. Palmview 88 K10
FORTIER
st. Pelican Wtr 109 L12
FORTITUDE
pl. Birtinya 90 C11
FORTUNE
av. Peachester 94 L16
ct. Nambour 66 K1
la. Palmview 88 M5
FOSSILWOOD
ct. Buderim 78 J9
FOUNTAIN
rd. Buderim 79 B1
FOURTH
av. Caloundra 100 D16
av. Marcoola 59 K10
av. Maroochydore 69 M11
FOURWINDS
av. Coolum Bch 39 E14
FOXTAIL
cct. Mountain Ck 80 A13
la. Nirimba 108 L7
ri. Doonan 17 G9
FRANCIS
ct. Pelican Wtr 109 K13
rd. Bli Bli 57 G8
rd. Peachester 94 N12
FRANGIPANI
cr. Nirimba 108 F2
pl. Mountain Ck 79 N12
st. Peregian Spr 29 D15
FRANGIPANNI
ct. Montville 74 Q6
FRANK
st. Coolum Bch 39 H15
FRANKLAND
av. Meridan Pl 99 K1
FRANKLIN
pl. Sippy Downs 78 M20
FRANKS
la. Mooloolah Vy 86 K19
FRANTI
st. Sippy Downs 89 C2
FRASCO
ct. Mt Coolum 49 G8
FRASER
av. Maroochydore 69 B16
ct. Little Mtn 99 N9
rd. Beerwah 106 D10
rd. Beerwah 106 H11
rd. Landsborough .. 106 K10
FRAWLEY
pl. Palmwoods 75 R7
FRAZER
la. Birtinya 90 A11
FRED CHAPLIN
cct. Corbould Park 98 L13
FREDERICK
st. Nirimba 108 L5
FREE
st. Beerwah 106 D20
FREEDOM
pl. Sunrise Bch 19 P1
FREEMAN
ct. Tewantin 7 P20
ct. Witta 73 M6
FREESIA
cl. Currimundi 89 R20
FREMANTLE
pl. Kuluin 68 M11
FRENCH
ct. Golden Bch 110 A6
FRESHWATER
ct. Glenview 87 R17
st. Mountain Ck 79 Q15
FREYCINET
row.Buderim 78 H11
FRIARBIRD
pl. Pomona 4 G11
pl. Twin Waters 59 C19
FRIENDSHIP
av. Marcoola 59 F7
av. Marcoola 59 G9
FRIZZO
rd. Glass Hse Mtn . 126 C5
FRIZZO CONNECTION
rd. Glenview 98 C2
rd. Palmview 88 E1
rd. Palmview 88 F20
rd. Tanawha 78 F19
rd. Tanawha 88 E1
FRODO
ct. Coolum Bch 39 E20
ct. Coolum Bch 49 E1
FROGMOUTH
cct. Mountain Ck 79 K15
la. L Macdonald 15 H5
FROST
la. Baringa 99 D16
FRYAR
ct. Landsborough 96 A16
FRYAY
cr. Yandina 45 Q9
FRYING PAN
tr. Noosa N Shore 8 R11
FUERTE
ct. Bli Bli 58 B14
FULLAGER
dr. Eumundi 25 P10
FULLER
ct. Noosaville 8 H19
st. Baringa 99 C20
FULLERTONS
rd. Glass Hse Mtn . 115 G20
FULLVIEW
cr. Buderim 68 K19
FULMAR
ct. Aroona 100 C9
FURL
st. Noosaville 18 R4
FURLONG
dr. Moffat Bch 100 L13
FURNESS
dr. Tewantin 7 L18
FUTURE
wy. Maroochydore 69 J12
FYNE
ct. Tewantin 7 J15

G

GABA
la. Maroochydore 69 J12
GABBIE
cr. Nirimba 108 J3
GADEN
rd. Montville 74 M4
GAINSBOROUGH
cr. Peregian Spr 28 Q13
GAIRDNER
st. Caloundra W 99 G13
GALAH
pl. Mountain Ck 79 R16
GALGATE
st. Sunrise Bch 19 Q3
GALLAGHERS
rd. Tanawha 77 J11
GALLEON
st. Tewantin 7 R11
GALLERY
dr. Bli Bli 57 E4
pl. Little Mtn 99 N7
GALLEY
st. Wurtulla 90 E13
GALLOWAYS
la. Cootharaba 1 H1
GALLOWS
pl. Palmwoods 75 P7
GALWAY
st. Caloundra W 99 J14
GAM
av. Currimundi 90 E19
GAMBAN
esp.Currimundi 90 F19
GANNAWARRA
st. Currimundi 90 E20
GANNET
cl. Wurtulla 90 J16
st. Peregian Bch 29 J11
GANTRY
rd. Landsborough 96 H18
GAP
rd. Bellthorpe 92 N16
rd. Booroobin 93 A14
GARCIA
ct. Peregian Spr 28 N20
GARDAK
st. Maroochydore 69 M14
GARDEN
av. Palmwoods 76 F3
ct. Buderim 68 P16
pl. Nambour 55 P14
GARDENIA
pl. Forest Glen 77 J1
st. Currimundi 90 A20
GARDENS
sq. Currimundi 100 D2
GARDENVALE
dr. Coes Creek 66 A7
GARDNER
st. Glass Hse Mtn . 116 B19
GARDNERS
la. North Maleny 74 H17
rd. Federal 4 A17
GARDS
rd. Ringtail Creek 1 E17
GAREMA
ct. Mountain Ck 79 H8
GARNET
st. Cooroy 14 Q3
st. Mountain Ck 79 N13
GARRAD
rd. Woombye 66 P19
GARRADS
rd. Glass Hse Mtn . 116 G15
GATEWAY
av. Landsborough 96 K17
dr. Diddillibah 67 N9
dr. Noosaville 18 E2
GATTERA
rd. Landsborough 96 A13
GAYANDI
st. Wurtulla 90 E18
GAYLARD
rd. Image Flat 55 D7
GAYOME
st. Pacific Pdse 59 D13
GAZA
ct. Aroona 100 E5
GAZANIA
st. Palmview 88 K11
GECKO
ct. Bli Bli 57 R8
GEEBUNG
ct. Meridan Pl 89 P14
la. Doonan 17 G11
GEEHI
ct. Buderim 79 E7
GEERIBAUCH
la. Yaroomba 49 M4
GEES
rd. Eerwah Vale 25 F20
GEM
la. Nambour 56 G15
st. Cooroy 14 R1
st. Cooroy 15 A1
GEMELLE
ct. Witta 73 M4
GEMSON
cr. Moffat Bch 100 K12
GENOA
cct. Birtinya 90 C12
ct. Noosaville 18 N2
GEOFF FLYNN
ri. Noosa Heads 9 K14
GEOFFREY
st. Caloundra W 99 R12
GEO HAWKINS
cr. Corbould Park 98 M8
GEORDY
cl. Beerwah 105 P19
GEORGE
st. Alexandra Hd 69 R19
st. Caloundra 100 J13
st. Cooran 3 Q5
st. Kenilworth 31 L12
st. Maroochydore 69 J11

Map Ref

st. Moffat Bch........100 K12
st. Nambour............56 F14
st. Noosaville...........8 P17
st. Tewantin...............7 Q9
st. Tewantin..............8 C10
st. Yandina.............46 A8
GEORGE WYER SCENIC
dr. Mapleton............53 R14
dr. Obi Obi..............53 R14
GEORGINA
pl. Beerwah..........115 N4
GERAGHTY
la. Wootha...............93 H5
GERAGHTY CREEK
rd. Conondale.........92 P6
GERBRA
pl. Bokarina............90 H6
GERRARD
rd. Eudlo.................85 A2
GERRYBELL
st. Golden Bch......110 B9
GERRYGONE
pl. Pomona...............4 G11
GEVERS
rd. Black Mountain..13 P7
GHARA
ct. Coolum Bch.......39 E20
GHEERULLA
rd. Gheerulla...........33 C17
GHOST GUM
av. Kuluin................68 J12
GHOSTGUM
cl. Little Mtn...........99 E14
ct. Tewantin...............7 Q11
GIBB
la. Banya..............108 F5
GIBBINS
wy. Chevallum.........77 G8
GIBBS
ct. Diddillibah..........67 E4
la. Palmview...........88 N6
GIBSON
av. Maleny..............94 B2
rd. Noosaville............8 J17
st. Buderim.............78 L2
st. Maroochydore....69 F7
st. Tewantin...............7 Q8
GIDGEE
ct. Caloundra W......99 Q8
ct. Doonan..............27 K7
GILBERT
st. Buderim.............78 P2
st. Maroochydore....69 F8
GILGHI
ct. Warana..............80 H14
GILLESPIE
st. Sippy Downs......89 A4
GILLIES
cl. Caloundra W......99 H12
GILLILAND
rd. Carters Ridge.....13 H12
GILLINGHAM
pl. Pelican Wtr.......109 N6
GILSONS
rd. Cootharaba..........1 K10
GIMBAL
ct. Wurtulla.............90 E12
GINGER
st. Caloundra W......99 L15
GINGER BELL
av. Bli Bli.................57 M9
GIPANNI
pl. Diddillibah..........67 F6
GIPPS
st. Caloundra W......99 F15
GIPPSLAND
pl. Caloundra W......99 F13
GIRRAWEEN
cr. Banya..............108 C8
ct. Sunshine Bch.......9 M20
dr. Image Flat..........56 K10
dr. Nambour.............56 K10
st. Warana..............80 H20
GIRUA
st. Bli Bli.................58 D14
GLADSTONE
pde.Moffat Bch........100 L11
GLASSHOUSE
dr. Little Mtn...........99 M12
pde.Maleny...............94 M2
GLASSHOUSE VIEW
ct. Buderim.............78 Q4
GLASS HOUSE-WOODFORD
rd. Beerburrum......125 A10
rd. Glass Hse Mtn.125 A10

Map Ref

GLASSWING
av. Palmview...........88 E11
GLASSY
la. Bokarina.............90 L10
GLEE
st. Birtinya..............90 D11
GLEN
ct. Marcoola............59 K7
rd. Mons..................77 Q10
GLEN ABBY
av. Peregian Spr......28 P14
GLENALPIN
ct. Buderim.............68 Q17
GLENBAR
av. Flaxton..............54 K18
GLENBRAE
ct. Buderim.............68 P16
GLENBROOK
dr. Nambour.............55 N13
GLENCON
ct. Buderim.............68 B17
GLENEAGLE
ct. Buderim.............78 K9
GLENEAGLES
dr. Tewantin...............7 M16
GLEN EDEN
ct. Flaxton..............54 L17
GLENELG
st. Nirimba............108 G3
GLENFERN
rd. W Woombye.......65 C18
GLENFIELDS
bvd.Mountain Ck.......79 G12
bvd.Mountain Ck.......79 M10
GLENFINNAN
ct. Forest Glen........67 E17
GLENHAVEN
ct. Palmview...........88 A16
GLENKEITH
pl. Eudlo.................85 J2
GLEN KYLE
dr. Buderim.............69 H19
GLENLEA
dr. Maroochydore....69 C7
GLENMORE
cl. Caloundra W, off McDyer St..........99 J14
GLENMOUNT
rd. Buderim.............78 B8
rd. Mons..................78 A11
rd. Tanawha.............78 B15
GLENNIE
cl. Caloundra W......99 H12
GLENN VISTA
pl. Chevallum..........77 F13
GLENOAK
av. Peregian Spr......29 A20
GLENRAY
av. Caloundra.........100 J13
GLENRIDGE
dr. Cooroibah............1 N19
GLENROWAN
cl. Kulangoor...........45 Q18
GLENS
rd.n,Balmoral Ridge..74 N19
GLENSIDE
cl. Burnside............55 M20
GLENTREE
st. Bokarina.............90 H8
GLENVIEW
cl. Buderim.............78 R6
rd. Glenview............86 Q16
rd. Glenview............87 L19
rd. Mooloolah Vy.....86 Q16
rd. Palmview...........88 B17
GLENWOOD
pl. Twin Waters.......59 C17
GLENYS
st. Burnside.............65 Q2
GLIDER
pl. Glass Hse Mtn.115 R16
GLORIA
cl. Glass Hse Mtn.115 R18
st. Maroochydore....69 J13
GLOUCESTER
rd. Buderim.............78 K3
GLOVER
ct. Montville.............74 N7
pl. Pelican Wtr.......109 P11
rd. Palmview...........89 B10
GOANNA
la. Palmview...........88 K8
GOBBERTS
rd. Yandina.............45 Q13

Map Ref

GODFREYS
av. Bli Bli.................68 N3
rd. Bli Bli.................58 P18
rd. Bli Bli.................68 Q3
rd. Pacific Pdse.......58 P18
rd. Pacific Pdse.......68 Q3
GODILLA
st. Coolum Bch.......39 H20
GODWIN
pl. Pelican Wtr.......109 Q6
GODWIT
pl. Peregian Spr......39 D1
GOLD
st. Aroona.............100 E7
GOLDBURG
ct. Noosaville..........17 R9
GOLD CREEK
rd. Eerwah Vale.......25 A18
rd. North Arm...........35 E1
GOLDCREST
ct. Sunrise Bch........19 M7
GOLDEN
cr. Palmview...........88 L5
st. Caloundra W......99 L16
GOLDENBELL
pl. Peregian Spr......28 R14
GOLDEN PINE
wy. Palmwoods........76 F10
GOLDEN RAIN
la. Eumundi.............25 M17
GOLDEN VALLEY
pl. Valdora..............37 D20
pl. Valdora..............47 C1
GOLDFINCH
cl. Peregian Spr......39 C4
ct. Wurtulla.............90 J13
GOLDSMITH
pl. Buderim.............69 F19
GOLF
st. Buderim.............68 M20
st. Maroochydore....69 J11
GOLF COURSE
dr. Tewantin...............7 K16
GOLF LINKS
rd. Buderim.............79 H3
rd. Mountain Ck.......79 H3
GOODCHAP
st. Noosaville...........8 F17
st. Tewantin...............8 F17
GOODEY
wy. Kureelpa............54 N6
GOODLA
rd. Sandy Creek......92 A16
GOODWILL
st. Birtinya..............90 C11
GOODWIN
st. Tewantin...............7 R14
st. Tewantin...............8 A10
GOODWOOD
ct. Buderim.............68 H18
GOOLOI
ct. Tewantin...............7 P17
GOOLOOWAN
cl. Kiels Mtn............67 C13
GOOLWA
st. Coolum Bch.......49 E1
GOOMBURRA
pl. Buderim.............78 J10
GOONAWARRA
dr. Mooloolaba........79 Q3
GOONGILLA
st. Yaroomba...........49 L5
GORDON
dr. Tanawha.............78 B12
pl. Glass Hse Mtn.115 R18
GOSFORD
ct. Buderim.............79 A2
GOSHAWK
bvd.Buderim.............78 L14
la. Ringtail Creek......1 N12
st. Glass Hse Mtn.115 Q16
GOSLING
st. Caloundra........100 F15
GOSSAMER
ct. Marcus Bch........19 M20
dr. Buderim.............79 E5
GOTHIC
pde.Currimundi..........90 G20
pde.Currimundi..........90 K20
GOULBURN
cr. Nirimba............108 H3
GOULD
dr. Glass Hse Mtn.115 E17
GOULDIAN
ct. Peregian Bch.....29 K7

Map Ref

GOURAMI
ct. Mountain Ck.......79 J11
GOWEN
dr. Landsborough..106 D4
GOWENS
rd. Peachester.........94 J20
GRACE
ct. Pelican Wtr.......109 Q6
ct. Yaroomba...........49 J1
GRACEMERE
bvd.Peregian Spr......29 A18
GRADOREAN
st. Pelican Wtr.......109 N9
GRADUATE
la. Sippy Downs......78 N16
GRADY
st. Twin Waters.......59 E14
GRAF
rd. Baringa...............98 Q19
GRAHAM
dr. Landsborough..106 E5
GRAHAMS
rd. Pinbarren.............4 G6
rd. Pomona................4 G6
GRAMMAR SCHOOL
wy. Forest Glen........77 G5
GRAMPION
dr. Caloundra W......99 F15
GRAND
pde.Parrearra...........80 B11
pde.Parrearra...........80 E15
pde.Parrearra...........80 E17
GRANDSTAND
dr. Nambour............56 H14
GRANDVIEW
dr. Coolum Bch.......39 H18
dr. Coolum Bch.......49 H1
dr. Yaroomba...........49 H1
dr. Yaroomba...........49 H2
la. Coolum Bch.......39 H18
rd. Balmoral Ridge..74 L20
GRANDVILLE
ct. Buderim.............79 C9
GRANGE
pl. Peregian Spr......29 B18
rd. L Macdonald.........5 R19
rd. Tinbeerwah...........5 R19
GRANITE
ct. Noosaville..........18 M2
la. Curramore..........32 Q14
st. Banya..............108 E6
GRANT
st. Battery Hl.........100 G5
st. Buderim.............69 B20
st. Noosa Heads.......9 G14
GRANVILLE
gdn.Moffat Bch........100 J12
GRASS GULLY
cr. Little Mtn...........99 J6
GRASS TREE
la. Palmview...........88 E10
GRASSTREE
ct. Pelican Wtr.......109 L10
ct. Sunrise Bch........19 M2
rd. Eumundi.............25 K2
GRASSY
st. Banya..............108 D6
GRAYS
rd. Doonan.............17 M19
rd. Doonan.............27 R4
GRAZIER
wy. Palmview...........88 L12
GREAT KEPPEL
cr. Mountain Ck.......79 P12
wy. Banya..............108 E6
GREBE
cr. Bli Bli.................57 K5
st. Aroona.............100 D10
st. Peregian Bch.....29 K13
GREBER
rd. Beerwah...........105 R17
GREEN
pl. Currimundi.......100 D1
GREENACRE
rd. Verrierdale.........26 M7
GREEN ACRES
la. Pomona................4 E7
GREENACRES
ct. Glenview...........97 C2
GREENFIELDS
ct. Maleny..............74 D20
la. Cootharaba..........1 L6
GREEN GATE
rd. Cooroibah............1 Q19

Map Ref

GREENHAVEN
cl. Burnside............66 A3
dr. Palmview...........88 G16
GREENHILLS
esp.Maleny...............74 F18
pl. Coolum Bch.......39 G19
GREENLEAF
ct. Buderim.............68 R15
GREENLEES
ct. Palmwoods........76 A6
GREENLINE
cct. Highworth..........55 N13
cct. Nambour............55 N13
GREENMOUNT
dr. Palmview...........88 G7
GREENOAKS
dr. Coolum Bch.......39 D18
GREENOCK
pl. Kiels Mtn...........67 D13
GREENRIDGE PINBARREN
rd. Cooran................3 K3
GREENRIDGE-PINBARREN
rd. Pinbarren.............4 B5
GREENSBORO
pl. Little Mtn...........99 Q4
GREENSHANK
st. Pelican Wtr.......109 P14
st. Peregian Bch.....29 K18
GREENSIDE
ct. Peregian Spr......29 A18
GREENS VISTA
pl. Yaroomba...........49 E2
GREEN TREE
pl. Doonan..............17 B14
GREENVALE
ct. Buderim.............68 Q16
ct. Little Mtn...........99 E5
GREENVIEW
av. Beerwah...........106 B19
cl. Coolum Bch.......39 F10
tce. Palmview...........88 M7
GREENWAY
ct. Baringa...............99 G19
ct. Tewantin...............7 K15
pl. Mountain Ck.......79 M10
GREENWOOD
cl. Buderim.............78 J9
pl. Little Mtn...........99 G5
GREER
la. Eumundi.............26 B9
GREGG
rd. Cooroy...............15 F13
GREG GREG
ct. Buderim.............79 E7
GREGORY
ct. Nambour............55 P17
rd. Traveston.............3 G3
st. Golden Bch......100 C20
GREGSON
pl. Caloundra........100 C15
GRENADA
wy. Parrearra...........80 F16
GRENFELL
ct. Kuluin...............68 N10
GRENVILLE
st. Pelican Wtr.......109 N10
GRETEL
ct. Sunrise Bch........19 P4
GREVILLEA
cl. Buderim.............78 N2
la. L Macdonald.........5 H20
st. Palmview...........88 L11
GREVILLIA
ct. Moffat Bch........100 L12
GREY
la. Nirimba............108 J2
GREY GUM
dr. Little Mtn...........99 P9
GREYGUM
ct. L Macdonald.........1 C19
ct. Mooloolaba........79 Q1
pl. Currimundi..........90 A17
GRIDLEY
st. Eumundi.............26 A12
GRIEG
st. Maroochydore....69 A11
GRIFFIN
cr. Caloundra W......99 G15
pl. Coes Creek........66 A5
GRIFFITH
av. Tewantin...............7 F16
la. Buderim.............79 C1
pl. Baringa...............99 C17

Map Ref

GRIGO
rd. Peachester.........94 M19
GRIGOR
rd. Conondale..........32 A19
st. Moffat Bch........100 L11
st.w,Moffat Bch........100 H10
GRIMES
tce. Burnside............55 K20
GROSVENOR
tce. Noosa Heads.......9 F16
GROVE
bvd.Mooloolah Vy......96 B2
ct. Yandina..............46 D11
GRUNDON
rd. Conondale..........73 A12
GUILFOYLE
cr. Mooloolah Vy.....86 R15
GULAI
st. Buddina..............80 K3
GULL
cl. Nambour............55 P16
pl. Parrearra...........80 G14
GUM BLOSSOM
ct. Sippy Downs......88 H2
GUMBOIL
rd. L Macdonald.........5 R17
rd. L Macdonald.........5 R8
rd. Tinbeerwah...........5 R17
rd. Tinbeerwah...........5 R8
GUMDALE
ct. Noosaville..........18 D4
GUMLAND
dr. Witta..................73 P9
GUMLEAF
cl. Doonan..............26 N5
GUMNUT
ct. Buderim.............69 B18
ct. Tewantin...............8 A9
st. Currimundi.......100 B1
GUM TREE
pl. Perwillowen........65 L3
GUMTREE
dr. Buderim.............79 C3
dr. L Macdonald.......15 G3
GUMTREE POCKET
ct. Little Mtn...........99 G4
GUMVIEW
pl. Little Mtn...........99 L4
GUNNAROO
la. Montville.............74 K3
GURNERS
dr. Tanawha.............78 B16
GUY
av. Buderim.............78 D7
GUYMER
ct. Caloundra W......99 F11
GWANDALAN
rd. L Macdonald.........5 K3
GWEN
ct. Landsborough..106 H3
GWENDA
av. Mt Coolum.........49 G6
GWENETH
rd. Peregian Bch.....28 Q6
GWYNORE
ct. Buderim.............79 B3
GYMEA
ct. Mountain Ck.......79 K8
GYMPIE
st. Tewantin...............7 Q10
st. Tewantin...............8 A11
st.n,Landsborough....96 E17
st.s,Landsborough....96 C20
tce. Noosaville...........8 K17
GYNDIER
dr. Tewantin...............6 P19
dr. Tinbeerwah...........6 P19
GYPSY
cl. Mt Coolum..........49 C9

H

HAAS
st. Bli Bli.................58 C14
HABITAT
pl. Noosa Heads.....19 C2
HADDYS
cl. Mountain Ck.......79 J7
HAFLINGER
rd. North Arm...........36 G8
HAGEN
pl. Bli Bli.................58 D14
HAIG
st. Golden Bch......110 C7

Map Ref

HAKEA
av. Maleny 74 C18
ct. Mountain Ck 79 M10
ct. Tewantin 7 K16
la. Palmview 88 L11
wy. Peregian Spr 28 Q20
HALCYON
pl. Coolum Bch 39 G20
wy. Bli Bli 57 N4
HALEY
st. Palmview 88 L8
HALIAD
dr. Mt Coolum 49 K10
HALIFAX
ct. Woombye 66 E7
HALL
ct. Burnside 65 P3
ct. Tewantin 7 P17
HALLEY
ct. Coolum Bch 39 E19
HALLMARK
ct. Buderim 78 Q7
HALSE
la. Noosa Heads 9 J12
HALYARD
dr. Wurtulla 90 G13
HAMERSLEY
ct. Yandina Ck 37 R10
la. L Macdonald 5 Q13
HAMIA
ct. Bli Bli 58 C11
HAMILTON
cl. Mooloolah Vy 86 M18
rd. L Macdonald 5 G7
rd. W Woombye 65 J16
st. Buderim 78 R3
st. Meridan Pl 99 M2
HAMLIN
cl. Woombye 66 G16
HAMPTON
cl. Baringa 99 F20
ct. Peregian Spr 29 A15
HANCOCK
st. Mooloolaba 80 D2
wy. Baringa 98 P17
HANKINSON
st. Golden Bch 110 B10
HANLON
st. Buderim 78 G2
HANNAH
cr. Baringa 99 C19
HANS
st. Caloundra W 100 A9
HANS BOYSEN
dr. Mudjimba 59 H12
HANSON
st. Bli Bli 56 P12
HANWELL
ct. Little Mtn 99 H5
HAPGOOD
rd. Landsborough 97 H20
HAPPY
la. Birtinya 90 E10
wy. Palmview 88 M5
HAPPY JACK CREEK
rd. Carters Ridge 13 F11
rd. Ridgewood 13 G9
HAPPY VALLEY
rd. L Macdonald 5 F2
HARBOUR
pde. Buddina 80 J5
HARBOUR HEIGHTS
la. Kuluin 68 M10
HARBOURLIGHTS
wy. Pelican Wtr 109 R10
HARCH
rd. Witta 74 A5
HARDINGS
rd. Hunchy 75 H5
HARDWOOD
ct. Buderim 79 D4
rd. Beerwah 106 J1
rd. Landsborough 96 G20
rd. Landsborough 106 J1
rd. Landsborough 106 M7
HARDY
st. Sunrise Bch 19 N2
HARGREAVES
st. Currimundi 90 J20
HARKER
ct. Little Mtn 99 P5
HARLEQUIN
rd. Palmview 88 L6
HARLEY
st. Glass Hse Mtn 116 E10

Map Ref

HARLOW
cr. Tewantin 7 E15
HARMONY
bvd. Palmview 88 M7
bvd. Palmview 88 P7
ct. Cooroibah 6 Q6
gln. Buderim 68 N17
HAROLD
pl. Peachester 94 M15
HARPER CREEK
rd. Conondale 73 A18
HARPERS
la. Pelican Wtr 109 P11
HARRIER
cr. Peregian Spr 39 C3
st. Aroona 100 B4
HARRIS
ct. Tewantin 7 Q19
dr. Palmwoods 76 F8
rd. Diamond Vy 85 D13
HARRISON
la. Baringa 99 D16
HARRY
pl. Beerwah 106 A17
st. Nirimba 108 L5
HARRYS
la. Buderim 68 G17
HART
cr. Bells Creek 108 P3
HARTLEY
cr. Pelican Wtr 109 L12
HARTWICKS
rd. Kiels Mtn 67 K7
HARVARD
ct. Sippy Downs 78 J19
HARVEST
dr. Palmview 88 K11
rd. Yandina 46 E6
st. Beerwah 116 G4
HARVEY
ct. Nambour 56 D12
la. Meridan Pl 89 M20
HASKINS
st. Baringa 99 B18
HASLEWOOD
cr. Meridan Pl 99 M2
HASSALL
la. Reesville 73 K15
HASTING
pl. Buderim 79 A8
HASTINGS
bvd. Noosa Heads 9 C18
cl. Battery Hl 100 H4
st. Noosa Heads 9 G11
HATCH
rd. Cootharaba 1 H3
HATFIELD
rd. Eumundi 25 P15
HATTEN
st. Mooloolah Vy 86 E19
HAUPTS
rd. Woombye 66 P11
HAVANA
rd.e, Coolum Bch 39 G2
rd.w, Peregian Spr 39 C3
HAVEN
ct. Mooloolah Vy 86 B20
pl. Yandina 45 N6
HAVENSIDE
ct. Pomona 4 F15
HAWK
la. Pomona 4 C7
rd. Pomona 4 C7
HAWKESBURY
ct. Bli Bli 58 C10
HAWLEY
ct. Sunrise Bch 19 M7
HAWTHORN
ct. Buderim 79 C10
gr. Marcus Bch 29 K1
HAY
st. Tewantin 8 C11
HAYDEN
st. Tewantin 7 R8
HAYMAN
ct. Buderim 69 F18
la. Meridan Pl 99 L2
st. Parrearra 80 D15
HAYWARD
rd. L Macdonald 5 M18
HAZEL
pl. Glenview 87 C17
HAZELDYNE
ct. Pelican Wtr 109 H13

Map Ref

HAZELTINE
ct. Maroochydore 69 H14
HAZELWOOD
ct. Noosaville 18 D6
HEADLAND
dr. Birtinya 90 C14
dr. Noosaville 8 J19
HEADLANDS
ct. Moffat Bch 100 M12
HEADWATERS
ct. Yandina 45 P6
HEATH
ct. Little Mtn 99 N10
la. Kureelpa 54 N6
rd. Stanmore 93 J19
HEATHERDALE
ct. Little Mtn 99 J5
HEATHFIELD
rd. Coolum Bch 39 G14
HEATHGLEN
ct. Little Mtn 99 L12
HEATHLAND
dr. Sunrise Bch 9 N20
dr. Sunrise Bch 19 N1
dr. Sunshine Bch 19 N1
HEATHWREN
st. Forest Glen 67 K19
HECTOR
st. Boreen Point 2 A3
HEDGE
rd. Glass Hse Mtn 125 R2
HEGARTY
cct. Bli Bli 58 C19
HEGGYS
ct. Buderim 79 E6
HEIDI
st. Kuluin 68 H12
HEIGHTS
rd. Beerwah 105 R19
HEILIG
ct. Glass Hse Mtn 126 F1
HELEN
st. Caloundra W 99 Q12
HELICONIA
st. Mountain Ck 79 R14
HELM
cr. Wurtulla 90 F13
ct. Noosaville 18 L1
HEM
la. Nirimba 108 J3
HEMDAN
ct. Nambour 56 A13
HEMPSALL
rd. Cootharaba 1 D1
HEMPSTOCK
st. Glass Hse Mtn 116 D16
HENDERSON
st. Buderim 78 F3
st. Sunshine Bch 19 R1
HENDRY
st. Tewantin 8 B12
HENEBERY
pl. Caloundra W 99 R14
rd. Burnside 55 F18
rd.n, Burnside 55 G15
HENNING
cr. Meridan Pl 89 M20
ct. Buderim 79 F1
ct. Mountain Ck 79 Q12
HENRI MARI
ct. Buderim 79 D9
HENRY
ct. Glass Hse Mtn 115 P17
st. Cooran 3 P4
st. Nirimba 108 M5
HENSLEY
la. Cooran, off Casey St 3 Q6
HENZELL
st. Dicky Beach 100 K8
HERACLES
ct. Buderim 79 G1
HEREFORD
dr. Kureelpa 54 R6
st. Sippy Downs 89 C4
HEREWARD
st. Pelican Wtr 109 N7
HERITAGE
dr. Glass Hse Mtn 126 E3
dr. Noosaville 8 G19
pl. Mons 77 N8
tce. Nambour 56 G14
wy. Burnside 65 K1

Map Ref

HERMITAGE
ct. Buderim 79 A10
HERMOSA
st. Mountain Ck 79 M5
HERON
ct. Tewantin 8 D9
dr. Aroona 100 C9
rd. Peregian Spr 28 N20
rd. Peregian Spr 38 N1
rd. Verrierdale 38 N1
st. Peregian Bch 29 K13
HERRON
av. Twin Waters 59 H20
HERVEY
ch. Maroochydore 69 B16
HESLOP
pl. Burnside 55 M20
HESPER
dr. Doonan 17 H9
HESSEN
pl. Ringtail Creek 4 R3
HETHERINGTON
dr. Twin Waters 59 E17
HEWITT
st. Coolum Bch 39 G12
HIBBERTIA
st. Mountain Ck 79 Q16
HIBISCUS
av. Beerburrum 136 C5
av. Mooloolaba 69 P20
av. Noosa Heads 9 H14
st. Beerwah 106 A20
st. Parklands 56 J8
HICKORY
ct. Beerwah 115 Q2
ct. Buderim 69 C19
pl. Tewantin 7 M19
HIDDEN
la. Palmview 88 C10
pl. Maroochydore 69 B14
HIDDEN VALLEY
rd. North Arm 36 G8
HIDDEN VALLEY
rd. Eumundi 36 G8
HIDEAWAY
ct. Yandina Ck 37 D10
la. Glenview 87 P19
la. Tinbeerwah 17 A11
pl. Mons 77 Q9
st. Birtinya 90 B15
HIGH
st. Peachester 94 M17
st. Sippy Downs 78 K17
HIGHCLARE
ct. Little Mtn 99 H7
HIGHFIELD
ri. Pomona 4 F15
st. Buderim 68 R17
HIGHGATE
pl. Maroochydore 69 A11
HIGHGROVE
cct. Peregian Spr 29 A19
HIGHLAND
dr. L Macdonald 5 G8
pl. Buderim 78 E7
tce. Little Mtn 99 K7
HIGHLANDS
rd. Eudlo 85 F4
HIGHLANDS HILL
rd. Maroochy R 57 G1
HIGH PARK
cr. Little Mtn 99 L5
HIGHTON
ct. Buderim 68 L20
HIGHVIEW
av. Nambour 55 L16
HILARY
cr. Woombye 66 K18
rd. Carters Ridge 13 G9
HILL
rd. Bli Bli 58 E4
st. Currimundi 100 G2
st. Nambour 56 E20
st. Palmwoods 76 C5
st. Pomona 4 F11
st. Sunshine Bch 19 Q1
st. Woombye 66 F12
HILLCREST
av. Nambour 55 M17
av. Tewantin 8 F18
ct. Beerwah 115 D2
rd. Kiamba 34 P15
HILLFOOT
la. Montville 74 N7

Map Ref

HILLGROVE
ct. Bli Bli 57 R14
HILLIARDS
la. Maroochydore 69 D14
HILLSBOROUGH
cct. Mountain Ck 79 N13
HILLSIDE
ct. Little Mtn 99 N7
ct. Sunrise Bch 19 M7
la. Bald Knob 94 R3
rd. Glass Hse Mtn 125 N4
wy. Highworth 55 K14
HILLSTON
st. Buderim 68 J19
HILLSVIEW
pl. Maroochy R 46 R9
HILLTOP
cr. Coolum Bch 49 D1
cr. Maleny 74 B19
cr. Maroochydore 68 Q11
ct. L Macdonald 5 P6
dr. Burnside 55 H18
HILLVIEW
cr. Little Mtn 99 K4
dr. Buderim 78 P6
la. Cooroy 15 H15
la. Pomona 4 F17
HILTON
esp. Tewantin 8 F16
tce. Noosaville 8 E15
tce. Tewantin 8 E15
HIMSTEDTS
rd. Kenilworth 31 F19
HINCHINBROOK
ct. Little Mtn 99 M9
HINKABOOMA
la. Gheerulla 33 E13
HINKLER
pde. Maroochydore 69 K11
HINLEY
av. Maroochydore 69 F7
HINTERLAND
cl. Tinbeerwah 16 Q10
dr. Little Mtn 99 M6
st. Palmwoods 76 H1
HISTED
tce. Bli Bli 58 A18
HI-TECH
dr. Kunda Park 67 Q16
HIXSON
wk. Pelican Wtr 109 P11
HOBBS
rd. Buderim 68 B14
rd. Kunda Park 68 B14
HOBSON
st. Palmwoods 76 D3
HOCKING
st. Nambour 56 F19
HODGENS
rd. Bald Knob 94 L9
rd. Crohamhurst 94 L9
rd. Peachester 94 L9
st. Caloundra 100 K14
HOFFMANN
cl. Montville 74 M2
HOFMANN
dr. Noosaville 18 G4
HOLBROOK
ct. Yaroomba 49 J2
HOLLAND
st. Landsborough 96 B16
wy. Mons 77 R3
HOLLETT
rd. Doonan 17 R9
rd. Noosaville 17 R9
HOLLINDALE
tr. Noosa Heads 9 K14
HOLLIS
rd. Pomona 4 D14
HOLLOWAY
st. Mountain Ck 79 R15
HOLLOWS
la. Birtinya 90 A12
HOLLY GREEN
cr. Palmwoods 76 E3
HOLLYHOCK
cr. Noosa Heads 19 B3
HOLMES
st. Currimundi 99 R2
HOLT
rd. Beerwah 116 M5
st. Currimundi 100 K1
HOLTS
rd. Cooroy 15 B12

Map Ref

HOLYN
cl. Woombye 66 D7
HOMEPORT
tr. Noosa N Shore 8 G12
HOMESTEAD
ct. Yandina 46 A9
dr. Little Mtn 99 F5
dr. Tewantin 7 F11
la. Tewantin 7 E11
pl. Woombye 66 D7
HONEY
st. Caloundra W 99 L16
HONEYBEE
ct. Burnside 65 R2
pl. Palmwoods 76 F9
HONEYDEW
pl. Ninderry 36 L16
HONEYEATER
av. Noosaville 18 C1
cl. Buderim 79 H3
cr. Peregian Spr 39 A2
la. Maleny 94 D3
pl. Bli Bli 57 L6
HONEY FARM
rd. Meridan Pl 98 P3
HONEY GEM
pl. Cooroibah 1 Q20
pl. Cooroibah 6 N1
HONEY MYRTLE
cl. Peregian Spr 38 R3
cl. Peregian Spr 39 A3
pl. Woombye 66 E17
rd. Noosa Heads 19 B3
HONEYMYRTLE
ct. Mountain Ck 79 L13
HONEYSUCKLE
ct. Buderim 78 J16
dr. Bokarina 90 H7
dr. Montville 74 Q5
la. Maleny 74 C19
la. Noosa Heads 9 K17
pl. Yandina 45 Q5
HONEYTREE
la. Ridgewood 14 B7
HONEYWELL
ct. Tewantin 7 G15
HONEYWOOD
ct. Currimundi 90 A19
HOOK
la. Banya 108 F6
HOOP
ct. Maroochydore 68 R11
HOOPER
cr. Tewantin 7 R16
ct. Landsborough 96 B16
la. Baringa 99 C18
rd. North Maleny 74 J12
HOOPERS
rd. Kunda Park 68 C12
HOOP PINE
ct. Buderim 79 E4
rd. Cooroy 15 B18
rd. Eerwah Vale 15 B18
HOPE
ct. Meridan Pl 99 K2
HOPPER
st. Maleny 74 E19
HORIZON
wy. Woombye 66 F16
HORIZONS
dr. Coolum Bch 39 H19
HORSESHOE
bnd. Buderim 68 J16
HORTON
pde. Maroochydore 69 H10
HOSPITAL
la. Cooroy 14 R3
rd. Nambour 56 B16
st. Pomona 4 E12
HOTSPUR
cr. Little Mtn 99 M8
HOUGHTONS
rd. Landers Shoot 75 D19
HOUSTON BRIDGE
Coolabine 31 Q13
HOVARD
rd. Bald Knob 94 R2
rd. Bald Knob 95 E6
HOVEA
cl. Buderim 78 N2
pl. Tewantin 7 Q8
rd. Carters Ridge 13 D9
st. Aroona 100 D7

Map Ref

KARALISE
ct. Buddina 80 H14
KARANNE
dr. Mooloolah Vy 86 E18
KARAWATHA
dr. Buderim 79 B11
dr. Mountain Ck 79 K6
st. Buderim 79 C7
KARDINIA
st. Minyama 80 D9
KAREELA
av. Noosa Heads 9 L11
KAREN
pl. Nambour 55 L16
KARIBU
st. Buderim 78 J15
KARINGAL
ct. Mt Coolum 49 G7
KARINYA
pl. Twin Waters 69 C1
KARKAWARRI
ct. Buddina 80 K4
KARLEE
ct. Coolum Bch 39 F19
KARLOO
ct. Mountain Ck 79 R11
KARNU
dr. Ninderry 36 P18
dr. Valdora 36 P18
KAROBEAN
pl. Wurtulla 90 E15
KAROME
st. Pacific Pdse 59 B13
KARRI
ct. Mapleton 54 F10
ct. Mountain Ck 79 L12
KARUMBA
pl. Beerwah 115 L2
pl. Maroochydore 69 C13
st. Warana 80 J18
KARUNDA
st. Wurtulla 90 F18
KATE
cr. Nirimba 108 M2
ct. Beerwah 115 C3
st. Alexandra Hd 69 Q18
KATEENA
st. Pomona 4 M7
KATHARINA
st. Noosa Heads 9 G14
KATHERINE
st. Beerwah 106 C18
st. Maroochydore 69 E8
KATHLEEN
dr. Bli Bli 58 B15
KATIE
cl. Coolum Bch 39 E18
KATOA
st. Alexandra Hd 69 P15
st. Buddina 80 J9
KAURI
cr. Peregian Spr 39 B5
dr. Montville 74 P6
la. Cooroy 15 B6
pl. Currimundi 90 B20
st. Cooroy 15 B4
st. Cooroy 15 B6
KAWANA
st. Alexandra Hd 69 N18
wy. Birtinya 90 C8
wy. Currimundi 89 R14
wy. Meridan Pl 89 R14
wy. Mountain Ck 79 J16
wy. Parrearra 80 B16
wy. Sippy Downs 79 J16
wy. Warana 90 D3
KAWANA ISLAND
bvd.Parrearra 80 F19
bvd.Warana 80 F19
KAWANNA
st. Mudjimba 59 L11
KAY
av. Bli Bli 58 C18
KAYLEIGH
dr. Buderim 69 G17
KEARNS
ct. Nambour 56 C13
KEEL
ct. Noosaville 8 N18
ct. Wurtulla 90 F13
KEELSON
st. Birtinya 90 D12
KEIL
st. Woombye 66 F13

Map Ref

KEIR
rd. Bellthorpe 92 L19
KEITH
ct. Marcoola 59 J9
KEITH ROYAL
dr. Marcoola 59 J7
KELKS HILL
rd. Nambour 66 F4
KELLEHERS
rd. Pomona 3 R12
KELLO
rd. Beerwah 116 D5
KELLY
ct. Buderim 69 G17
ct. L Macdonald 5 F2
ct. Landsborough 96 L17
KELMAN
st. Palmview 88 K9
KELS
la. Reesville 73 E18
KEMBLA
ct. Chevallum 77 F6
KENELAND
av. Little Mtn 99 E8
KENEWIN
av. Maroochydore 69 E8
KENILWORTH BROOLOO
rd. Brooloo 31 H1
rd. Kenilworth 31 L7
KENILWORTH SKYRING CREEK
rd. Carters Ridge 13 E10
rd. Ridgewood 13 E10
rd. Tuchekoi 3 A16
rd. Tuchekoi 13 A1
KENMAN
rd. Traveston 3 A2
KENNEDY
pde.Golden Bch 100 D19
rd. Bli Bli 58 C15
rd. Conondale 92 M6
KENNEDYS
rd. Cooroy 4 Q18
rd. L Macdonald 5 A9
rd. Pomona 4 Q18
rd. Pomona 4 R13
rd. Pomona 5 A7
KENNY
ct. Landsborough 96 F15
KENSINGTON
dr. Cooroy 5 B19
dr. Minyama 80 E11
st. Palmwoods 75 R8
KENT
ct. Buderim 78 L1
KENTIA
st. Highworth 55 J14
KENTISH
rd. Kiels Mtn 67 B11
KENTUCKY
ct. Little Mtn 99 F8
KEPPEL
la. Buderim 79 F2
KEPPLE
st. Meridan Pl 99 L1
KEPPLEGROVE
dr. Sippy Downs 88 H4
KERADA
rd. Nambour 66 J1
rd. Rosemount 66 J1
KERENJON
av. Buderim 68 J15
KERLIN
la. Woombye 66 M16
KERRI
pl. Sunshine Bch 19 M4
KERRS
la. Coes Creek 65 Q7
KERRYL
st. Kunda Park 68 D12
KESSLER
st. Baringa 99 D19
KESSLING
av. Kunda Park 68 A16
KESTEVEN
st. Palmview 88 M9
st. Pelican Wtr 109 N7
KESTRAL
ct. Buderim 78 D6
KESTREL
cr. Peregian Bch 29 L6
st. Aroona 100 D9
KESWICK
pl. Buderim 69 G19
st. Meridan Pl 89 L20

Map Ref

KETCH
pl. Noosaville 8 Q18
st. Wurtulla 90 E13
KEVDON
st. Golden Bch 110 B10
KEVLAR
ct. Sunrise Bch 19 N3
KEW
pl. Minyama 80 F11
KEY
ct. Noosa Heads 9 E13
KEY WEST
av. Coolum Bch 39 G16
KHANCOBAN
dr. Buderim 79 D8
KIAH
ct. Cooran 3 R4
KIAMA
st. Battery Hl 100 G3
st. Coes Creek 65 Q6
KIAMBA
ct. Sunshine Bch 10 A16
rd. Cooloolabin 45 A11
rd. Kiamba 34 Q20
rd. Kiamba 45 A11
rd. Kiamba 54 Q1
KIANGA
st. Pelican Wtr 109 P11
KIARA
rd. Eerwah Vale 25 A18
KIATA
ct. Mt Coolum 49 E13
ct. Noosa Heads 9 G19
KIDAMAN CREEK
rd. Curramore 53 J20
rd. Kidaman Creek 53 C12
rd. Obi Obi 53 J20
KIDD
rd. Pomona 4 M10
KIEL MOUNTAIN
rd. Diddillibah 67 B10
rd. Kiels Mtn 67 B10
rd. Woombye 66 L15
KIKUYU
rd. Chevallum 77 F9
st. Bli Bli 57 P9
KILBRIDE
ct. Caloundra W 99 J15
KILCOY
la. Conondale 92 H4
KILCOY-BEERWAH
rd. Beerwah 105 Q20
rd. Beerwah 116 B1
rd. Cedarton 93 P20
KILDEYS
rd. Cootharaba 1 H1
KILKIE
av. Bli Bli 57 N7
KILLARA
av. Coolum Bch 39 F12
KILLARNEY
cr. Nambour 66 C4
KILLAWARRA
rd. L Macdonald 5 M4
KILLEEN
cl. Buderim 79 C8
KILLICK
st. Kunda Park 68 B14
KILNER
dr. Valdora 47 J3
KIM
cl. Mt Coolum 49 F7
KIMBAH
ct. Cooroibah 6 N7
KIMBARRA
ct. Buderim 79 C6
KIMBERLEY
ct. Doonan 17 H9
ct. Eumundi 15 P19
KIMBERLY
ct. Buderim 68 L20
KINDAL
ct. Palmwoods 75 P9
KING
rd. Mooloolah Vy 95 Q4
st. Buderim 78 L3
st. Cooran 3 P4
st. Kings Beach 100 N14
st. Maroochydore 69 M10
st. Shelly Bch 100 N14
st. Traveston 3 F1
KING CREEK
rd. Eerwah Vale 14 R20
KINGFISH
ct. Mountain Ck 79 K12

Map Ref

KINGFISHER
av. Caloundra W, off Kookaburra Dr 99 Q10
cr. Palmview 88 C9
ct. Kuluin 68 L13
dr. Bli Bli 57 K6
dr. Peregian Bch 29 L12
rdg.Kureelpa 54 L5
st. Aroona 100 D9
KINGFISHER LOOKOUT
Landsborough 96 P5
KING ORCHID
dr. Little Mtn 99 H4
KING PARROT
av. Glass Hse Mtn 115 Q17
la. Black Mountain 14 F10
la. Ridgewood 14 F10
KINGS
la. Maleny 73 R18
la. Reesville 73 R18
pl. Burnside 65 Q1
rd. Glass Hse Mtn 116 E15
rd.n,Cooroy Mtn 16 B9
rd.s,Cooroy Mtn 16 B13
KINGS BAY
st. Yaroomba 49 L9
KINGSFORD SMITH
pde.Maroochydore 69 M12
pde.Moffat Bch 100 M9
KINGSGATE
dr. Tinbeerwah 16 P3
KINGSGROVE
ct. Buderim 68 M14
KINGSLEY
ct. Little Mtn 99 E6
KINGSMILL
cct. Peregian Spr 28 N13
KINGSTON
ct. Mooloolah Vy 86 Q19
st. Peregian Spr 39 D3
KINGSVIEW
ct. Little Mtn 99 K5
dr. Flaxton 54 J13
KINMOND CREEK
rd. Cootharaba 1 C1
KINROSS
ct. Caloundra W 99 J15
KINSALE
ct. Kuluin 68 N11
KINSHIP
la. Birtinya 90 E10
st. Palmview 88 M5
KIPPARA
la. Maroochydore 69 L11
KIRBY
ct. Tanawha 78 G15
rd. Montville 74 R8
rd. Montville 75 A14
rd. Obi Obi 53 P17
rd. Palmwoods 75 A14
rd. Stanmore 93 F20
KIRI
ct. Buderim 78 L7
KIRRA
rd. Maroochy R 47 H19
rd. Maroochy R 57 J2
rd. Maroochy R 57 L2
KIRRAWOOD
ct. Maroochy R 57 L3
KIRSTEN
cct. Nirimba 108 K3
ct. Maroochydore 69 E8
dr. Glass Hse Mtn 115 R18
KIRSTY
dr. Tanawha 77 Q13
KITCHENER
st. Golden Bch 110 D5
KITE
pl. Parrearra 80 G13
st. Mountain Ck 79 R12
KITNEY
cl. Tanawha 77 M12
KITTYHAWK
cl. Marcoola 59 G9
KLINAIN
st. Coes Creek 65 R6
KLOTZ
rd. Yandina 46 K12
KNOWLES
pl. Glass Hse Mtn 115 M19
KNOX
av. Caloundra 100 K17
rd. Mooloolah Vy 86 E15

Map Ref

KOALA
cr. L Macdonald 1 C20
ct. Little Mtn 99 C14
ct. Mooloolaba 69 M20
ct. Witta 73 P9
KOALA HILL
dr. Rosemount 57 B18
KOCHO
rd. Image Flat 55 R10
KOEL
cct. Peregian Spr 39 C1
st. Noosaville 9 A20
KOKI
ct. Mountain Ck 79 L7
KOKODA
av. Bli Bli 58 D18
KOKOMO
st. Peregian Spr 29 D15
KOLORA
pl. Palmwoods 76 F4
KOMBI
st. Bokarina 90 H10
KOMODO
ct. Parrearra 80 D14
KONA
ct. Mountain Ck 79 L7
KONDALILLA FALLS
rd. Flaxton 54 J19
rd. Montville 54 J19
KONONDA
ct. Mooloolaba 80 A6
KOOKABURRA
cl. Bli Bli 58 C13
cr. Bokarina 90 H5
cst. Montville 74 P10
dr. Caloundra W 99 Q10
dr. Palmview 88 C11
la. Noosa Heads 19 E2
pl. Kulangoor 46 D16
KOOLENA
st. Buddina 80 J8
KOOLINDA
st. Warana 80 J15
KOONGALBA
st. Yandina 46 D10
KOOPA
pl. Pelican Wtr 109 L11
KOORALBYN
ct. Nambour 66 D4
KOORAWATHA
la. Palmwoods 76 E3
KOORIN
dr. Buddina 80 H14
dr. Warana 80 H14
KOORINGA
ct. Maroochydore 69 C10
KOORINGAL
cr. Buddina 80 H6
KOOYONGA
ct. Nambour 66 E4
KOWALD
rd. Landsborough 96 L9
KOWANDI
st. Wurtulla 90 D18
KOWONGA
st. Pacific Pdse 59 B15
KOWREE
cr. Maroochydore 69 A12
KRAUSE
rd. Ninderry 36 H14
rd. North Arm 36 H14
KRESS
rd. Tuchekoi 3 A19
KRIS
ct. Bli Bli 58 B16
KRISTEN
cl. Buderim 79 F10
KROMES
rd. North Arm 35 H6
KULANDA
st. Wurtulla 90 H11
KUMALA
st. Battery Hl 100 G4
KUMBADA
ct. Minyama 80 F7
KUMBAR
st. Pacific Pdse 59 B15
KUNARI
st. Buddina 80 J9
KUNDART
st. Coes Creek 65 P6
KUPARRA
ct. Currimundi 100 F1
KUPIANO
dr. Bli Bli 58 D14

Map Ref

KURACCA
st. Wurtulla 90 D16
KURAN
st. Maroochydore 68 P5
KUREELPA FALLS
rd. Kureelpa 54 N3
rd. Kureelpa 55 A15
KU-RING-GAI
ct. Kuluin 68 M13
KURRAJONG
cct. Peregian Spr 38 R4
cl. Mooloolah Vy 96 B2
cr. Meridan Pl 89 M14
ct. Beerwah 106 A7
ct. Montville 74 P6
pl. Tewantin 7 N11
KURRIMINE
cr. Mountain Ck 79 M16
KUSKOPF
pl. Woombye 66 G15
KUTHAR
st. Pelican Wtr 109 J11
KWILA
cr. Peregian Spr 38 R5
pl. Little Mtn 99 J3
KYAMBA
ct. Mooloolaba 80 B4
KYEEMA
st. Buddina 80 J13
KYLE
ct. Doonan 17 H17
KYLEE
cr. Maroochydore 69 M14
KYLEMORE
ct. Caloundra W 99 J15
KYLIE
ct. Pomona 4 G9

L

LABURNUM
cr. Noosaville 8 K17
gr. Parklands 56 H7
LACEBARK
st. Meridan Pl 89 P14
st. Mountain Ck 79 L11
LACEWING
dr. Sippy Downs 88 L2
LACEY
la. Yandina 46 A9
LACHLAN
av. Nambour 55 P17
cl. Caloundra W, off McDyer St 99 J14
cr. Beerwah 115 C2
LADY ELLIOT
av. Banya 108 H6
st. Mountain Ck 79 N12
LADY MUSGRAVE
dr. Mountain Ck 79 N5
LAGODA
dr. Mt Coolum 49 G6
LAGOON
dr. Palmwoods 76 F3
LAGOONA
dr. Noosa Heads 9 D13
LAGUNA
ct. Coolum Bch 39 G11
gr. Doonan 27 C6
st. Boreen Point 1 R3
LAIDLAW
rd. Woombye 66 A8
rd.n,Coes Creek 66 A8
LAKE
ct. Maroochydore 69 D12
ct. Tewantin 7 Q15
st. Tewantin 8 D14
LAKE COOROIBAH
rd. Cooroibah 7 E2
LAKEDRIVE
cr. Marcoola 49 J15
LAKE DUNETHIN
rd. Maroochy R 47 H15
LAKE EDGE
dr. Noosa Heads 19 B4
LAKE ENTRANCE
bvd.Noosaville 18 D7
LAKEFIELD
cr. Beerwah 115 L1
LAKE FLAT
rd. Boreen Point 1 R1
rd. Cootharaba 1 H1
LAKEHEAD
dr. Sippy Downs 78 G19
LAKE KAWANA
bvd.Birtinya 90 C9
bvd.Bokarina 90 C9
bvd.Wurtulla 90 C9

MOUNTAINDALE

Map Ref
rd. Cooroy Mtn 15 J15
rd. Eumundi 15 J15
MARTINS CREEK
rd. Buderim 68 H18
MARY
st. Alexandra Hd 69 Q19
st. Caloundra 100 J14
st. Cooran 3 R5
st. Kenilworth 31 L12
st. Landsborough 96 C15
st. Nambour 56 C20
st. Noosaville 8 N17
st. Palmwoods 76 C4
MARYANN
st. Golden Bch 109 R11
MARY ANNE
dr. Peregian Bch 29 C9
MARYBELL
dr. Baringa 99 B18
MARY CAIRNCROSS
av. Maleny 94 M3
MARY RIVER
rd. Black Mountain .. 14 M2
rd. Cooroy 14 M2
MARY RIVER BRIDGE
rd. Cambroon 32 C2
MASON
ct. Noosaville 8 B20
la. Baringa 99 D19
MASTHEAD
qy. Noosaville 18 P1
MATHESON
st. Baringa 98 Q17
MATHEW
st. Nambour 56 E16
MATILDA
cr. Battery Hl 100 H5
MATTHEW
cr. Pelican Wtr 109 M7
st. Beerwah 106 A19
MAUD
st. Caloundra 100 J14
st. Maroochydore 69 J14
st. Maroochydore 69 K11
st. Nambour 56 D18
MAUI
ct. Parrearra 80 F20
st. Peregian Spr 29 C14
MAURICE HARVEY
cr. Corbould Park 98 P13
MAURITIUS
cr. Parrearra 80 E16
MAVARRA
st. Maroochydore 69 K12
MAWARRA
av. Buddina 80 J7
MAWHINNEY
rd. Glenview 88 C18
st. Beerwah 106 D20
MAWSON
rd. Beerwah 116 K3
st. Sippy Downs 78 M16
MAX
la. Nirimba 108 M5
MAXIMILLIAN
rd. Noosa N Shore 8 D4
MAXWELL
ct. Coolum Bch 39 J19
MAY
st. Maroochydore 69 L13
MAYDENA
st. Warana 80 J19
MAYERS
rd. Coes Creek 65 H6
rd. Perwillowen 65 H6
rd. Towen Mtn 65 H6
MAYES
av. Caloundra 100 E16
MAYFAIR
cr. Baringa 99 G20
la. Buderim 69 B20
la. Buderim 69 C20
MAYFIELD
st. Alexandra Hd 69 R19
st. Buderim 78 L2
st. Nambour 66 E1
MAYO
st. Caloundra W 99 H14
MEA
st. Coolum Bch 49 E4
MEADOW
ct. Doonan 17 C18
rd. Reesville 73 L18
st. Palmview 88 Q8

Map Ref
MEADOWOOD
ri. Mapleton 54 E8
MEADS
rd. Tanawha 78 G12
MEAGAN
ct. Witta 73 N4
MEANDER
ct. Buderim 68 H20
MEANDERSEA
ct. Mountain Ck 79 J8
MEARS
la. Booroobin 93 B14
MEASBERG
rd. Witta 73 P4
MEDINAH
pl. Peregian Spr 28 N18
MEDINDIE
ct. Bli Bli 58 B17
MEDITATION
ct. Nambour 55 M11
MEELGAN
st. Coolum Bch 39 D19
MEHER
rd. Kiels Mtn 67 D10
MEISNER
ct. Mountain Ck 79 K12
MELALEUCA
av. Buderim 68 L14
la. Cootharaba 1 D1
st. Kuluin 68 L13
st. Marcus Bch 29 M3
st. Moffat Bch 100 M12
MELANIE
ct. Buderim 78 R3
MELCAR
ct. Diddillibah 68 A7
MELIA
ct. Mapleton 54 H9
ct. Tewantin 7 H16
la. Pomona 4 C14
MELINDA
ct. Buderim 78 K6
MELJAREN
pl. Buderim 79 H5
MELLUM
ct. Dicky Beach 100 H8
st. Landsborough 96 G20
MELLUMBROOK
dr. Landsborough 96 B16
MELLUMVIEW
dr. Beerwah 106 B18
MELODY
ct. Warana 80 G18
MELOS
pl. Parrearra 80 E14
MELROSE
pde.Maroochydore 69 N12
MELVILLE
ct. Mt Coolum 49 J9
MEMORIAL
av. Maroochydore 69 K10
av. Pomona 4 E11
av. Tewantin 8 D14
cl. Montville 74 N2
dr. Eerwah Vale 25 J4
dr. Eumundi 25 J4
dr. Eumundi 25 Q15
dr. Eumundi 26 A11
la. Kings Beach 100 Q15
MENARY
rd. Coes Creek 65 M10
rd. W Woombye 65 M10
MENARY BRIDGE
W Woombye 65 Q12
MENOROA
pl. Parrearra 80 E15
MENYAN
st. Currimundi 90 F20
MENZIES
dr. Pacific Pdse 59 C12
MERA
gr. Buderim 78 M1
MERCHANTS
pde.Marcoola 49 J14
MEREDITH
cr. Baringa 99 D20
MERGARD
ct. Eumundi 25 R14
MERI
ct. Pt Arkwright 49 K2
MERIBEL
la. Mons 77 P4
MERIDAN
ct. Pomona 4 F9
wy. Meridan Pl 89 L17

Map Ref
MERIDIAN
st. Bokarina 90 G9
MERIDIEN
dr. Maroochydore 69 B12
MERIMIST
wy. Kiels Mtn 67 H9
MERINDA
av. Palmwoods 75 L4
MERION
ct. Buderim 79 G8
MERKARA
cr. Twin Waters 69 C2
MERLOT
ct. Buderim 79 B9
MERMAID
cl. Caloundra W, off Eagle View Dr 99 Q10
qy. Noosaville 8 L19
MEROPE
st. Sunrise Bch 19 P5
MERRIGUM
st. Currimundi 100 H2
MERRIMA
av. Kings Beach 100 M17
MERRIMAN
ct. Palmwoods 76 D6
MERRY
st. Palmview 88 L5
MERVAL
ct. Mons 77 R2
MESSINES
rd. Aroona 100 E5
MESTON
ct. Pelican Wtr 109 P6
META
st. Mooloolaba 70 A20
METIER LINKWAY
Birtinya 90 D4
MEYRICKS
rd. Glass Hse Mtn . 125 A4
MIA
ct. Yandina 45 Q7
la. Landsborough 96 G16
MICHAEL
st. Golden Bch 109 R12
st. Golden Bch 110 A12
MICRANTHA
pl. Mountain Ck 79 L13
MIDDEN
ct. Bli Bli 58 C11
pl. Pelican Wtr 109 K11
MIDDLE CREEK
rd. Federal 3 J17
rd. Federal 13 P1
rd. Little Mtn 99 L6
MIDDLE PARK
ct. Coes Creek 65 P8
st. Little Mtn 99 K5
MIDDLESPRING
ct. Sippy Downs 88 K2
MIDDLETON
cr. Buderim 78 G3
rd. Witta 73 R8
MIDYIM
ct. Meridan Pl 89 P14
tce. Palmview 88 K12
MILBONG
st. Battery Hl 100 F7
MILIEU
pl. Birtinya 90 C4
pl. Warana 90 C4
MILJEE
ct. Buderim 69 C18
MILKWOOD
la. Pomona 4 H16
MILL
la. Nambour 56 C19
rd. Buderim 78 L1
st. Landsborough 96 E17
st. Nambour 56 C18
st. Noosaville 8 J16
st. Pomona 4 F10
MILLEN
ct. Coolum Bch 39 H18
MILLENNIUM
cct. Pelican Wtr 109 J10
MILLER
pl. Eumundi 25 N9
MILLGROVE
pl. Buderim 78 N1
MILL HILL
rd. Montville 74 N8
MILLIE
la. Nirimba 108 J3

Map Ref
MILLSTREAM
ct. Buderim 78 H1
pl. Glenview 88 A17
MILLWELL
rd. Maroochydore 68 R12
rd.e,Maroochydore 69 E11
MILLWOOD
st. Nambour 55 N13
MILPERA
la. Buderim 78 D7
rt. Noosa Heads 9 H19
MIMBA
pl. Wurtulla 90 D18
MIMOSA
cr. Currimundi 90 A18
st. Marcus Bch 29 K4
st. Peregian Bch 29 K4
MINCHENTONS CROSSING
Conondale 73 B13
MINCHINTON
st. Caloundra 100 J17
MINDA
cl. Tanawha 78 B16
MINDEE
st. Coolum Bch 39 E19
MINDI
rd. Doonan 16 L18
rd. Eumundi 16 L18
MINER
pl. Parrearra 80 G13
MINERVA
pl. Bli Bli 57 N3
MINESHAFT
rd. Eerwah Vale 14 P13
MING
ct. Nambour 55 Q11
MINGLE
st. Palmview 88 L6
MINGUS
st. Sippy Downs 89 B2
MINKARA
st. Warana 90 H1
MINKER
rd. Caloundra W 99 H13
MINNOW
ct. Currimundi 100 E3
MINT
st. Caloundra W 99 F16
MINTI
st. Maroochydore 69 A6
MINTO
pl. Currimundi 100 G2
MINURA
ct. Doonan 17 E10
MINYA
st. Buddina 80 J6
MINYAMA ISLAND
Minyama 80 E4
MIRABELLA
ct. Peregian Spr 39 B5
MIRAN
rd. Image Flat 55 C6
MIRANDA
st. Aroona 100 A6
MIRANG
st. Battery Hl 100 G4
MIRBELIA
pl. Doonan 17 L12
MIRNOO
st. Currimundi 100 F1
MIRRABOOK
ct. Noosa Heads 9 H19
MIRROOL
st. Warana 80 J15
MISSING LINK
rd. Glenview 87 B13
rd. Ilkley 87 B12
MISTRAL
av. Coolum Bch 39 E14
MISTY
ct. Yandina 46 P8
la. Cooroibah 1 N19
MISTY RISE
rd. Image Flat 55 P8
MITCHELL
ct. Cooran 3 N9
la. Witta 73 R8
st. Nambour 56 C19
MITCHELLI
ct. Little Mtn 99 P10
MITTELSTADT
rd. Glass Hse Mtn . 115 Q14

Map Ref
MITTI
st. Noosa Heads 9 L10
MIVA
st. Cooroy 15 B5
st. L Macdonald 15 B6
st. Maleny 74 D18
MIZZEN
cl. Wurtulla 90 E14
ct. Noosaville 18 M2
pl. Twin Waters 69 C2
MOANA
ct. Mountain Ck 79 M8
MOFFAT
st. Moffat Bch 100 N10
MOFFATT
rd. Glass Hse Mtn . 126 D6
MOFFITT
ct. Maleny 74 A17
MOHR
cl. Sippy Downs 88 Q4
MOILOW
ct. Tewantin 7 Q16
MOLAKAI
dr. Mountain Ck 79 L6
MOLOKAI
la. Parrearra, off Sumatra Ct 80 D16
MONA
ct. Bli Bli 58 C17
MONAK
rd. North Arm 36 A9
rd. Peregian Bch 28 K8
MONARCH
cl. Yandina 45 R8
ct. Peregian Spr 38 R4
pl. Beerwah 116 A2
pl. Mons 77 L9
rd. Carters Ridge 13 D9
MONASH
st. Golden Bch 110 C6
MONA VISTA
cr. Coolum Bch 39 K19
ct. Coolum Bch 39 J19
MONK
pl. Tewantin 7 R17
MONKS
cr. Buderim 78 N3
MONKS BRIDGE
Noosaville 18 R2
MONOMEET
cl. Eumundi 26 B1
MONOMEETH
st. Buderim 78 P2
MONS
rd. Buderim 77 M5
rd. Forest Glen 77 E1
rd. Forest Glen 77 G5
rd. Mons 77 M5
MONSCOTT
pl. Forest Glen 77 L6
MONS SCHOOL
rd. Buderim 68 A20
rd. Mons 77 N4
MONTAGE
ct. Buderim 68 B18
MONTEGO
ct. Bli Bli 58 B12
wy. Peregian Spr 29 D15
MONTERAY
st. Mountain Ck 79 M6
MON TERRE
dr. Little Mtn 99 K7
MONTGOMERY
cr. Golden Bch 110 D7
MONTREAL
dr. Peregian Spr 38 Q1
MONTROSE
st. Beerwah 106 B16
MONTSERRAT
cr. Caloundra W 99 H12
MONTVILLE-MAPLETON
rd. Flaxton 54 H12
rd. Mapleton 54 H12
MOODIE
ct. Woombye 66 E7
MOOLOO
cr. Nambour 55 Q16
MOOLOOLABA
esp.Mooloolaba 70 B20
rd. Buderim 79 A2
MOOLOOLAH
dr. Minyama 80 D9
dr. Minyama 80 E5
rd. Eudlo 86 D5

Map Ref
rd. Mooloolah Vy 86 F19
st. Landsborough 96 H19
MOOLOOLAH ISLAND
Minyama 80 D8
MOOLOOLAH MEADOWS
dr. Diamond Vy 85 R14
dr. Mooloolah Vy 85 R14
MOOMBA
st. Pacific Pdse 59 E15
MOONAH
ct. Mountain Ck 79 N5
MOONARE
cr. Noosa Heads 9 F20
MOONBEAM
cr. Castaways Bch .. 19 N13
MOONDARA
dr. Wurtulla 90 H13
MOONDARRA
cr. Mooloolaba 79 R2
MOORABINDA
st. Buderim 78 P1
MOORHEN
pl. Noosaville 8 B18
st. Palmview 88 H6
MOORHOUSE
rd. Woombye 66 J12
MOORINDIL
st. Tewantin 8 B13
MOORINGS
cct. Twin Waters 69 D1
MOORSHEAD
av. Golden Bch 110 B7
MOOYA
st. Battery Hl 100 G7
MORA
ct. Coolum Bch 49 E5
MORETON
cl. Little Mtn 99 N12
pde.Caloundra 100 L17
pde.Kings Beach 100 L17
st. Sippy Downs 88 R3
MORETON BAY
dr. Caloundra W 99 Q9
MORGAN
cl. Yaroomba 49 F1
MORIAC
st. Currimundi 100 B3
MORINDA
cct. Noosaville 8 B19
MORK
ct. Doonan 16 L18
MORNING DEW
cl. Cooroibah 6 M1
MORNING GLORY
dr. Cooroibah 2 E19
MORNINGTON
cr. Peregian Spr 28 R14
ct. Little Mtn 99 P4
MOROBE
cr. Bli Bli 58 C14
MORONEY
pl. Beerwah 116 E2
MORRELL
ct. Doonan 27 J5
MORRISON
rd. Glass Hse Mtn . 115 Q8
st. Sippy Downs 89 A2
MORRISONS
rd. Peachester 94 P13
MORROW
ct. Burnside 55 J16
MORVEN
pl. Maleny 74 E16
MORWONG
dr. Noosa Heads 9 J12
st. Noosa N Shore 2 P2
MOSS DAY
pl. Burnside 55 H15
MOSSMAN
ct. Noosa Heads 9 E13
MOSSY BANK
rd. Diamond Vy 85 L7
rd. Eudlo 85 L6
MOUNTAIN
cl. Mountain Ck 79 H8
st. Pomona 4 D12
MOUNTAIN ASH
dr. Mountain Ck 79 K14
MOUNTAIN BREEZE
ct. Coes Creek 65 Q8
MOUNTAIN CREEK
rd. Buderim 79 F10
rd. Mountain Ck 79 H9
MOUNTAINDALE
ct. Mooloolah Vy 86 A14

Map Ref

STATION
rd. Birtinya 90 A9
rd. Birtinya 90 C7
sq. Nambour 56 D17
st. Pomona 4 F12
st. Pomona 4 K17
STAVE
rd. Obi Obi 53 M14
STAVEWOOD
st. Meridan Pl 89 M15
STAYSAIL
pl. Twin Waters 69 C2
STEGGALLS
rd. Yandina 45 P5
STEINER
cr. Baringa 99 A17
STELARNI
pl. Buderim 79 E1
STELLAR
st. Palmview 88 L5
STEPHANIE
cl. Mudjimba 59 J12
STEPHEN
cr. Nirimba 108 M6
st. Buderim 78 J1
st. Tewantin 8 E10
STEPHEN BURTON
wy. Pelican Wtr 109 K15
STEPHENS
st. Landsborough 96 F19
STEPHENSON
ct. Beerwah 106 E8
la. Belli Park 33 Q7
STERN
dr. Wurtulla 90 F12
STERNBERG
rd. Witta 73 M5
STERNLIGHT
st. Noosaville 18 N3
STEVE
la. Baringa 99 C18
STEVE IRWIN
wy. Beerburrum 126 C17
wy. Beerburrum 136 D1
wy. Beerwah 106 D11
wy. Beerwah 116 D7
wy. Elimbah 136 E11
wy. Glass Hse Mtn 116 D18
wy. Glass Hse Mtn 126 C14
wy. Glenview 97 M5
wy. Landsborough 96 F20
wy. Landsborough 106 D9
STEVENS
rd. Glenview 97 J2
st. Sunshine Bch 10 A18
st. Yandina 46 B8
STEWART
ct. Doonan 27 B6
ct. Tewantin 8 D7
wy. Shelly Bch 100 P13
STILLMANS
rd. Cooran 3 N1
STILLWATER
dr. Twin Waters 69 B1
pl. Noosaville 8 M18
STING-RAY HARBOUR
ct. Pelican Wtr 109 M10
STINT
st. Peregian Bch 29 K19
STIRLING
dr. Eumundi 26 G3
rd. Peachester 94 P19
STIRLING CASTLE
ct. Pelican Wtr 109 R7
STOCKMAN
ct. Pomona 4 F14
STOCKWHIP
ct. Cooroibah 6 N5
STONE
cr. Baringa 99 F19
STONEHAVEN
la. Glass Hse Mtn 115 M18
STONELEIGH
pl. Burnside 55 H19
STONEYBROOK
pl. Peregian Spr 38 R1
STONEY WHARF
rd. Bli Bli 58 H6
STORE
rd. Maroochy R 47 Q17
STORMBIRD
dr. Noosa Heads 19 E2
STORNAWAY
av. Caloundra W 99 J15

STORRS
rd. Peachester 94 M17
STRADBROKE
ct. Little Mtn, off Glasshouse Dr 99 M12
dr. Little Mtn 99 M9
st. Mountain Ck 79 P13
STRAKER
dr. Cooroy 14 P5
STRATFORD PARK
dr. Pomona 4 M7
STRATHFORD
av. Nambour 55 P14
STRAWBERRY
la. Eumundi 26 A15
rd. Beerwah 106 B6
STREZLECKI
cl. Buderim 78 J10
STRINGYBARK
ct. Tewantin 7 Q11
rd. Buderim 78 L14
rd. Sippy Downs 78 L16
STRONG
ct. Montville 74 P7
la. Eerwah Vale 25 J6
rd. Baringa 98 R16
STUART
pl. Nambour 55 Q17
pl. Tewantin 8 A10
STUMERS CREEK
rd. Coolum Bch 39 J11
SUBLIME
st. Palmview 88 L6
SUBWAY
av. Pomona 4 G12
SUDHOLZ
rd. Verrierdale 27 A17
SUE
st. Burnside 65 Q4
SUGAR
rd. Alexandra Hd 69 J15
rd. Buderim 69 K19
rd. Maroochydore 69 J15
rd.n,Maroochydore 69 H14
SUGAR BAG
rd. Aroona 99 R8
rd. Caloundra W 99 R8
rd. Little Mtn 99 L8
SUGAR CANE
la. Sippy Downs 89 B4
SUGAR COAST
dr. Glass Hse Mtn 126 A1
SUGAR GLIDER
la. Tinbeerwah 17 A2
pl. Pomona 4 E12
SUGAR GUM
dr. Mooloolah Vy 86 J17
SUGARGUM
pl. Black Mountain 4 K19
SUGAR MILL
dr. Palmview 88 K11
SUGAR VIEW
la. Rosemount 57 C16
SUGARWOOD
st. Aroona 100 B7
SULLER
st. Caloundra 100 G15
SULLIVANS
rd. Eudlo 85 F4
SULO
ct. Mudjimba 59 L11
SUMATRA
ct. Parrearra 80 D16
SUMMER
dr. Maroochydore 69 A6
SUMMERFIELD
ct. Bli Bli 58 B11
SUMMERLAND
st. Peregian Spr 29 C15
SUMMER RIDGE
pl. Buderim 68 C19
SUMMIT
cl. Glass Hse Mtn 125 R3
rd. Pomona 4 G10
st. Flaxton 54 J13
SUNBIRD
ch. Parrearra 80 F13
la. Peregian Spr 38 R4
SUNBURST
ct. Mountain Ck 79 L10
SUNBURY
pl. Peachester 94 P14
SUNCOAST
bvd.Marcoola 59 K4

SUNCOAST BEACH
dr. Mt Coolum 49 E11
SUNCREST
ct. Wurtulla 90 G16
SUNDAY CREEK
rd. Kenilworth 31 A16
SUNDEW
pl. Peregian Spr 39 B4
st. Mudjimba 59 K14
SUNDIAL
ct. Tewantin 7 M18
SUNDOWN
cl. Tanawha 78 B17
ct. Sunrise Bch 19 M7
SUNFLOWER
st. Nirimba 108 G3
SUNHAVEN
ct. Nambour 56 A17
SUNJEWEL
bvd.Currimundi 90 A20
SUNLAND
ct. Beerwah 116 D7
SUNNINGDALE
ct. Nambour 66 D4
SUNNY
la. Birtinya 90 C12
st. Palmview 88 L5
SUNNYRIDGE
ri. Buderim 78 Q6
SUNNYSIDE
ct. Maleny 74 E16
SUNORCHID
pl. Twin Waters 59 C17
SUNPOINTE
st. Maroochydore 69 A6
SUNRAY
av. Palmview 88 K8
SUNRIDGE
rd. Eudlo 75 K17
rd. Landers Shoot 75 K17
SUNRISE
av. Coolum Bch 39 G14
av. Tewantin 8 F18
dr. Maroochydore 69 C13
rd. Doonan 16 L16
rd. Eumundi 26 E1
rd. Tewantin 6 N19
rd. Tinbeerwah 6 N19
rd. Tinbeerwah 16 P11
rd. Tinbeerwah 17 A7
tce. Little Mtn 99 K6
SUNSEEKER
cl. Noosaville 8 M18
pde.Maroochydore 69 H10
SUNSET
av. Buderim 78 C7
dr. Little Mtn 99 N7
dr. Noosa Heads 19 D2
rd. Beerwah 106 A19
wy. Cooroibah 2 D19
SUNSET BEACH
av. Yaroomba 49 L10
SUNSET STRIP
Marcoola 59 L7
SUNSHINE
cl. Mudjimba 59 K10
ct. Maroochydore 69 D10
mwy.Alexandra Hd 68 P13
mwy.Bli Bli 58 R19
mwy.Buderim 68 P13
mwy.Buderim 79 A15
mwy.Coolum Bch 49 B7
mwy.Kuluin 68 P13
mwy.Marcoola 59 A4
mwy.Maroochydore 68 P9
mwy.Mooloolaba 79 M12
mwy.Mountain Ck 79 M12
mwy.Mt Coolum 49 B7
mwy.Pacific Pdse 58 R19
mwy.Pacific Pdse 68 P9
mwy.Peregian Bch 39 A13
mwy.Sippy Downs 78 F19
mwy.Tanawha 78 F19
SUNSHINE BEACH
rd. Noosa Heads 9 H16
rd. Sunshine Bch 9 K17
SUNSHINE COAST
pde.Maroochydore 69 H12
SUNSHINE COVE
wy. Maroochydore 69 A14
SUNSHINE GROVE
pl. Yandina 45 P7
SUNSTONE
ct. Yaroomba 49 G2

SUNVIEW
dr. Twin Waters 59 C19
SUPPLEJACK
ct. L Macdonald 1 F20
SURF
rd. Alexandra Hd 69 M15
rd. Maroochydore 69 M15
st. Sunshine Bch 9 Q18
SURFRIDER
pl. Mudjimba 59 K10
SURFSIDE
ct. Sunshine Bch 10 A17
la. Mt Coolum 49 K14
SUSES POCKET
rd. Mapleton 54 E12
SUTHERLAND
st. Buderim 68 N17
st. Dicky Beach 100 H7
SUTTON
la. Moy Pocket 33 A9
rd. Coolabine 53 C3
SUZANNE
cl. Mudjimba 59 J13
SUZEN
ct. Mooloolah Vy 86 E17
SWALLOW
st. Nambour 55 K17
st. Wurtulla 90 H15
SWALLOWTAIL
st. Noosa N Shore 2 Q2
SWAN
av. Sunshine Bch 19 Q2
cr. Banya 108 F5
st. Beerwah 116 E2
st. Noosaville 9 A19
SWANBOURNE
wy. Noosaville 18 B2
SWEEP
ct. Birtinya 90 D12
SWEETBRUSH
pl. Mountain Ck 79 L11
SWEETGUM
ct. Currimundi 90 B19
SWEETLIP
cct. Mountain Ck 79 N15
SWEET PEA
av. Nirimba 108 H1
SWEET WATER
st. Woombye 66 G15
SWELL
la. Bokarina 90 K10
SWIFT
dr. Cooroy 15 D1
la. Burnside 55 K19
pl. Peregian Spr 39 C4
SWIFTLET
pl. Forest Glen 67 L19
SWINBOURNE
la. Maroochydore 69 E7
SWITCHFOOT
st. Bokarina 90 J9
SWORD
st. Aroona 100 D7
SYCAMORE
dr. Currimundi 90 A16
st. Mudjimba 59 L11
SYDAL
st. Little Mtn 99 N13
SYD LINGARD
dr. Buderim 79 J1
SYDNEY
av. Pelican Wtr 109 L13
st. Nambour 56 D19
st. Tewantin 8 G16
SYKES
av. Kings Beach 100 N14
SYLVAN
st. Buderim 68 K16
SYLVANIA
cl. Bli Bli 57 N7
SYLVIA
st. Noosaville 8 M17
SYLVIE
st. Pelican Wtr 109 K15
SYMONDS
wy. Baringa 98 R20
SYMPHONY
wy. Palmview 88 H10

T

TABLELANDS
rd. Cooran 3 R4
TADOMA
st. Palmview 88 H7

TAGERA
st. Warana 90 H2
TAHITI
st. Parrearra 80 D15
TAILOR
st. Noosa N Shore 2 Q2
TAILSLIDE
cr. Bokarina 90 H9
TAINE
st. Noosaville 9 A20
TAINTONS
rd. Woombye 66 E16
TAIT
st. Tewantin 8 D9
TALANA
dr. Dulong 54 Q10
TALARA
ct. Tewantin 7 R18
st. Currimundi 100 C3
TALINGA
st. Buddina 80 K10
TALLANGATTA
st. Nambour 56 K10
TALLAWA
pl. Wurtulla 90 J12
TALLAWONG
cl. Beerwah 106 B7
TALLGRASS
av. Tewantin 7 J13
TALLGUM
av. Doonan 26 N9
av. Doonan 26 P3
av. Verrierdale 26 N9
TALLOWOOD
cl. Little Mtn 99 N5
ct. Peregian Spr 39 A3
TALLOW WOOD
dr. Kuluin 68 J12
TALLOWWOOD
pl. Black Mountain 14 H1
pl. Palmwoods 76 E10
st. Maleny 74 D20
wk. Landsborough 97 E4
TALL TREES
wy. Little Mtn 99 L3
TAMALA
st. Warana 80 H18
TAMARIN
dr. Mapleton 54 G8
TAMARIND
ct. Woombye 66 F16
pl. Twin Waters 59 E19
st. Maleny 74 D17
st. Meridan Pl 89 M15
TAMARINDUS
st. Marcoola 49 K17
TAMARINE
ct. Cooroibah 6 Q5
TAMBORINE
cl. Mountain Ck 79 R13
cr. Banya 108 D6
TAMI
ct. Mt Coolum 49 F6
TAMIN
pl. Maroochy R 47 M20
TAMINGA
st. Wurtulla 90 H11
TAMLYN
rd. Kenilworth 31 M15
TAMPER
st. Nambour 56 C19
TANA
st. Maroochydore 69 B6
TANAH
st.e,Mt Coolum 49 K9
st.e,Yaroomba 49 K9
st.w,Mt Coolum 49 G7
st.w,Yaroomba 49 G7
TANAWHA
rd. Tanawha 78 D15
TANAWHA TOURIST
dr. Mons 77 J9
dr. Tanawha 77 J9
dr. Tanawha 78 B15
TANDARA
st. Buderim 78 P1
st. Warana 90 H3
TANDEM
av. Warana 90 F3
TANDERRA
dr. Cooran 3 R4
TANDUR TRAVESTON
rd. Traveston 3 D1
TANGELO
rd. Palmwoods 76 F1

TANGERINE
pl. Palmwoods 75 Q9
TANGLEWOOD
cl. Pomona 4 H15
tr. Noosa Heads 9 N10
TANGMERE
ct. Noosa Heads 9 G19
TANIA
av. Palmwoods 76 E14
TANNA
st. Caloundra W 99 F14
TANTULA
rd.e,Alexandra Hd 69 M18
rd.w,Alexandra Hd 69 L18
TARAWA
st. Parrearra 80 C12
TARCOOLA
av. Mooloolaba 80 B3
TARCUTTA
la. Nirimba 108 E3
la. Nirimba 108 F3
TAREE
ct. Kuluin 68 L10
TAREEL
st. Wurtulla 90 F17
TARGOO
rd. Valdora 37 D15
TARINA
st. Noosa Heads 9 G20
TARNKUN
st. Alexandra Hd 69 M17
TARO
pl. Aroona 100 B7
TARONGA
pl. Palmwoods 76 G2
st. Palmwoods 76 F2
TAROONA
ct. Peachester 94 N18
TARRA-BULGA
ct. Buderim 78 J10
TARSHAW
st. Bli Bli 57 N8
TARVER
st. Aroona 100 B5
TARWARRI
cr. Mooloolaba 80 A3
TARWHINE
pl. Mountain Ck 79 P15
TARWINE
st. Noosa N Shore 2 Q2
TARYN
cl. Glass Hse Mtn 115 P19
TASHI
pl. Little Mtn 99 H3
TASMAN
st. Banya 108 D8
TASOL
st. Bli Bli 58 D15
TASSEL
pl. Twin Waters 59 C17
TATIARA
ct. Nambour 56 C12
TAU
ct. Maroochydore 69 B6
TAY
av. Caloundra 100 G17
TAYHA
cr. Nirimba 108 J3
TAYLOR
av. Golden Bch 110 C5
av. Golden Bch 110 D3
ct. Cooroy 15 B13
ct. Mooloolah Vy 86 B18
dr. Pomona 4 C10
st. Marcoola 59 J10
tce. Marcoola 59 J9
TAYLORS
rd. Buderim 78 D12
rd. Tanawha 78 D12
TEAK
ct. Mountain Ck 79 K14
st. Maleny 74 E18
TEAL
ct. Wurtulla 90 J15
la. Palmview 88 P7
st. Caloundra W 99 F17
st. Peregian Bch 29 L9
TEASEL
ct. Mountain Ck 79 L9
sq. Currimundi 100 D2
TEA TREE
ct. Little Mtn 99 J4
gr. Peregian Spr 38 R3
la. Tinbeerwah 16 R4
pl. Twin Waters 59 E20

ZOMMER

Map Ref

WERIN
st. Tewantin 8 A13
st. Tewantin 8 B8
WERITA
ct. Sunrise Bch 19 M5
WERONA
st. Buddina 80 J8
WESLEY
ct. Noosa Heads 9 F13
WEST
tce. Caloundra 100 D15
WESTAWAY
pde. Currimundi 90 G19
pde. Currimundi 90 H19
rd. Little Mtn 99 C5
rd. Meridan Pl 99 C5
WEST COOLUM
rd. Coolum Bch 48 P12
rd. Mt Coolum 48 P12
WESTERN
av. Montville 54 F20
dr. Banya 108 C8
WEST EUMUNDI
rd. Eerwah Vale 25 L7
rd. Eumundi 25 L7
WESTHOLME
cct. Pelican Wtr 109 Q3
WESTLAKE
ct. Sippy Downs 88 K1
WESTMINSTER
av. Golden Bch 110 A4
WESTVIEW
cr. Nambour 55 Q13
WEXFORD
pl. Caloundra W 99 K14
WEYBA
esp. Noosa Heads 9 D20
rd. Noosaville 8 R18
st. Sunshine Bch 9 P19
WEYBA PARK
dr. Noosa Heads 19 D1
WHALE
dr. Noosa Heads 9 R15
dr. Sunshine Bch 9 R15
WHALLEY CREEK
cl. Burnside 55 R20
WHARF
rd. Bli Bli 58 B17
st. Maroochydore 69 J8
st. Yandina 46 C12
WHEELDON
ct. Cooroy 14 P6
WHEELER
cr. Caloundra W 99 G15
WHELAN
rd. Bollier 13 A18
WHIMBREL
ct. Pelican Wtr 109 N14
WHIPBIRD
pl. Doonan 17 H13
pl. Glenview 87 M18
st. Buderim 79 J3
WHIPTAIL
ct. Maleny 74 C19
WHISPERING GUM
av. Eumundi 26 J1
WHISTLER
la. Peregian Spr 39 A4
pl. Beerwah 116 A4
st. Bli Bli 58 C12
wy. Pomona 4 G11
WHISTLER RIDGE
dr. Yandina Ck 37 D11
WHITBY
la. Sippy Downs 78 R19
pl. Pelican Wtr 109 M9
st. Glass Hse Mtn 116 F20
WHITE
st. Nirimba 108 J2
WHITEASH
pl. Currimundi 90 A17
WHITE BEECH
rd. Noosa Heads 19 B3
WHITEBEECH
st. Meridan Pl 89 N13
WHITECAP
cr. Bokarina 90 J9
WHITE CEDAR
dr. Meridan Pl 89 N14
pl. W Woombye 65 M11
WHITE CLOUD
la. Palmwoods 76 B9
WHITECROSS
rd. Bli Bli 57 N10
WHITE-DOVE
ct. Wurtulla 90 J14
WHITE FIG
pl. Burnside 55 J19
WHITE GUMS
st. Landsborough 96 J20
WHITEHAVEN
dr. Buderim 69 F20
pde. Yaroomba 49 L10
wy. Pelican Wtr 110 B2
WHITE OAK
pl. Perwillowen 65 K2
st. Sippy Downs 89 E4
WHITES
rd. Buderim 67 R18
rd. Forest Glen 67 P16
rd. Kunda Park 67 P16
rd. Landsborough 95 L16
rd. Mt Mellum 95 L16
WHITEWOOD
ct. L Macdonald 5 K1
ct. Mountain Ck 79 L10
WHITING
rd. Glass Hse Mtn 116 H17
st. Maroochydore 69 G6
st. Noosa N Shore 2 Q2
WHITLEY
av. Bells Creek 108 P4
WHITSUNDAY
dr. Pacific Pdse 59 A13
st. Parrearra 80 C15
WHITTLE
rd. Tuchekoi 13 C1
WHYALLA
st. Wurtulla 90 H13
WHYANDRA
cl. Doonan 17 A18
WIAN
st. Buderim 78 F3
WICKERSON
cr. Bli Bli 58 C18
WIDGEE
pl. Caloundra W 99 H12
WILBUR
ct. Glass Hse Mtn 116 G14
WILCOX
rd. Kenilworth 31 M6
rd. Kenilworth 31 P3
WILD
rd. Bald Knob 95 H12
rd. Crohamhurst 94 H8
rd. Landsborough 95 H12
WILD APPLE
ct. Noosa Heads 19 B5
WILDERNESS
cct. Little Mtn 99 J6
tr. Noosa N Shore 2 P15
WILDFLOWER
st. Sunshine Bch 19 Q1
wy. Little Mtn 99 J2
WILD HONEY
pl. Buderim 67 R19
WILDWOOD
pl. Mooloolah Vy 86 A18
WILGA
ct. Mapleton 54 H9
WILGAN
pl. Buderim 79 E1
WILGEE
ct. Cooroy 5 C20
WILGUY
cr. Buderim 78 C7
WILKES
ct. Tinbeerwah 16 P1
la. Eumundi 26 D9
rd. Woombye 66 G8
WILKIEA
st. Meridan Pl 89 M16
WILKINS
la. Palmwoods 75 R13
rd. Glass Hse Mtn 115 F15
WILKINSON
st. Baringa 99 A17
WILKINSONS
ct. Cooroy 14 P6
WILLANDRA
pl. Kureelpa 54 L7
WILLAROO
ct. Wurtulla 90 J14
wy. Maleny 74 C19
WILLAWONG
pl. Cooran 4 B4
WILLETT
rd. Bellthorpe 92 F17
WILLIAM
rd. Eumundi 25 Q11
st. Alexandra Hd 69 Q18
st. Buderim 78 C8
st. Cooran 3 P5
st. Landsborough 96 C16
st. Moffat Bch 100 H11
st. Mons 78 C8
st. Nambour 56 E19
st. Noosaville 9 A15
st. Shelly Bch 100 L12
st. Tewantin 7 P16
WILLIAM PARKER
pl. Buderim 69 K20
WILLIAMS
st. Coolum Bch 39 H14
WILLIAMSON
la. Caloundra 100 J17
WILLIS
rd. Bli Bli 57 R9
rd. Bli Bli 58 B12
WILLOW
cr. Marcoola 49 K18
la. Maleny 74 E18
st. Bli Bli 57 R13
WILLOWOOD
cr. Highworth 55 M12
cr. Nambour 55 M12
WILLS
av. Golden Bch 100 D20
rd. Weyba Downs 18 F18
WILSHIRE
pl. Pelican Wtr 110 A1
WILSON
av. Dicky Beach 100 M8
av. Woombye 66 G12
la. Woombye 66 E5
rd. Ilkley 87 B5
rd. Tanawha 77 R20
rd. Tanawha 88 E1
WILSONS
la. Eerwah Vale 25 H12
rd. Tanawha 78 D19
WILUNA
st. Warana 90 H3
WIMBIN
st. Pacific Pdse 59 D15
WIMBREL
ct. Wurtulla 90 J15
WIMMERS
la. Cooroy 14 R3
WIN
rd. Peregian Bch 29 C6
WINBIRRA
wy. Noosa Heads 9 F19
WINCH
st. Wurtulla 90 F13
WINCHESTER
rd. Little Mtn 99 G9
WINDERMERE
wy. Sippy Downs 78 R20
WINDRED
la. Conondale 92 P9
WINDSOR
av. Moffat Bch 100 N12
av. Shelly Bch 100 N12
rd. Burnside 55 J16
rd. Burnside 55 L19
rd. Nambour 55 L19
WINDSOR VALLEY
dr. Burnside 55 L19
WINDSURF
pl. Noosaville 8 K20
WINGARA
pl. Pomona 4 L9
st. Buddina 80 H8
WINJEEL
ct. Currimundi 100 B3
WINKARA
st. Wurtulla 90 E15
WINSTON
ct. Landsborough 106 D3
rd. Palmwoods 76 K2
rd.s, Chevallum 76 L4
rd.s, Palmwoods 76 L4
WINTERFORD
pl. Coes Creek 66 B6
WINTERGREEN
wy. Peachester 94 N13
WINTZLOFF
rd. Landsborough 106 K4
WIRRA
pl. Tewantin 7 M6
WIRRAWAY
st. Alexandra Hd 69 N14
st. Maroochydore 69 N13
WIRRUNA
dr. Cooran 3 N7
WISES
rd. Buderim 68 R18
rd. Buderim 69 D17
WISHART
cr. Baringa 99 C20
WISTERIA
cr. Sippy Downs 89 E3
pl. Currimundi 90 A18
WITCHWOOD
cl. Coolum Bch 39 G12
WITHAM
rd. Maleny 94 C1
WITTA
cir. Noosa Heads 9 G12
rd. Witta 73 P12
WITTABERG
rd. Witta 73 P5
WOLLEMI
st. Beerburrum 136 C7
WOLLOMIA
wy. Sunrise Bch 19 N5
WOMBAT
pl. Ninderry 36 J15
WONGA
cct. Beerwah 115 Q2
st. Maroochydore 69 K13
WONGABEL
st. Maleny 74 E16
WOOD
ct. Baringa 99 A19
rd. Beerwah 116 N10
WOODBROOK
dr. Buderim 78 J15
WOODCHESTER
cl. Rosemount 57 H16
la. Rosemount 57 H16
WOODCUTTER
ri. Pomona 4 G15
WOOD DUCK
la. Tinbeerwah 16 Q1
WOODGROVE
bvd. Beerwah 115 R3
WOODHAVEN
pl. Glass Hse Mtn 126 A1
wy. Cooroibah 1 R19
WOODHILL
ct. Buderim 68 R16
WOODLAND
ct. Tewantin 7 G14
dr. Peregian Bch 29 C9
dr. Peregian Bch 29 J12
pl. Dulong 54 P11
WOODLANDS
bvd. Currimundi 89 P15
bvd. Meridan Pl 89 P15
cr. Buderim 68 P16
ct. Mooloolah Vy 86 M20
ct. Mooloolah Vy 96 M1
WOODLARK
ri. Sunrise Bch 19 P6
WOODLOT
ct. Buderim 68 Q16
ri. Tewantin 7 H14
WOODPECKER
cl. Maleny 74 C19
wy. Coolum Bch 49 D7
WOODROFFE
st. Little Mtn 99 H9
WOODS
ct. Palmwoods 75 Q10
la. Noosa N Shore 8 D2
pl. Landsborough 96 E11
WOODSWALLOW
cr. Bli Bli 57 L7
la. Black Mountain 4 F18
WOODWOOD
rd. Landsborough 106 G3
WOOLLAHRA
ct. Pomona 4 M7
WOOLUMBA
st. Tewantin 7 R17
WOOMBA
pl. Mooloolaba 80 B4
WOOMBYE
st. Meridan Pl 89 M15
WOOMBYE-PALMWOODS
rd. Palmwoods 76 E4
rd. Woombye 66 K20
WOONGAR
st. Boreen Point 2 A3
WOONUM
rd. Alexandra Hd 69 L17
WOORILLA
cr. Mountain Ck 79 N11
WOORIM
st. Landsborough 96 J18
WOOROI FOREST
dr. Tewantin 17 C6
dr. Tinbeerwah 17 C6
WOOROOKOOL
pl. Noosaville 9 B15
WORBA
la. Tinbeerwah 6 E20
WORENDO
ct. Caloundra W 99 G14
WOTAMA
ct. Mooloolaba 80 B7
WOYIN
st. Alexandra Hd 69 N18
WRAY
wk. Bli Bli 58 D16
WREN
cr. Buderim 79 J2
st. Baringa 99 D18
WRIGHT
ct. Bli Bli 57 R13
pl. Baringa 99 D20
st. Maroochydore 69 G8
WRIGLEY
st. Maroochydore 69 J15
WUNNUNGA
cr. Yaroomba 49 L4
WURLEY
dr. Bokarina 90 H11
dr. Wurtulla 90 H11
WURLI
ct. Cooroy 14 M2
WURTULLA
st. Maroochydore 69 K16
WUST
rd. Cooroy 14 N10
rd. Doonan 16 Q14
WYANDA
dr. Bokarina 90 H4
dr. Warana 90 H4
WYANDRA
st. Noosa Heads 9 H17
WYBALENA
rd. Pomona 4 G16
WYGANI
dr. Noosa N Shore 8 M15
WYLAH
st. Noosaville 9 A19
WYNDLORN
av. Buderim 78 J1
WYONA
dr. Noosa Heads 9 G19
WYREEMA
tce. Caloundra 100 K16
WYUNA
dr. Noosaville 9 D15
WYWONG
st. Pacific Pdse 59 D14

X

XANADU
gr. Buderim 78 Q6
pl. Mooloolah Vy 96 B2

Y

YAKOLA
pde. Alexandra Hd 69 L17
YALLANGA
pl. Mooloolaba 79 R3
YALLARA
ct. Noosa Heads 9 G19
YALTARA
st. Wurtulla 90 D16
YANDINA-BLI BLI
rd. Bli Bli 57 P1
rd. Maroochy R 47 A18
rd. Yandina 46 G11
YANDINA-COOLUM
rd. Coolum Bch 39 C18
rd. Maroochy R 47 C10
rd. Valdora 47 M13
rd. Yandina 46 E8
rd. Yandina Ck 47 M13
YANGO
st. Pacific Pdse 59 D15
YANGUBBI
la. Cooroibah 7 F5
YARA
st. Alexandra Hd 69 M15
YARINGA
av. Buddina 80 K6
av. Buddina 80 K7
YAROOMBA
dr. Yaroomba 49 L9
YARRA
wy. Nirimba 108 F4
YARRAN
rd. Peregian Spr 29 B19
YARRAWAH
st. Coes Creek 65 P5
YARROCK
st. Coolum Bch 49 D2
YATAMA
pl. Cooroibah 7 A3
YEATES
rd. Beerwah 115 A3
YELLOW CEDAR
pl. Palmwoods 76 A10
YELLOW FIN
cct. Mountain Ck 79 N14
YELLOWOOD
cl. Tewantin 7 M11
YERAMBA
pl. Buderim 79 A5
YERRANYA
row. Yaroomba 49 M5
YEW
ct. Buderim 79 F4
YIDNEY
st. Maroochydore 69 B17
YILLEEN
ct. Mooloolaba 79 Q3
YINDI
st. Buderim 78 P1
YINNEBURRA
st. Yaroomba 49 M4
YINNI
st. Maroochydore 69 A5
YOOMBA
cr. Alexandra Hd 69 M17
YORK
pl. Mountain Ck 79 Q11
rd. Buderim 78 N2
YORKEYS
la. Maroochydore 69 C12
YORLAMBU
pde. Maroochydore 69 K16
YOUNGS
dr. Doonan 26 Q3
dr. Doonan 27 A1
rd. Glass Hse Mtn 116 A12
YOUTH
av. Burnside 66 A1
YUCCA
ct. Mountain Ck 79 R14
YULONG
st. Maroochydore 69 A12
YULUNGA
pl. Mooloolaba 80 B3
YUNGAR
st. Coolum Bch 39 E17
YUROL FOREST
dr. Pomona 4 G11
YURUGA
st. Mooloolaba 79 Q3
YVONNE
st. Highworth 55 H13

Z

ZANTE
la. Parrearra 80 E14
ZANZIBAR
ct. Parrearra 80 F17
ZARA
ct. Buderim 78 K5
ZEAL
st. Birtinya 90 C12
ZEALEY
rd. Nambour 56 E12
ZEIL
cr. Banya 108 C7
ZENITH
st. Glass Hse Mtn 116 B20
ZEPHYR
st. Palmview 88 L8
ZGRAJEWSKI
rd. Verrierdale 37 N6
rd. Yandina Ck 37 N6
ZINNIA
cl. Peregian Spr 39 A4
ZOMMER
dr. Palmwoods 76 E7

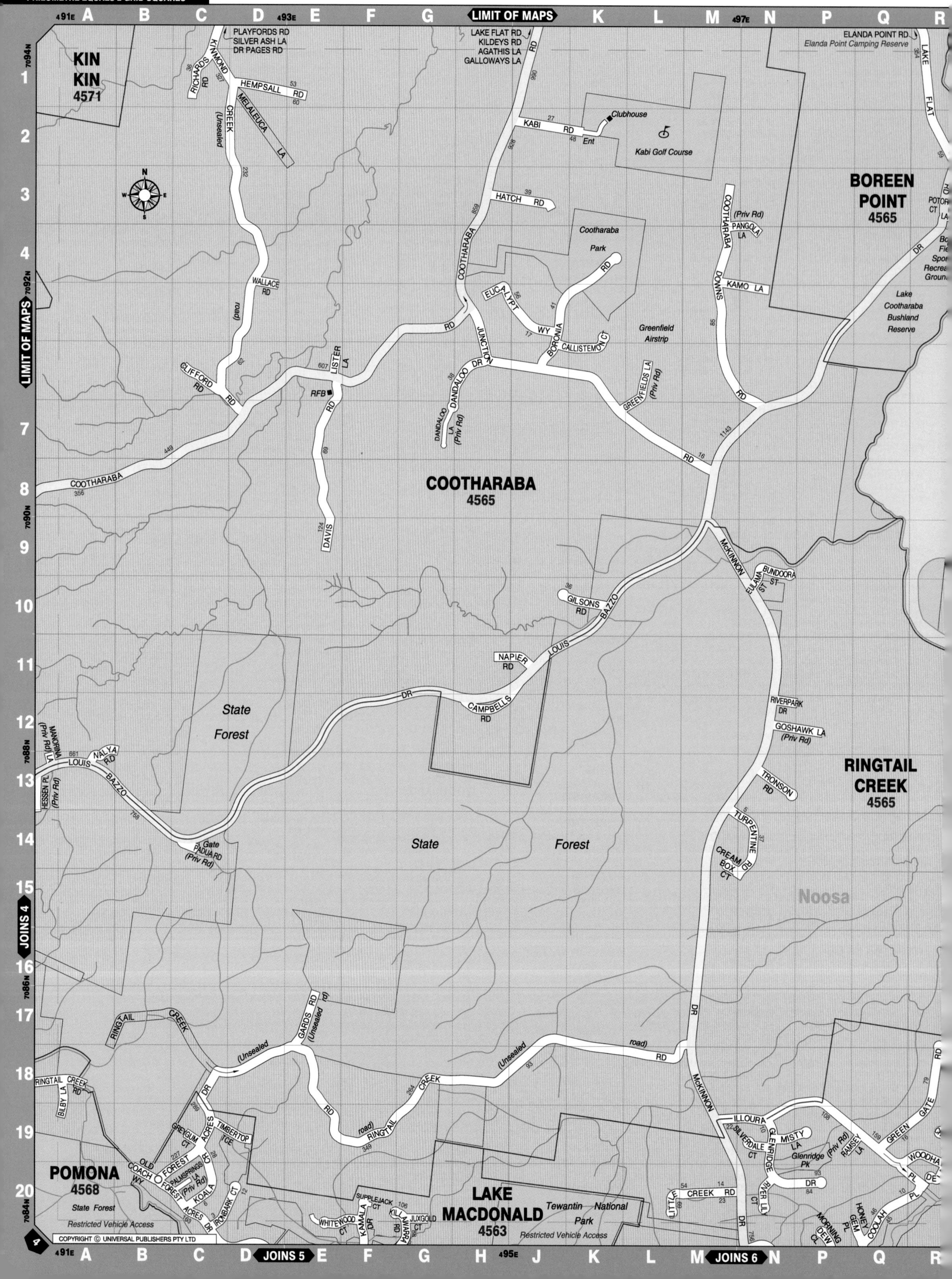

MAP 1
1 KILOMETRE EQUALS 2 GRID SQUARES

LIMIT OF MAPS

KIN KIN 4571

BOREEN POINT 4565

PLAYFORDS RD
SILVER ASH LA
DR PAGES RD

LAKE FLAT RD
KILDEYS RD
AGATHIS LA
GALLOWAYS LA

ELANDA POINT RD.
Elanda Point Camping Reserve

HEMPSALL RD

RICHARDS RD
KINMOND
MELALEUCA LA
CREEK (Unsealed)

KABI RD
Ent
Clubhouse

HATCH RD

Kabi Golf Course

COOTHARABA
PANGOLA LA
(Priv Rd)

WALLACE RD

Cootharaba Park

DOWNS
KAMO LA

Lake Cootharaba Bushland Reserve

EUCALYPT
WY
BORONIA
CALLISTEMON CT

Greenfield Airstrip

LISTER LA
(road)

CLIFFORD RD

RFB

JUNCTION DR
DANDALOO LA
DANDALOO LA (Priv Rd)

GREENFIELDS LA (Priv Rd)

RD

COOTHARABA

DAVIS

COOTHARABA 4565

RD

McKINNON
EUMA
BUNDOORA ST

GILSONS RD
BAZZO
LOUIS

NAPIER RD

RIVERPARK DR
GOSHAWK LA (Priv Rd)

State Forest

CAMPBELLS RD

DR

RINGTAIL CREEK 4565

TRONSON RD

MANNION LA (Priv Rd)
HESSEN PL (Priv Rd)
LOUIS
NALYA RD
BAZZO

TURPENTINE RD
CREAM BOX CT

Gate
PADUA RD (Priv Rd)

State Forest

Noosa

RINGTAIL CREEK

RINGTAIL CREEK RD
BLBY LA

GARDS RD (Unsealed)

(Unsealed)

road
CREEK

(Unsealed)

road
RD

McKINNON
DR

ILLOURA
SILVERDALE CT
GLENRIDGE
MISTY LA
RAMSEY LA

Glenridge PK

GREEN GATE RD

WOODHA

POMONA 4568

GREYGUM CT
ACRES
TIMBERTOP TCE
DR FOREST
OLD COACH
FOREST WY
PALMSPRINGS
KOALA
PONBARR CT (Priv Rd)
ACRES

SUPPLEJACK CT
WHITEWOOD CT
KAMALA DR
KILL MARRA
JUXGOLD CT

LAKE MACDONALD 4563

Tewantin National Park
Restricted Vehicle Access

LITTLE CREEK RD
RIVER CT
DR

MORNING DEW PL
HONEY GEM PL
COOLAH

State Forest
Restricted Vehicle Access

JOINS 5
JOINS 6
JOINS 4

MAP 2
1 KILOMETRE EQUALS 2 GRID SQUARES

LIMIT OF MAPS

Lake

Cootharaba

Great Sandy

National Park

Laguna

**NOOSA
NORTH
SHORE
4565**

Bay

NOOSA

RIVER

Johns Landing
Camping Ground
(Private)

Great Sandy

National Park

**COOROIBAH
4565**

Great Sandy

National Park

Noosa
North
Shore
Wilderness
Beachfront
Camping
Area

AMAROO

MURCHISON LA

LANCASTER

JOHNS RD
376

RD
378

WILDERNESS

Lake

Cooroibah

Noosa North Shore Retreat

Eco Centre

Noosa North Shore
Retreat Tourist Park

BEACH RD

Lakeside
Bushland
Reserve

LAKESIDE DR

LAKEWAY

COOROIBAH

JIRRIMA

Great
Sandy
National
Park

NOOSA RIVER

MAXIMILLIAN

QUARRY TR

Teewah

TR

RD

Beach

MAP 3
1 KILOMETRE EQUALS 2 GRID SQUARES

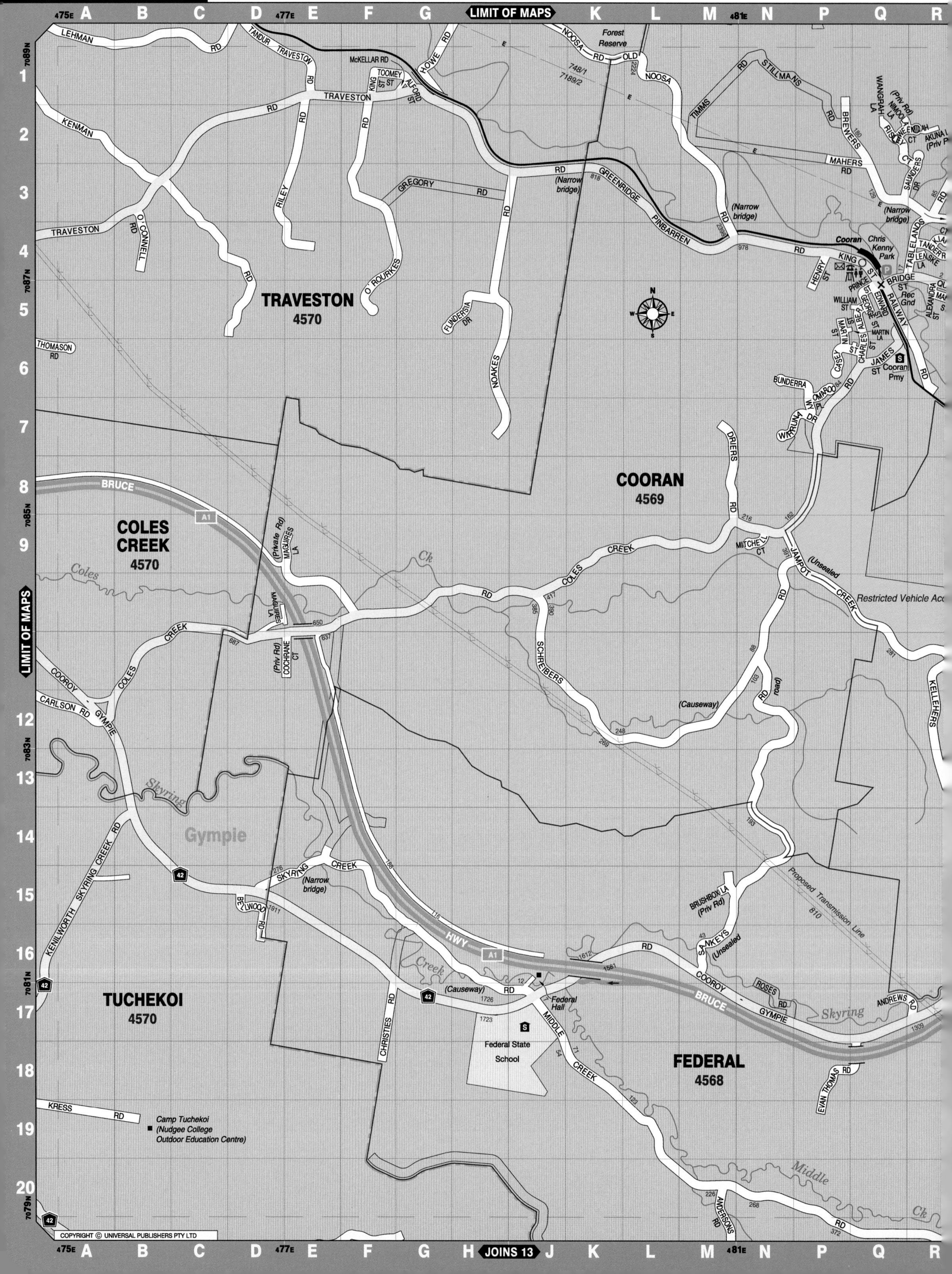

LIMIT OF MAPS

TRAVESTON
4570

COORAN
4569

COLES CREEK
4570

TUCHEKOI
4570

FEDERAL
4568

Gympie

Federal State School

Federal Hall

Camp Tuchekoi
(Nudgee College
Outdoor Education Centre)

Forest Reserve

Chris Kenny Park

Cooran

Restricted Vehicle Acc

Proposed Transmission Line

(Narrow bridge)

(Causeway)

(Unsealed)

LIMIT OF MAPS

JOINS 13

MAP 4
1 KILOMETRE EQUALS 2 GRID SQUARES

A B C D 485E E F G **LIMIT OF MAPS** K L M 489E N P Q R 491E

LIMIT OF MAPS

State Forest

COOTHARABA
4565

PINBARREN
4568

RINGTAIL CREEK
4565

State Forest
Restricted Vehicle Access

Noosa

Noosa District High S Pomona Campus

Pomona Showground

Cooroora Ck Museum

POMONA
4568

Cooroora Mountain Pk

Forest Reserve

Restricted Vehicle Access

DOLLARBIRD DR 2
FRIARBIRD PL 4
GERRYGONE PL 3
SONGBIRDS DR 1
WHISTLER WY 5

Pomona Pmy

Palm Lake Resort

State Forest

State Forest
Restricted Vehicle Access

COOROY
4563

BLACK MOUNTAIN
4563

State Forest

COPYRIGHT © UNIVERSAL PUBLISHERS PTY LTD

JOINS 1 / JOINS 5

1 2 3 4 7089N 7087N 7085N 5 7 8 9 10 7083N 11 12 13 14 7081N 15 16 17 18 7079N 19 20

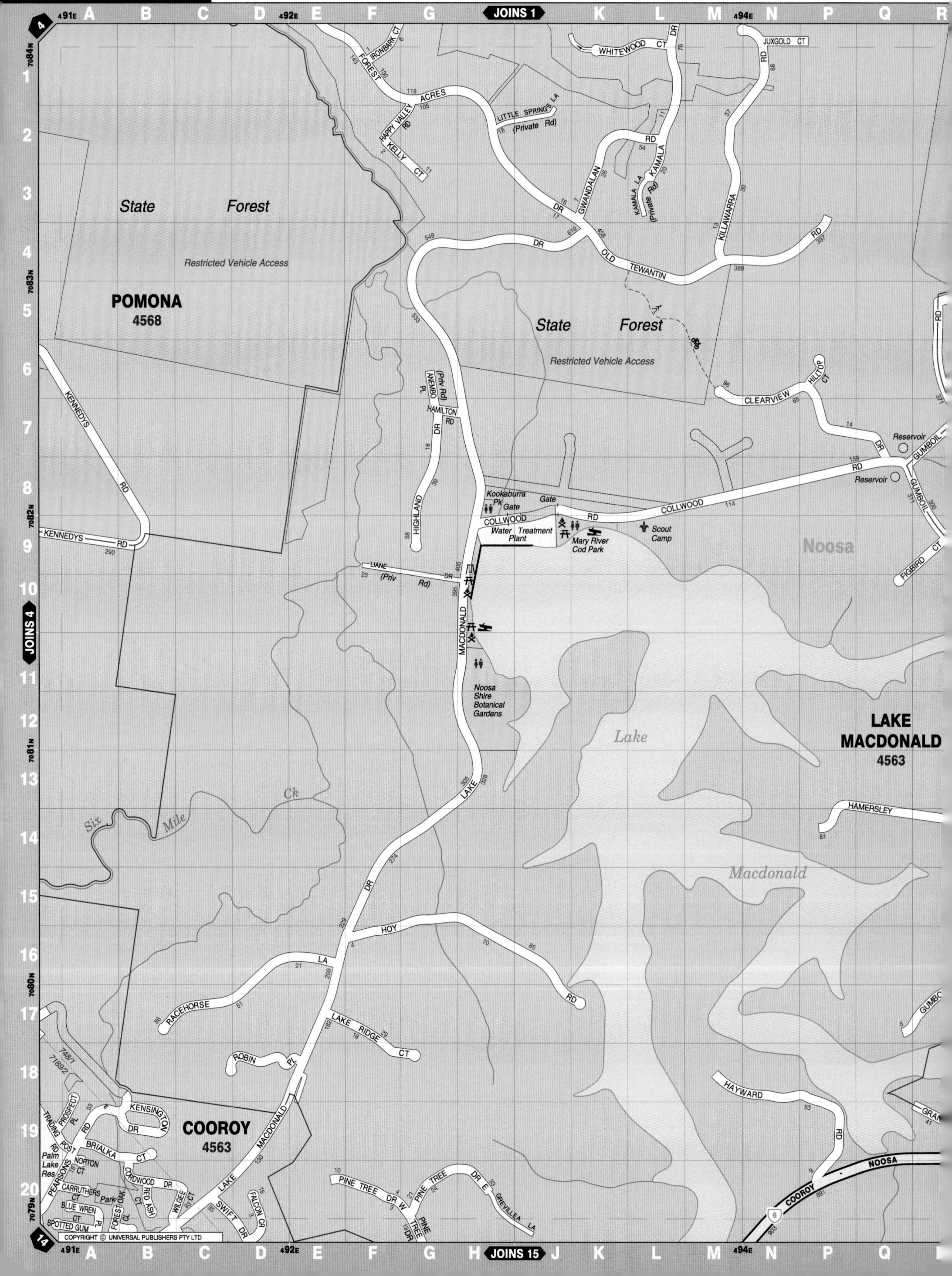

MAP 5
1 KILOMETRE EQUALS 4 GRID SQUARES

JOINS 1

4

491E

A B C D 492E E F G K L M 494E N P Q R

1

JOINS 4

State Forest

Restricted Vehicle Access

POMONA
4568

KENNEDYS RD

KENNEDYS RD

State Forest

Restricted Vehicle Access

IRONBARK CT

FOREST

HAPPY VALLEY RD

KELLY CT

ACRES

LITTLE SPRINGS LA
(Private Rd)

WHITEWOOD CT

JUXGOLD CT

GWANDALAN DR

KANALA LA
(Private Rd)

KAMALA RD

OLD TEWANTIN

KILLAWARRA RD

CLEARVIEW

HILLTOP CT

DR

Reservoir

Reservoir

GUMBOIL CT

FIGBIRD CT

Noosa

(Priv Rd)
ANEMBO PL

HAMILTON RD

HIGHLAND DR

Kookaburra
Pk Gate

Gate

COLLWOOD

Water Treatment
Plant

RD

Mary River
Cod Park

COLLWOOD RD

Scout
Camp

LIANE
(Priv Rd)

DR

MACDONALD

Noosa
Shire
Botanical
Gardens

Lake

LAKE

LAKE
MACDONALD
4563

Lake

Macdonald

Six Mile Ck

HAMERSLEY

DR

HOY

LA

RACEHORSE

LAKE RIDGE CT

RD

ROBIN PL

GUMBOI

HAYWARD

GRAN

COOROY
4563

MACDONALD

KENSINGTON DR

BRIALKA CT

PEARSONS RD
PROSPECT RD
TRADING POST
NORTON CT
CORDWOOD DR
RED ASH
WILGEE CT
Palm
Lake
Res
CARRUTHERS CT
Park
BLUE WREN CT
SPOTTED GUM CT
FOREST OAK CT

LAKE

SWIFT DR

FALCON CR

PINE TREE DR W

PINE TREE

PINE TREE DR E

GREVILLEA LA

RD

HAYWARD RD

COOROY NOOSA

COOROY

14

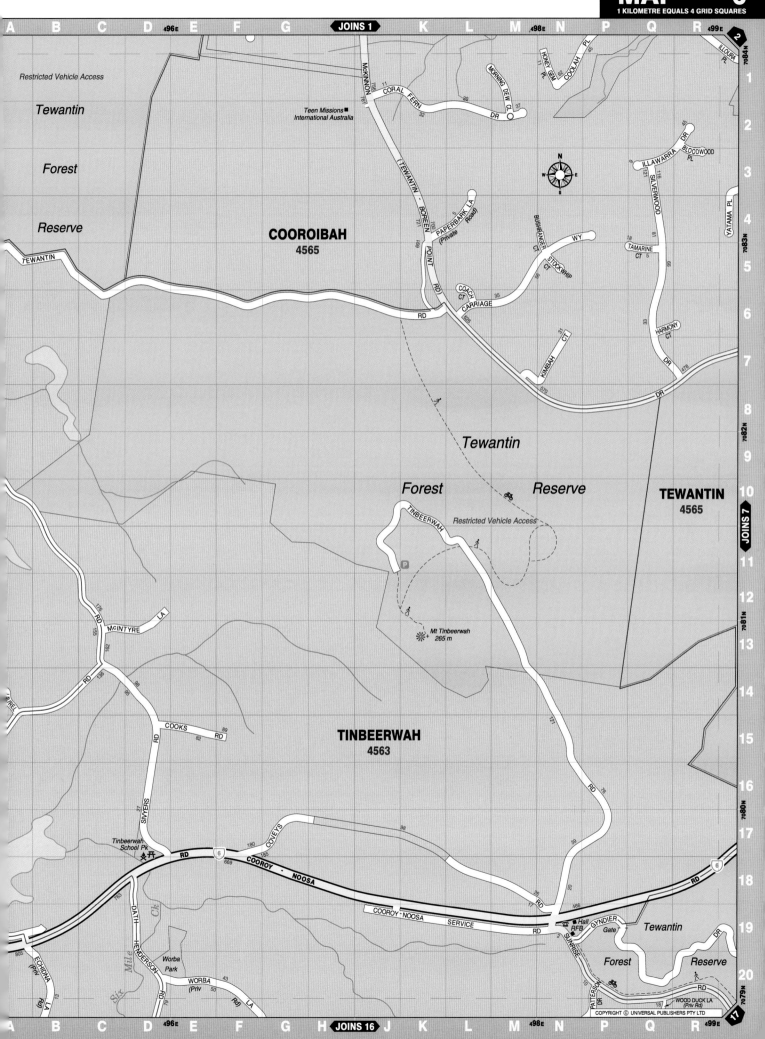

MAP 6
1 KILOMETRE EQUALS 4 GRID SQUARES

JOINS 1

Restricted Vehicle Access

Tewantin

Forest

Reserve

COOROIBAH
4565

Teen Missions
International Australia

Tewantin

Forest   *Reserve*

TEWANTIN
4565

Restricted Vehicle Access

TINBEERWAH

Mt Tinbeerwah
265 m

TINBEERWAH
4563

Tinbeerwah
School Pk

COOROY - NOOSA

COOROY - NOOSA SERVICE

Tewantin

Worba
Park

Forest   *Reserve*

WOOD DUCK LA
(Priv Rd)

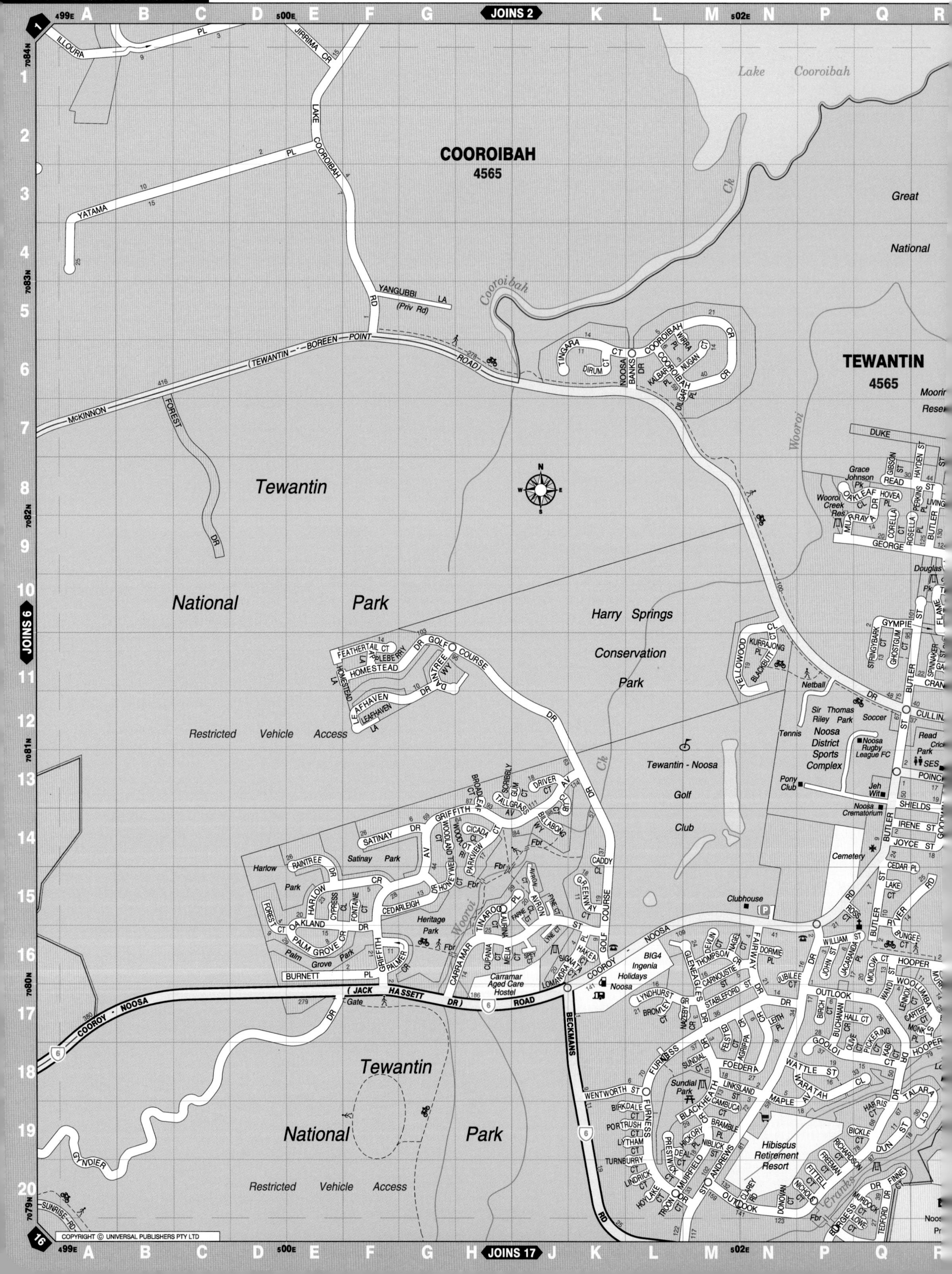

MAP 7
1 KILOMETRE EQUALS 4 GRID SQUARES

JOINS 2

COOROIBAH
4565

TEWANTIN
4565

Lake Cooroibah

Great

National

Tewantin

National Park

Harry Springs

Conservation

Park

Tewantin - Noosa

Golf

Club

Tewantin

National Park

Restricted Vehicle Access

Restricted Vehicle Access

Noosa District Sports Complex

Noosa Rugby League FC

Sir Thomas Riley Park

Pony Club

Noosa Crematorium

Cemetery

Clubhouse

Carramar Aged Care Hostel

BIG4 Ingenia Holidays Noosa

Hibiscus Retirement Resort

Sundial Park

Heritage Park

Satinay Park

Harlow Park

Harlow

ILLOURA
YATAMA
McKINNON
FOREST DR
JIFRIMA CR
LAKE COOROIBAH PL
YANGUBBI LA (Priv Rd)
TEWANTIN — BOREEN — POINT ROAD
COOROY - NOOSA
JACK HASSETT (DR) ROAD
BECKMANS RD
GYNDIER
SUNRISE RD

TINGARA
NOOSA BANKS
COOROIBAH DR
KALBAROIBAH PL
DIRUM CT
NUGAN CT
WIRRA CR
DUKE
GIBSON
HAYDEN ST
READ
OAKLEAF
HOVEA
CORELLA
ROSELLA
PERKINS
BUTLER
LIVING
MURRAY
GEORGE
GYMPIE
FLAME
STRINGYBARK
GHOSTGUM
SPINNAKER
CRAN
KURRAJONG PL
BLACKBUTT
YELLOWOOD
CULLIN
BUTLER DR
SHIELDS
IRENE ST
JOYCE ST
POINC
CEDAR PL
LAKE CT
PIER
BUNGEE
WILLIAM ST
HOOPER
JACARANDA
MOLOW CT
WANDI
LENNOX
CARTER
MURI
FEATHERTAIL CT
PLEBERRY
HOMESTEAD
LEAFHAVEN
LEAFHAVEN LA
DAINTREE WY
GOLF COURSE DR
BROADLEAF CT
SCRIBBLY GUM
TALLGRASS AV
DRIVER CT
GUM AV
GRIFFITH DR
WOODLAND
CICADA CT
PARKVIEW
SATINAY DR
RAINTREE DR
CYPRESS
FONTAINE
CEDARLEIGH
AKLAND CT
HARLOW CR
FOREST CT
PALM GROVE CR
GRIFFITH
PALMER
BURNETT
CARRA MAR
CUPANIA
MELIA
TINAROO
SIGNAL CT
LOMANDRA
SPEY
LYNE CT
COOROY
BILLABONG WY
ARROW
AVRON
FARNE
GREENWAY
HAVEN
CADDY CL
GOLF COURSE
FINEST
FAIRWAY PL
DORMIE PL
DEVLIN
NAGLE
THOMPSON
GLENEAGLES
CARNOUSTIE
STABLEFORD
NAZEBY
BROMLEY
LYNDHURST
CLIVE
BIRCH
JOHN ST
LEITH
HALL CT
BUCHANAN
PICKERING
KABI
GOOLOI
OUTLOOK DR
HOOPER
WATTLE ST
WARATAH
MAPLE
FURNESS
FELSTED
GRIPPA
FOEDERA
LINKSLAND
CAMBUCA
BLACKHEATH
BRAMBLE PL
HICKORY
NIBLICK
DEAL
ANDREWS
DONOVAN
NICHOLS
FITTEL
FREEMAN
RICHARDSON
BICKLE CT
HARRIS
DUN ST
TALARA
MURFORD
LONE
TEDFORD
FINNEY
BIRKDALE CT
PORTRUSH
LYTHAM
TURNBURY
PRESTWICK
LINDRICK CT
HOYLAKE CT
TROON CT
MURFIELD
WENTWORTH ST
FURNESS

JOINS 17

MAP 8
1 KILOMETRE EQUALS 4 GRID SQUARES

JOINS 2

JOINS 18

JOINS 9

Sandy

Park

NOOSA
NORTH
SHORE
4565

Great   Sandy

National   Park

Noosa

Sheep
Island

Sheep Island
Conservation
Park

Goat
Island

Goat Island
Conservation
Park

Makepeace
Island

Teewah
Laguna
Bay

Beach

ECHELON ESP

RIVER

Doonella

Lake

Noosa
Convention
Exhibition
Centre

Wallace
House

Noosa
Leisure
Cntr

Noosa
Hospital

Wallace
Park

NOOSAVILLE

4566

Keyser I

Keyser I
Conservation
Park

Laguna
Estate

Noosa Waters
Ret Estate

Noosa Yacht
& Rowing Club

Liberty
Swing
Lions Park

Apex
Park

Quota
Park

Pelican Beach
Park

Massoud Pk

Jetty

Noosa
Homemaker
Centre

Noosa
Village

Noosaville
Substn

Riverlands

Noosa
Nursing Cntr

Ingenia
Holidays
Noosa Nth

Ferry

Big
Shell

Lakeside
Pk

Ward
Park

Art
Gallery
Cncl
Marina

Jetty
Swim
Pool

MAP 9
1 KILOMETRE EQUALS 4 GRID SQUARES

507E 508E 509E 510E

NOOSA NORTH SHORE 4565

Teewah Beach
ECHELON ESP
FRYING PAN TR

Laguna Bay

Laguna Bay

North Head
Inlet
Breakwater
Coastguard Tower
Noosa Spit
CLAUDE BATTEN DR

Dolphin Pt
The Stairway
Boiling Pot
Tea Tree Bay
Noosa Hill
Coastal
Grar Ba

Little Cove
Noosa Hill (147 m)

Noosa National Park

SLSC
HASTINGS ST
Lions Park
Noosa Sound
Ravenwood Park
Sounds Park
Picture Point
Bunya
Laguna Lookout
Reservoir
Hollindale Tr

Noosa Spit Recreation Reserve

Munna Pt
Coast Guard (VM-4GW)
Munna Pk

GYMPIE TCE
WILLIAM ST
RUSSELL ST
HOWARD ST
WOORO
DOLPHIN CR
NOOSA

Nancy Cato Pk
PARK CT

Keyser I
NOOSAVILLE 4566
Keyser Island Conservation Park
Hay I

NOOSA HEADS 4567

Noosa Fair
Plaza
Cinema
MAINSAILS SQ
Pinnaroo Rotary Park
RACV Resort Noosa
Ross I

SUNSHINE BEACH
Noosa National Park

Sunshine Beach
Noosa District Rugby Union Club
Cmnty Centre
St Thomas More Catholic Primary
BICENTENNIAL
PARKEDGE RD
SOLWAY
NEBULA
OCEANIA
PACIFIC

HASTINGS BVD 3
LITTLE COVE CR 4
SANCTUARY DR 1
THOMPSON DR 2

WEYBA RD
Noosa Arts Theatre
Noosa AFC
Australian Rules Ovals
Laguna Estate
Ret Est
NANNYGAI ST
WYLAH ST
TAINE ST
SWAN ST
KOEL
CRAB

A W Dan Park
GIRRAWEEN CT
Noosa Aquatic Centre
Tennis
EENIE CREEK RD
HEATHLAND DR

JOINS 8
JOINS 19
JOINS 18

COPYRIGHT © UNIVERSAL PUBLISHERS PTY LTD

7084N 7083N 7082N 7081N 7080N 7079N

MAP 13
FOLLOWS

10

1 KILOMETRE EQUALS 4 GRID SQUARES

A B C D s12E E F G H s13E J K L M s14E N P Q R s15E

1 2 3 4 5 6 7 8 9 10 11 12 13 14 15 16 17 18 19 20

7084N 7083N 7082N 7081N 7080N 7079N

CORAL

SEA

Fairy
Pools

*Picnic
Cove*

Track

Track

Noosa
Head

Hells
Gates

Beach

Alexandria

Bay

Track

Alexandria

Oyster
Rocks

Roaring Caves
(Blowhole)

Lion
Rock

Harrys

Devils
Kitchen

Cooks
Monument

Paradise
Caves

CANALLY CT

DR

ESPLANADE

ARAKOON RD

26

27

28

29

30

31

32

Beach

Sunshine

SLSC

**SUNSHINE
BEACH**

4567

A B C D s12E E F G H J K L M s14E N P Q R s15E

A B C D E F G H JOINS 3 J K L M N P Q R

JOINS 3

FEDERAL
4568

TUCHEKOI
4570

KENILWORTH

WHITTLE RD

CHINAMANS OLSENS RD

SKYRING CREEK

RD

312

150

ANDERSONS RD

268

MIDDLE CREEK

378

447

Middle

TUCHEKOI RD

VIC OLSEN BRIDGE

1189

119

IRONSTONE CREEK

37

78

1131

1018

RIVER

BLACK MOUNTAIN RD

BLACK MOUNTAIN RD

984

978

190

179

902

630

718

RD

PADJPA RD

BOLLIER
4570

Gympie

RD

N
W E
S

CRAWFORDS RD

40

1061

GETERS RD

82

CRAWFORDS LA

Jack Ck Happy

MARY

HOVEA RD

SARUS RD

RD

40

MONARCH RD

15

CARTERS RIDGE
4563

Mary Fereday Pk

JUBILEE

RD

42

POULSEN

KENILWORTH

SKYRING CREEK

763

WALLABY CT

MARY RD

HAPPY JACK CREEK

HAPPY JACK CREEK

373

OLD MILL

678

100

157

120

CRAWFORDS RD

RD

RD

1596

1352

1327

COOROY BELLI CREEK

1164

1145

RD

RIDGEWOOD
4563

POULSEN RD

144

144

OAK CT

137

GILLILAND RD

56

DONNELLYS RD

25

1440

Hall

RD

BELLI CREEK

1460

Blackfellow Creek

LIMIT OF MAPS

RIVER

ASPENNELL RD

RD

NEWSPAPER HILL

27

LAWRENCE RD

1528

COOROY

476

1531

SKYRING CREEK

388

State

WHELAN

RD

BELLI PARK
4562

292

MARY

Belli Ck

RD

NEWSPAPER HILL

(Narrow bridge)

892

205

178

Sunshine Coast

SPILLER RD

BOYLE

BELLI OAK TREE RD

10

65

60

Belli Ck

83

RD

RD

366

Restricted Vehicle Access

A B C D E F G H JOINS 33 J K L M N P Q R

JOINS 33

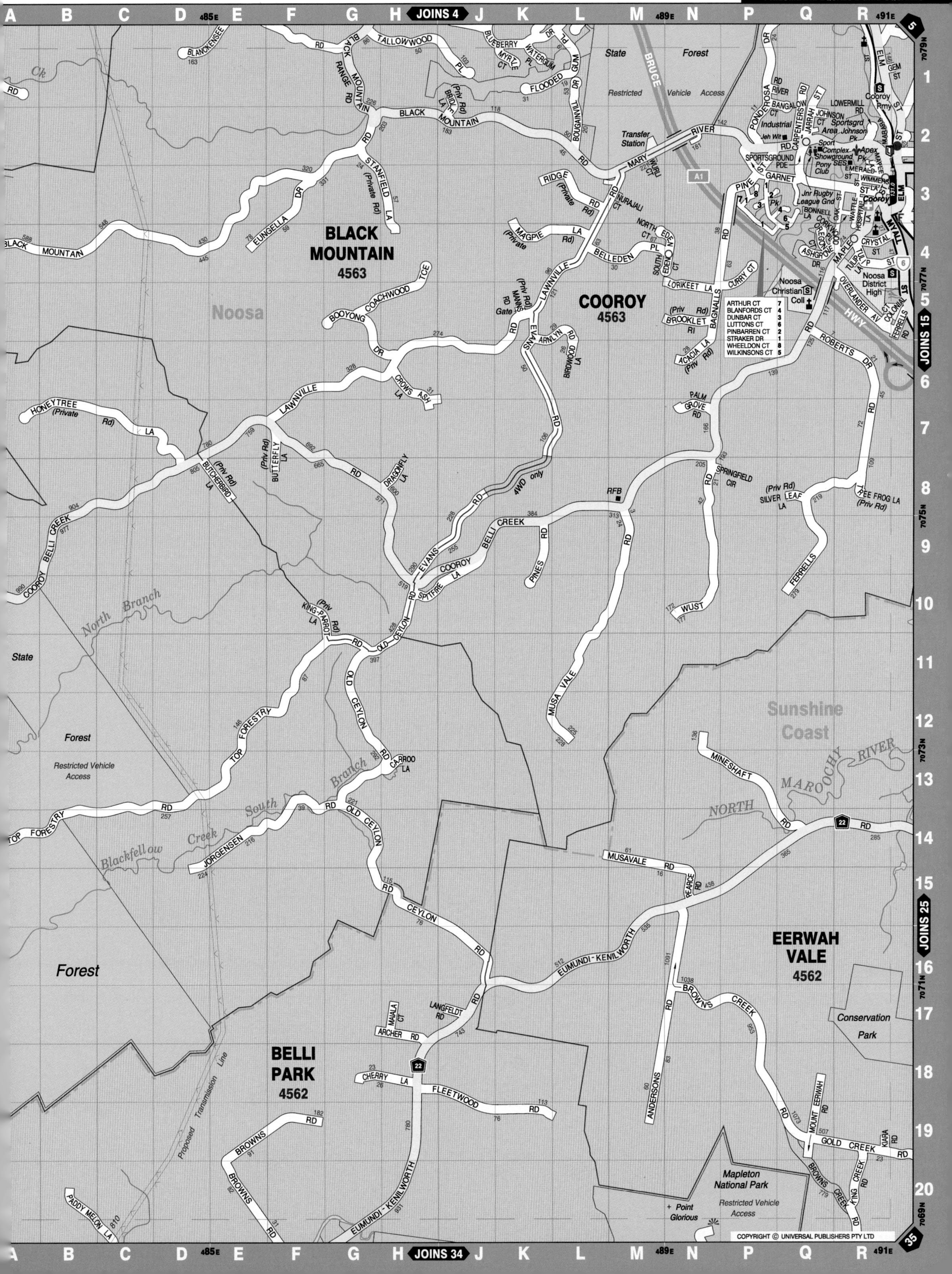

MAP 14
1 KILOMETRE EQUALS 2 GRID SQUARES

BLACK
MOUNTAIN
4563

COOROY
4563

Noosa

State Forest
Restricted Vehicle Access

EERWAH
VALE
4562

BELLI
PARK
4562

Forest

State Forest

Forest
Restricted Vehicle Access

Sunshine Coast

Mapleton
National Park
Restricted Vehicle Access
+ Point Glorious

Conservation Park

Blackfellow Creek

North Branch

South Branch

MAROOCHY RIVER
NORTH

Proposed Transmission Line

ARTHUR CT	7
BLANFORDS CT	4
DUNBAR CT	3
LUTTONS CT	6
PINBARREN CT	2
STRAKER DR	1
WHEELDON CT	8
WILKINSONS CT	5

JOINS 4
JOINS 15
JOINS 25
JOINS 34
JOINS 35

MAP 15
1 KILOMETRE EQUALS 4 GRID SQUARES

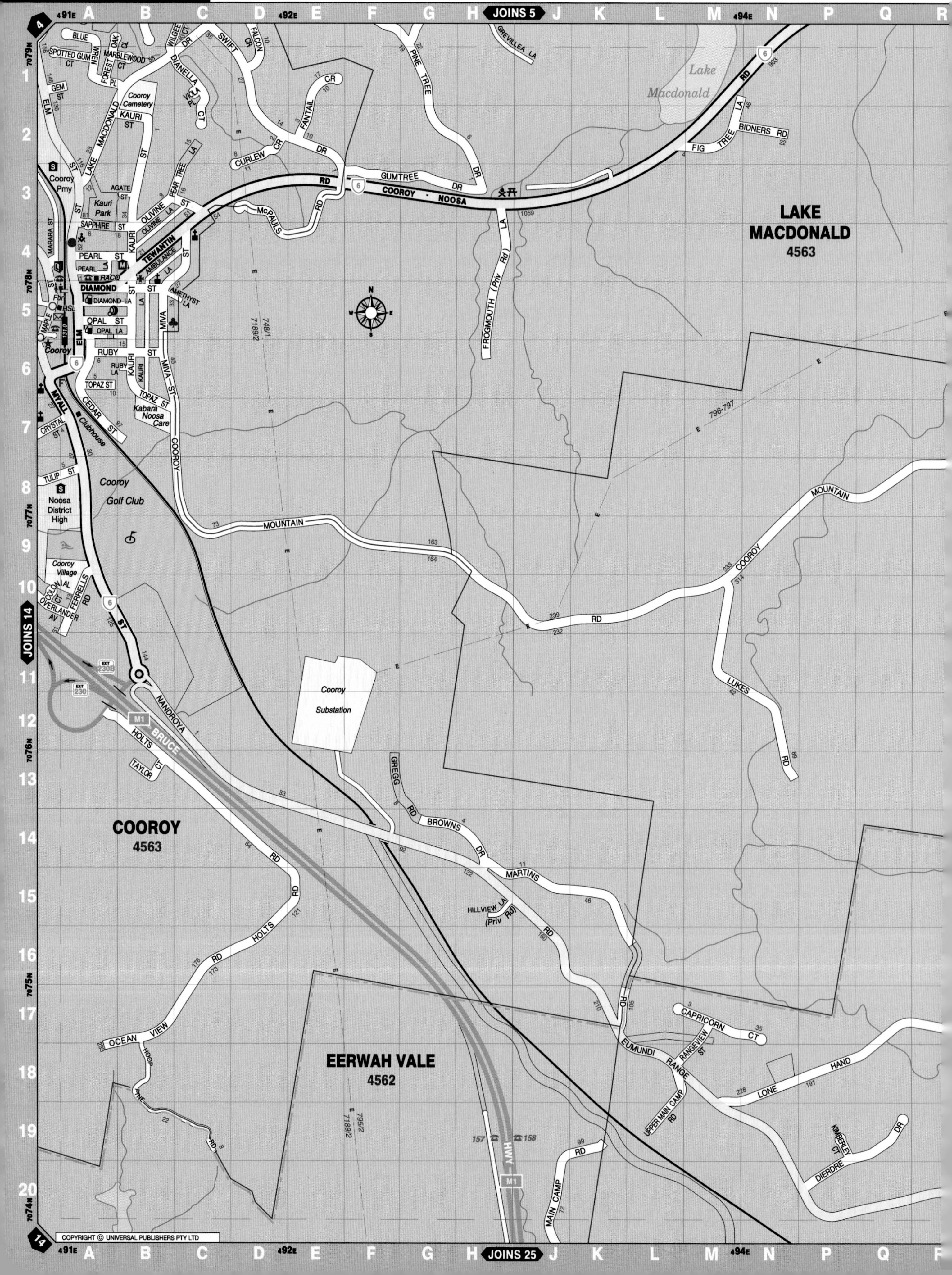

JOINS 5

LAKE MACDONALD
4563

Lake Macdonald

COOROY
4563

EERWAH VALE
4562

Cooroy Cemetery
Cooroy Pmy
Kauri Park
Cooroy Golf Club
Noosa District High
Cooroy Village
Cooroy Substation
Kabara Noosa Care
Cooroy Clubhouse

Street names:
BLUE, SPOTTED GUM CT, MARBLEWOOD CT, FOREST OAK CT, GEM ST, ELM ST, MARABA ST, KAURI ST, LAKE MACDONALD DR, WILGEE DR, DIANELLA DR, VIOLA CT, SWIFT, FALCON, CURLEW CR, FANTAIL DR, PEAR TREE LA, OLIVINE LA, AGATE ST, SAPPHIRE ST, PEARL ST, DIAMOND LA, OPAL LA, OPAL ST, RUBY ST, RUBY LA, KAURI LA, TOPAZ ST, MIVA ST, AMETHYST LA, TEWANTIN, AMBULANCE, MYALL ST, CEDAR ST, CRYSTAL ST, TULIP ST, COLONIAL, FERRELLS RD, OVERLANDER AV, MAPLE, PINE TREE, GREVILLEA LA, GUMTREE DR, COOROY - NOOSA, McPAULS, FROGMOUTH (Priv Rd), FIG TREE LA, BIDNERS RD

MOUNTAIN RD, COOROY RD, LUKES RD, NANDROYA, BRUCE, HOLTS, TAYLOR CT, HOLTS RD, OCEAN VIEW, HOOP PINE, GREGG RD, BROWNS DR, MARTINS, HILLVIEW LA (Priv Rd), CAPRICORN CT, RANGEVIEW ST, EUMUNDI RANGE RD, UPPER MAIN CAMP RD, LONE HAND, MAIN CAMP RD, KIMBERLEY CT, DIERDRE DR

HWY M1

JOINS 14
JOINS 25

70 79 N 70 78 N 70 77 N 70 76 N 70 75 N 70 74 N

491E 492E 494E

EXIT 230B EXIT 230

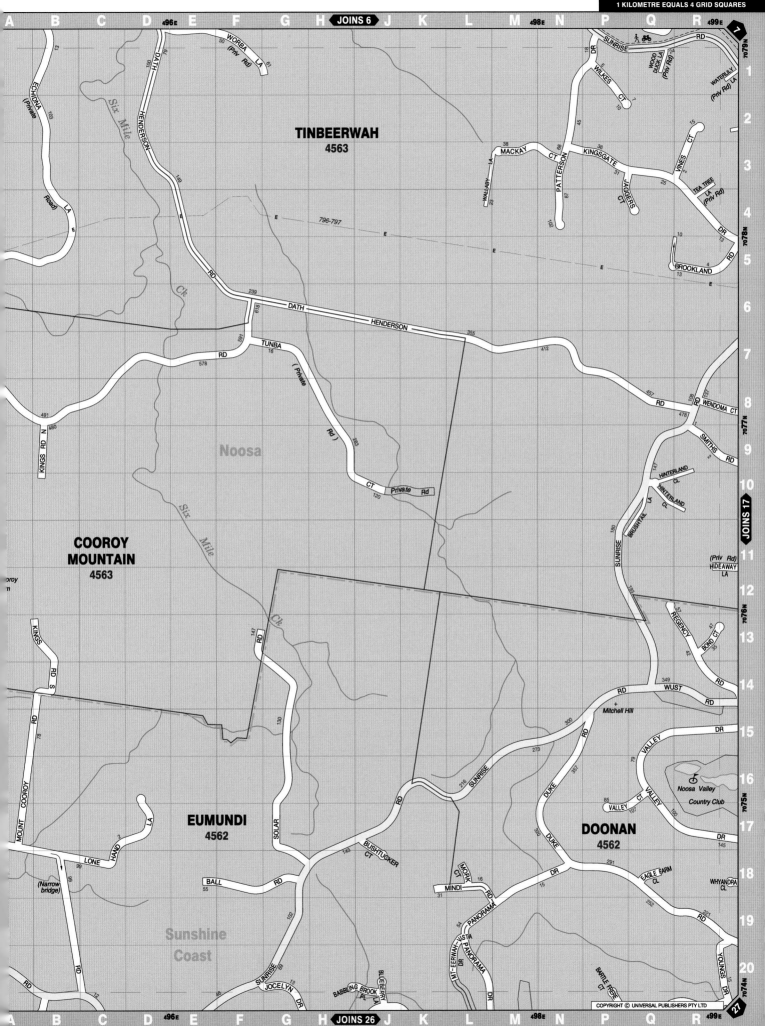

MAP 16
1 KILOMETRE EQUALS 4 GRID SQUARES

TINBEERWAH
4563

Noosa

COOROY
MOUNTAIN
4563

EUMUNDI
4562

DOONAN
4562

Sunshine
Coast

Noosa Valley
Country Club

Mitchell Hill

MAP **17**
1 KILOMETRE EQUALS 4 GRID SQUARES

JOINS 7

JOINS 16

JOINS 27

Tewantin

National *Park*

TEWANTIN
4565

Restricted   Vehicle   Access

TINBEERWAH
4563

Noosa

DOONAN
4562

Sunshine
Coast

Noosa Valley
Country Club

Col
Swift
Park

Pony
Club

RFB

RSPCA

Resource
Recovery

EMU   MOUNTAIN

Sunrise Hills
Substn

Cranks

Noosaville
Pmy

Clubhouse

SUNRISE
WATERLILY LA (Priv Rd)
SUGAR GLIDER LA (Priv Rd)
TEA TREE LA (Priv Rd)
KINGSGATE DR
BROOKLAND RD
WOOROI FOREST DR
PACIFIC
ASHDOWN CT
VIEW
UPLAND CT
WENDOMA CT
WENDOMA CL (Priv Rd)
SMITHS
HIDEAWAY (Priv Rd) LA
BUSHY PARK LA (Priv Rd)
AVIAN CT
ARBOUR PL
MINYURA CT
WY
NYLANA LA
PHEASANT
BEDDINGTON RD
GEEBUNG LA
LENEHANS RD
FOXTAIL RI
HESPER RI
KIMBERLEY CT
SENEGAL
PICCABEEN ST
LIVISTONA DR
SOLITAIRE ST
RAFFIA DR
MIRBELIA PL
WARD WY (Priv Rd)
WHIPBIRD DR
CALANTHE
CASSOWARY CT
WATTLEBIRD
PERSONIA LA
PAIGE CT
KYLE
ECHIDNA PL
BOND CT
REGENCY RD
GREEN TREE PL
TRAFALGAR CT
WUST
VALLEY DR
MEADOW CT
WHYANDRA CL
TEMPLETON WY
DUKE
YOUNGS DR
COCOS CT
LITTLERIDGE RD
EUMUNDI · NOOSA RD
GRAYS RD
NYELL RD
RUTCH RD
FELLOWSHIP
CHARLES DUKE MEMORIAL DR (Priv Rd)
HOLLETT-RL
OLD HOLLE
EUMUNDI · NOOSA
BECKMANS
ST ANDREWS
OUTLOOK
DONOVAN DR
BURGESS
TEDFO
MURDOCK DR
LOWE CT

MAP 18
1 KILOMETRE EQUALS 4 GRID SQUARES

JOINS 8

NOOSAVILLE
4566

Noosa
National Park

Noosa
Airstrip
(Private)

Noosa Hills
Golf Course

Clubhouse

Eenie Creek
Bushland
Reserve

Noosa
Civic

Business
Cntr

Business
Centre

Good
Shepherd
Lutheran
College

Noosa
Domain
Village

Noosa
Croquet
Club

Shorehaven
Park

Laguna
Estate

Noosa
Waters
Retirement
Estate

MONKS
BRIDGE

Lake

Weyba

Lake

Weyba

Weyba
Nature
Refuge

WEYBA DOWNS
4562

Waste
r Station

Noosa

National Park

Noosa Pengari
Steiner School

JOINS 28

JOINS 19

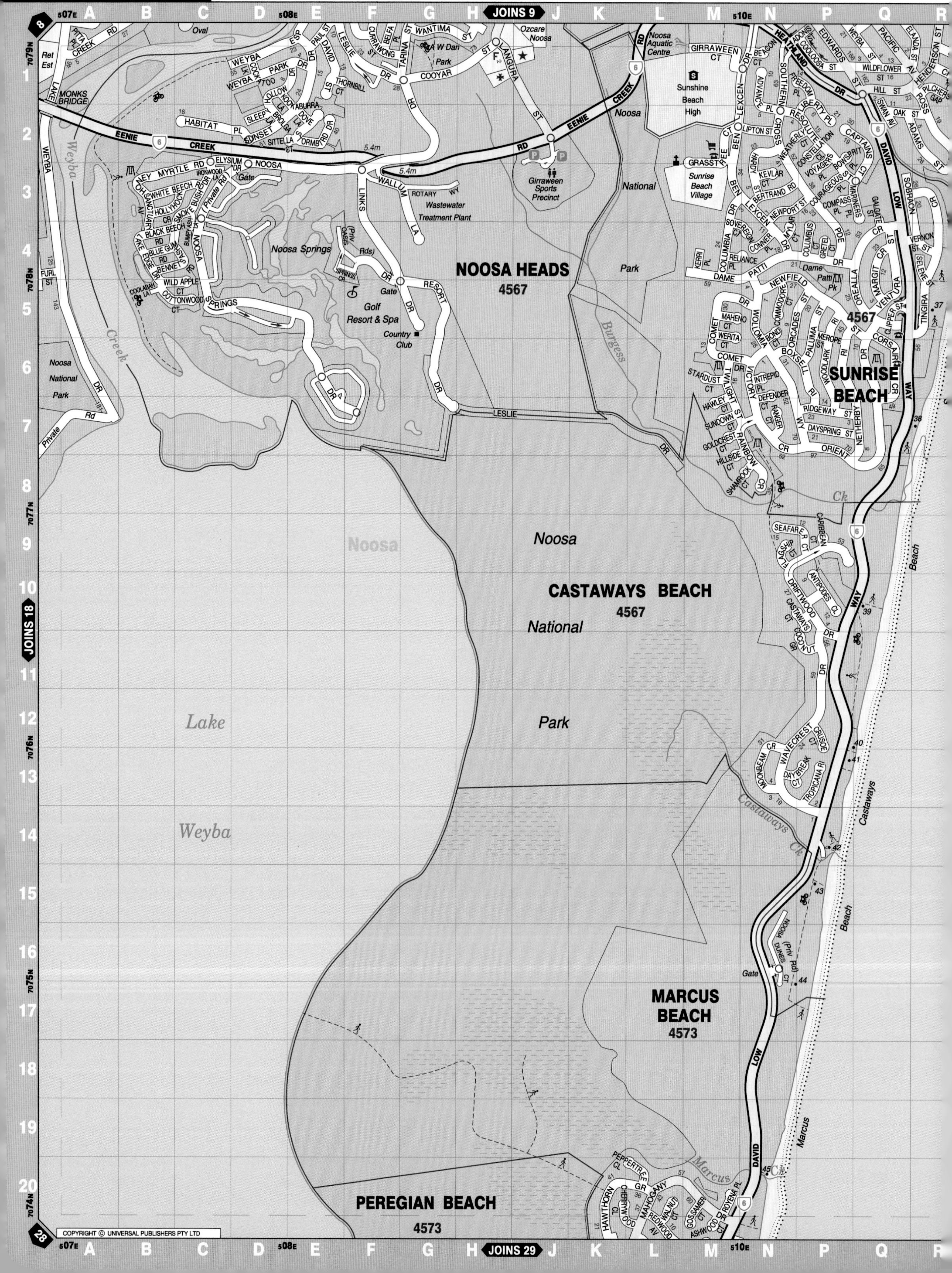

MAP 19
1 KILOMETRE EQUALS 4 GRID SQUARES

JOINS 9

NOOSA HEADS
4567

CASTAWAYS BEACH
4567

SUNRISE BEACH
4567

MARCUS BEACH
4573

PEREGIAN BEACH
4573

Noosa National Park

Noosa Springs

Golf Resort & Spa
Country Club

Wastewater Treatment Plant

Girraween Sports Precinct

Noosa Aquatic Centre

Sunshine Beach High

Sunrise Beach Village

Lake Weyba

Weyba Creek

JOINS 18

JOINS 28

JOINS 29

MAP 25 FOLLOWS

20

1 KILOMETRE EQUALS 4 GRID SQUARES

A B C D s12E E F G H JOINS 10 J K L M s14E N P Q R s15E

Sunshine Beach

**SUNSHINE
BEACH**
4567

N
W E
S

CORAL

SEA

7079N
1
2
3
7078N
5
6
7
8
7077N
9
10
11
12
7076N
13
14
15
16
7075N
17
18
19
20
7074N

A B C D s12E E F G H JOINS 30 J K L M s14E N P Q R s15E

14

JOINS 15

JOINS 14

EERWAH VALE
4562

Sunshine Coast

NORTH ARM
4561

JOINS 35

24

EUMUNDI RANGE RD

RIVER

NORTH

MAROOCHY

NEERAWAY

LA

LARNEYS

EUMUNDI

KENILWORTH

22

STRONG LA

CHAMBERS LA

MEMORIAL

BRUCE

MAIN

CAMP

GRASSTREE

RD

RD

EXIT 224

5.8m RD

5.8m

WEST EUMUNDI

MEMORIAL

HWY

Sandy Ck

ST

FINLE

BALKIN

BLACK STUMP RD

Eumundi
Showgrounds
& Sports
Complex

FULLAGER DR

MILLER PL

CLARK ST

BURRELL ST

COWELL ST

HULL AV

BOWMAN CT

VIV AV

SALE ST

ELIZABETH

RACECOURSE RI

Hall

BARLEE ST

CRESCENT

WILLIAM

Reservoir

POWERS CT

BRUSHBOX PL

CLIFTON PL

SANDERSON

Tatnell

COLEUS

WILSONS

14

795/2

71/89/2

N

Conservation

Park

Caplick Ck

GOLDEN RAIN LA

Cemetery

HATFIELD RD

BALSAM RD

RD

Ped Upass 5.5m

EUMUNDI

12

5.5m

EXIT 224

MEMORIAL

22

BRUCE HWY

M1

KIARA RD

GOLD CREEK

GEES RD

RD

BUNYA

M1

MAP 26
1 KILOMETRE EQUALS 4 GRID SQUARES

DOONAN
4562

* Eumundi Bicentennial Lookout

EUMUNDI
4562

VERRIERDALE
4562

Conservation Park

Restricted Vehicle Access

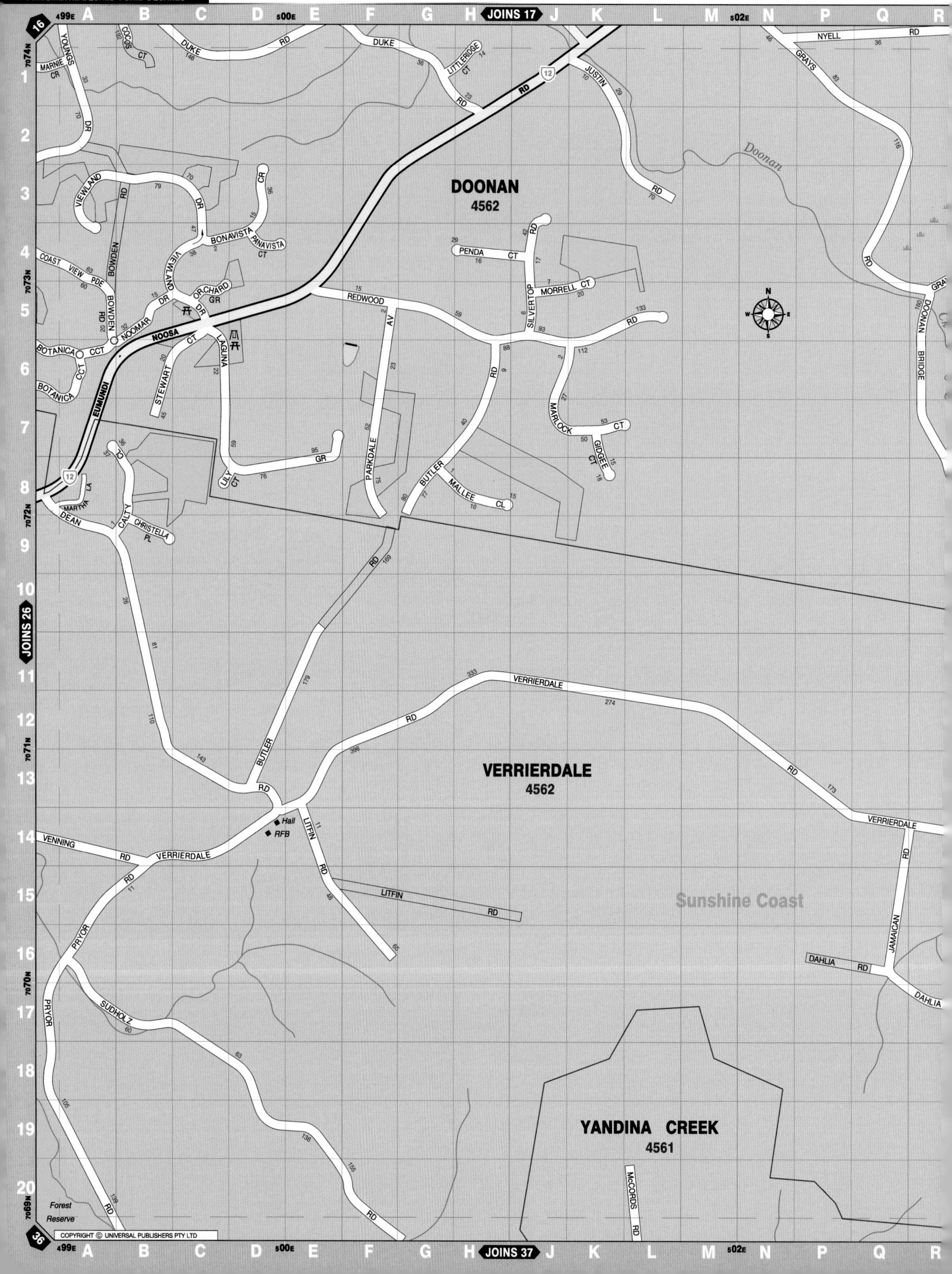

MAP 27

1 KILOMETRE EQUALS 4 GRID SQUARES

JOINS 17

DOONAN
4562

VERRIERDALE
4562

YANDINA CREEK
4561

Sunshine Coast

Doonan

Forest
Reserve

JOINS 26

JOINS 16

JOINS 36

MAP 28
1 KILOMETRE EQUALS 4 GRID SQUARES

A B C D s04 E F G H **JOINS 18** J K L M s06 E N P Q R s07 E

19

Noosa Pengari
Steiner School

EMU MOUNTAIN RD
RUTCH

Lake Weyba

Noosa

National Park

LAKESHORE PL

WEYBA
DOWNS
4562

Iona
College
Camp

Private Road

BARBARA RD

LAKE VISTA

LAKEWOOD

GWENETH RD

CLARENDON DR

ANNIE

MONAK

PEREGIAN
BEACH
4573

RD

Doonan

ROAD

EMU MOUNTAIN

RD

MURDERING CREEK

OLD EMU MOUNTAIN

JOINS 29

Peregian Beach
College

Noosa

DOONAN BRIDGE

ROAD

RD N

DOONAN BRIDGE EAST

Substation

PEREGIAN SPRINGS

Peregian-Springs DR

GAINSBOROUGH

Grove
Park

Gate

Conservation
Area

**PEREGIAN
SPRINGS
4573**

BELLERIVE

RIVIERA

SPYGLASS

SELKIRK

BONVILLE

WATERVILLE

BAHRANSE

COBBITY

GOLDEN BELL DR

CRENSHAW

LONGCOVE PL

BALGOWNIE DR

AVENUE

WESTVIEW

ROTHBURY

NICKLAUS

EAGLEFORD

PENNANT

Gate

Clubhouse

Peregian Springs

Gate

MEDINAH

INVERNESS PL

JACKSON

THE

Peregian Springs
Golf
Club

NOTTINGHAM LA

FOREST RIDGE

LAKESIDE DR

HERON

PARKWOOD

BUNKER WY

SAWGRASS

FAIRWAY PDE

PUTTERS

NOTTINGHAM

LONGCOVE

PARKVIEW

COPYRIGHT © UNIVERSAL PUBLISHERS PTY LTD

A B C D s04 E F G H **JOINS 38** J K L M s06 E N P Q R s07 E

39

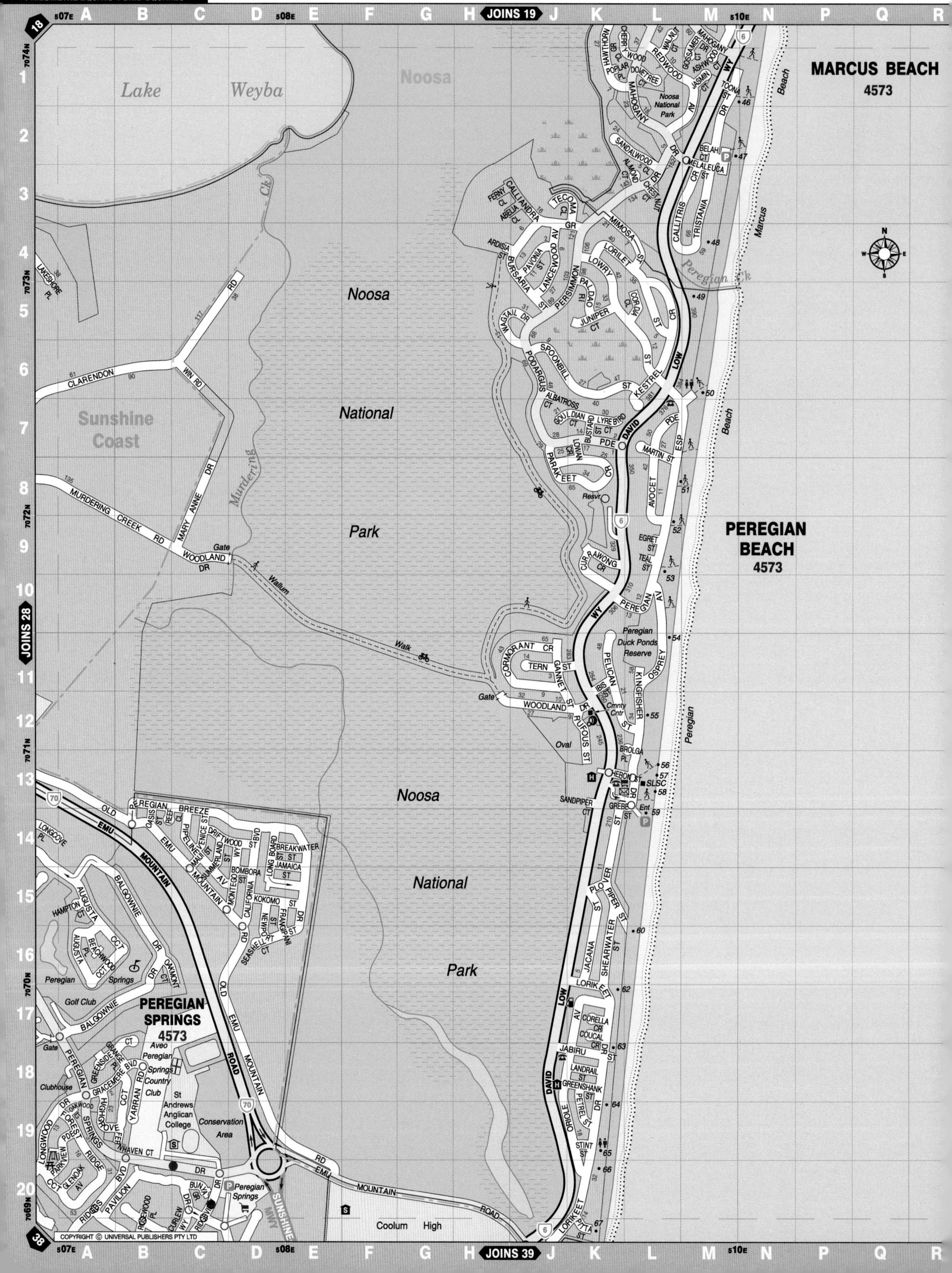

MAP 29
1 KILOMETRE EQUALS 4 GRID SQUARES

JOINS 19

JOINS 39

JOINS 28

MARCUS BEACH
4573

PEREGIAN BEACH
4573

PEREGIAN SPRINGS
4573

Lake Weyba

Noosa

Sunshine Coast

Noosa National Park

Noosa National Park

Murdering Ck

Noosa National Park

Peregian Golf Club

Peregian Springs

Aveo Peregian Springs Country Club

St Andrews Anglican College

Conservation Area

Peregian Springs

Coolum High

COPYRIGHT © UNIVERSAL PUBLISHERS PTY LTD

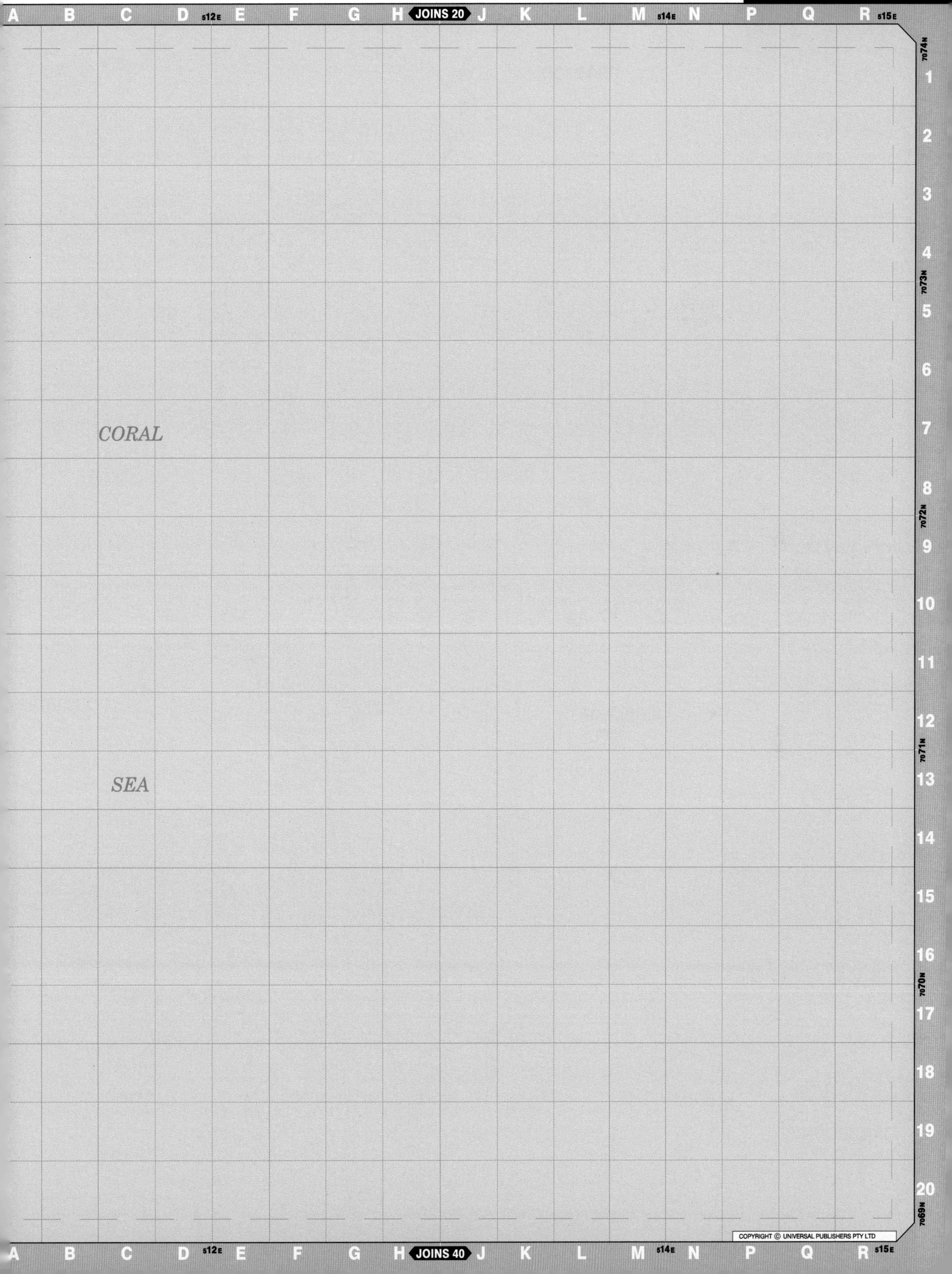

MAP 30
1 KILOMETRE EQUALS 4 GRID SQUARES

A B C D s12E E F G H JOINS 20 J K L M s14E N P Q R s15E

7o74N
1

2

3

7o73N
4

5

6

7

8

7o72N
9

10

11

12

7o71N
13

14

15

16

7o70N
17

18

19

20

7o69N

CORAL

SEA

JOINS 40

COPYRIGHT © UNIVERSAL PUBLISHERS PTY LTD

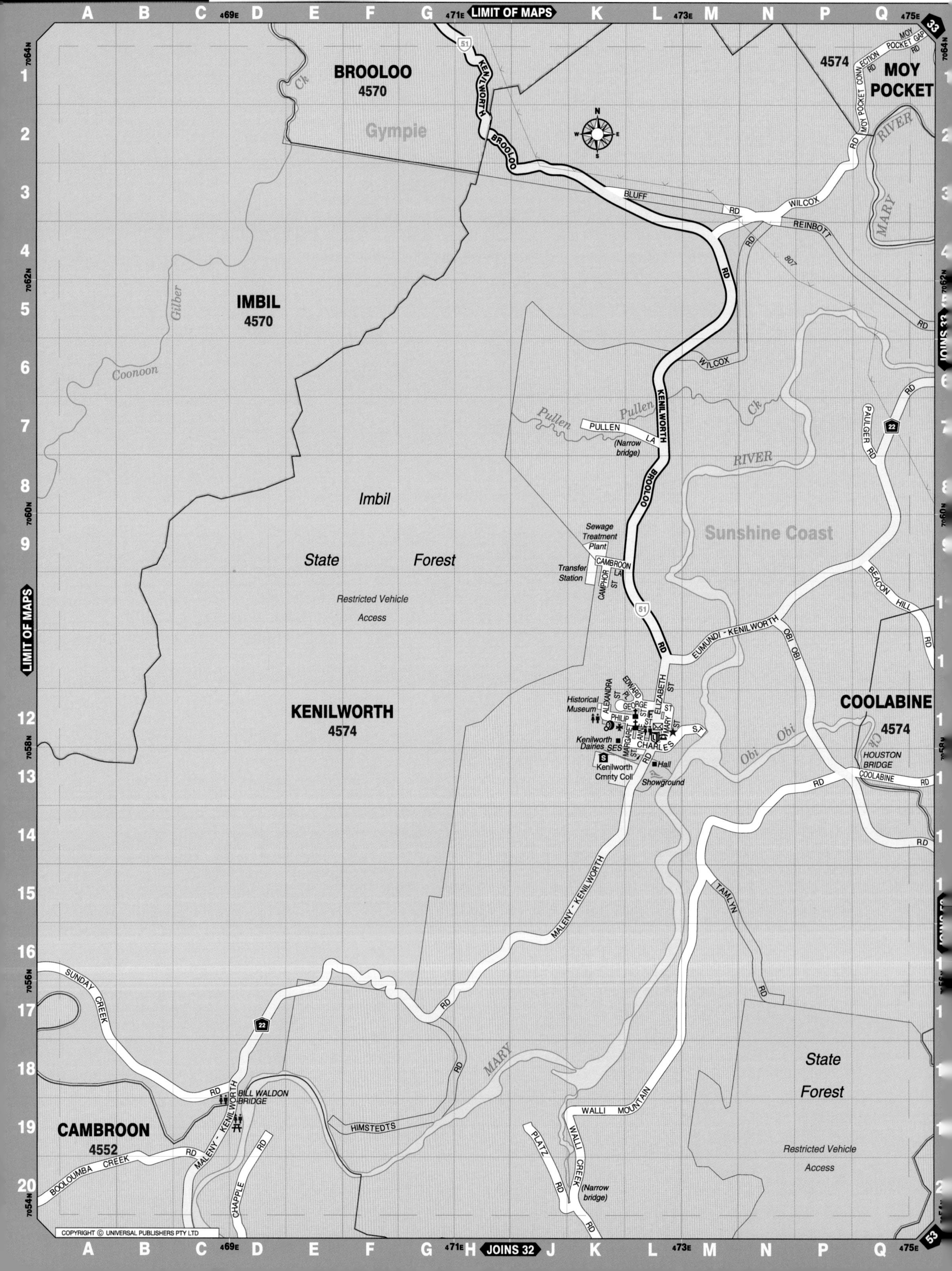

MAP 31
1 KILOMETRE EQUALS 2 GRID SQUARES

LIMIT OF MAPS

BROOLOO
4570

Gympie

IMBIL
4570

Gilber

Coonoon

Ck

51

KENILWORTH

BROOLOO

BLUFF

RD

WILCOX

REINBOTT

RD

807

WILCOX

4574

MOY POCKET

MOY POCKET CONNECTION RD

MOY POCKET GAP

MARY RIVER

33

PAULGER RD

22

RD

Pullen

Pullen

PULLEN LA

(Narrow bridge)

RIVER

Ck

Imbil

State Forest

Restricted Vehicle

Access

Sewage Treatment Plant

CAMBROON LA

Transfer Station

CAMPHOR ST

Sunshine Coast

51

RD

EUMUNDI - KENILWORTH

OBI OBI RD

BEACON HILL RD

KENILWORTH
4574

Historical Museum

ALEXANDRA ST

EDWARD ST

PHILIP ST

GEORGE ST

ELIZABETH ST

MARGARET ST

MARY ST

CHARLES

RD

Kenilworth Dairies

SES

S

Kenilworth Cmnty Coll

Hall

Showground

COOLABINE
4574

Obi - Obi

HOUSTON BRIDGE

COOLABINE RD

RD

RD

MALENY - KENILWORTH

TAMLYN RD

State Forest

Restricted Vehicle Access

MARY

SUNDAY CREEK

RD

22

BILL WALDON BRIDGE

MALENY - KENILWORTH RD

CAMBROON
4552

BOOLOUMBA CREEK RD

CHAPLE RD

HIMSTEDTS RD

PLATZ RD

WALLI CREEK RD

WALLI MOUNTAIN RD

(Narrow bridge)

LIMIT OF MAPS

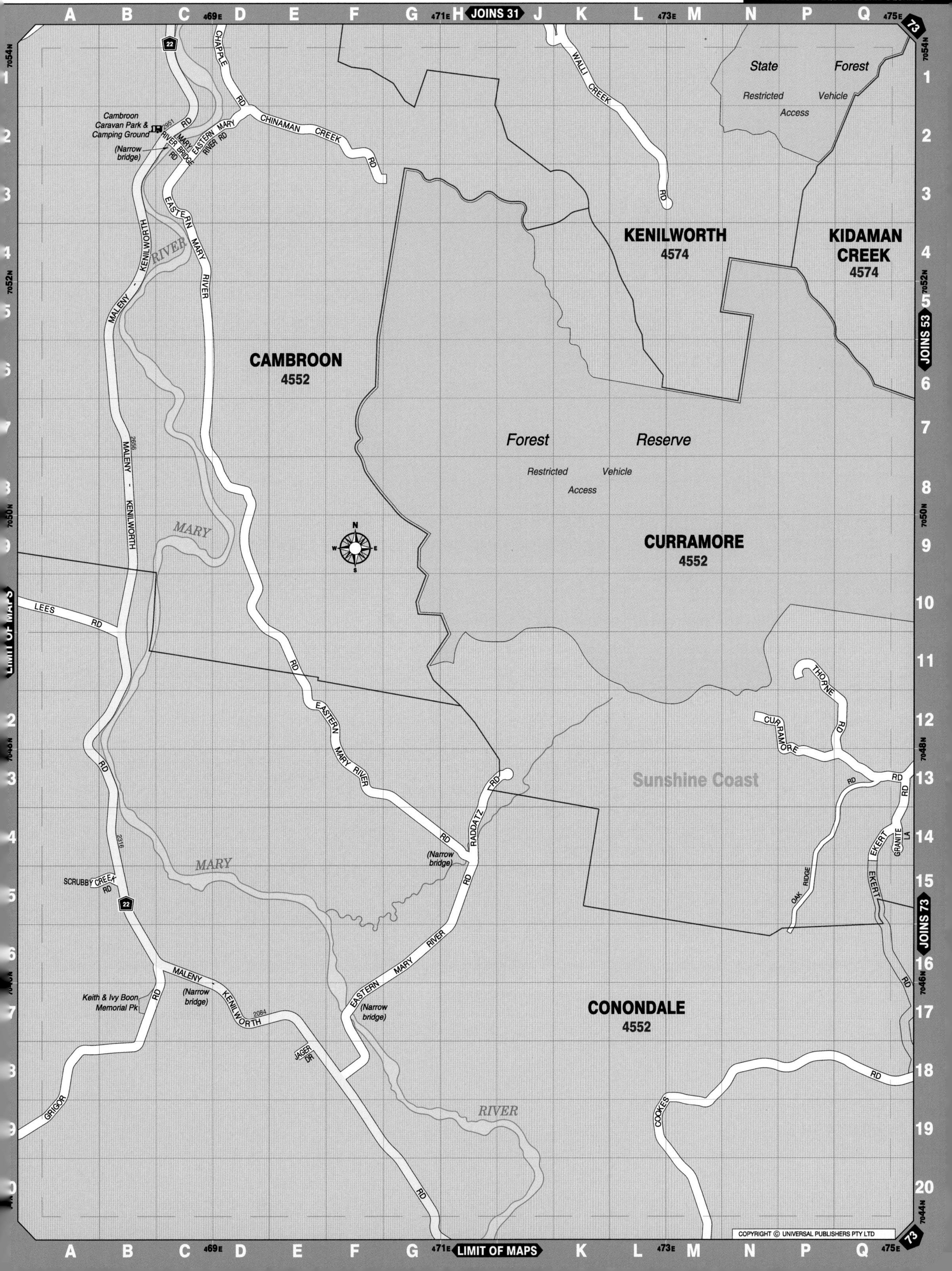

MAP 32
1 KILOMETRE EQUALS 2 GRID SQUARES

JOINS 31

JOINS 53

JOINS 73

LIMIT OF MAPS

State Forest
Restricted Vehicle Access

KENILWORTH
4574

KIDAMAN CREEK
4574

CAMBROON
4552

Forest Reserve
Restricted Vehicle Access

CURRAMORE
4552

Sunshine Coast

CONONDALE
4552

Cambroon Caravan Park & Camping Ground
(Narrow bridge)

Keith & Ivy Boon Memorial Pk

CHAPPLE RD

EASTERN MARY RIVER RD

CHINAMAN CREEK RD

MARY RIVER BRIDGE

KENILWORTH

MALENY

EASTERN MARY RIVER

MARY

RIVER

MALENY - KENILWORTH

LEES RD

WALL CREEK RD

EASTERN MARY RIVER RD

RADDATZ RD

(Narrow bridge)

THORNE RD

CURRAMORE RD

RD

EKERT RD

GRANITE LA

EKERT RD

OAK RIDGE RD

RD

SCRUBBY CREEK RD

MALENY RD

(Narrow bridge)

MALENY - KENILWORTH

JAGER DR

EASTERN MARY RIVER

(Narrow bridge)

RIVER

GRIGOR

COOKES RD

RD

22

73

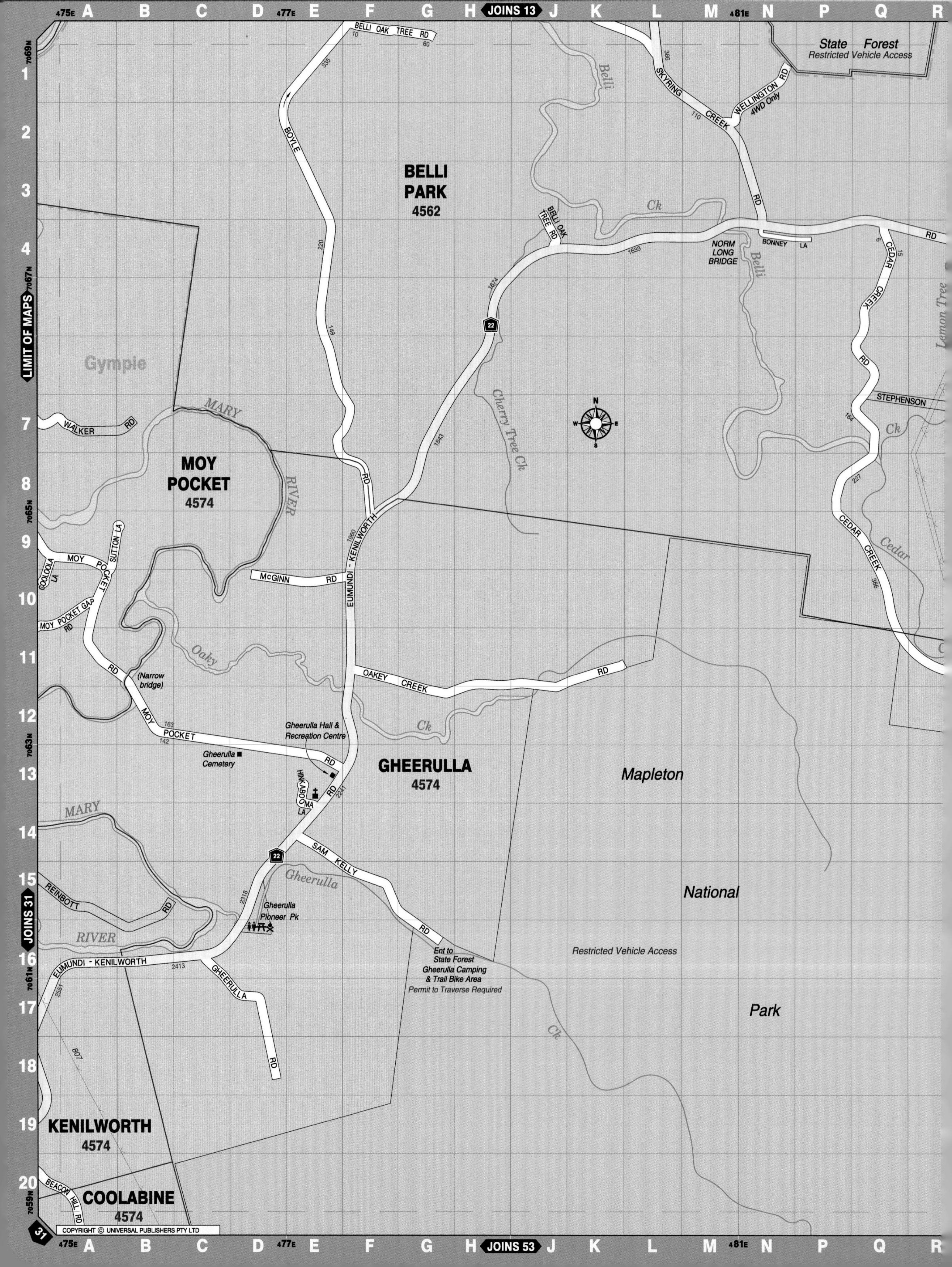

MAP 33
1 KILOMETRE EQUALS 2 GRID SQUARES

A B C D 477E E F G H **JOINS 13** J K L M 481E N P Q R

JOINS 13

LIMIT OF MAPS

BELLI PARK 4562

State Forest
Restricted Vehicle Access

BELLI OAK TREE RD

BOTLE

NORM LONG BRIDGE

BONNEY LA

SKYRING CREEK

WELLINGTON RD
4WD Only

CEDAR CREEK RD

Gympie

MARY RIVER

WALKER RD

MOY POCKET 4574

SUTTON LA

MOY POCKET LA

COOLOOLA LA

MOY POCKET GAP RD

McGINN RD

EUMUNDI - KENILWORTH RD

STEPHENSON

Cherry Tree Ck

Belli

Ck

Cedar

Oaky

OAKEY CREEK RD

MOY POCKET

(Narrow bridge)

Gheerulla Hall & Recreation Centre

Gheerulla Cemetery

HINKABOOMA LA

RD

GHEERULLA 4574

Mapleton

Ck

National

MARY RIVER

REINBOTT RD

Gheerulla Pioneer Pk

SAM KELLY RD

GHEERULLA RD

Gheerulla

Ent to State Forest Gheerulla Camping & Trail Bike Area
Permit to Traverse Required

Restricted Vehicle Access

Park

EUMUNDI - KENILWORTH

KENILWORTH 4574

BEACON HILL RD

COOLABINE 4574

MAP 34
1 KILOMETRE EQUALS 2 GRID SQUARES

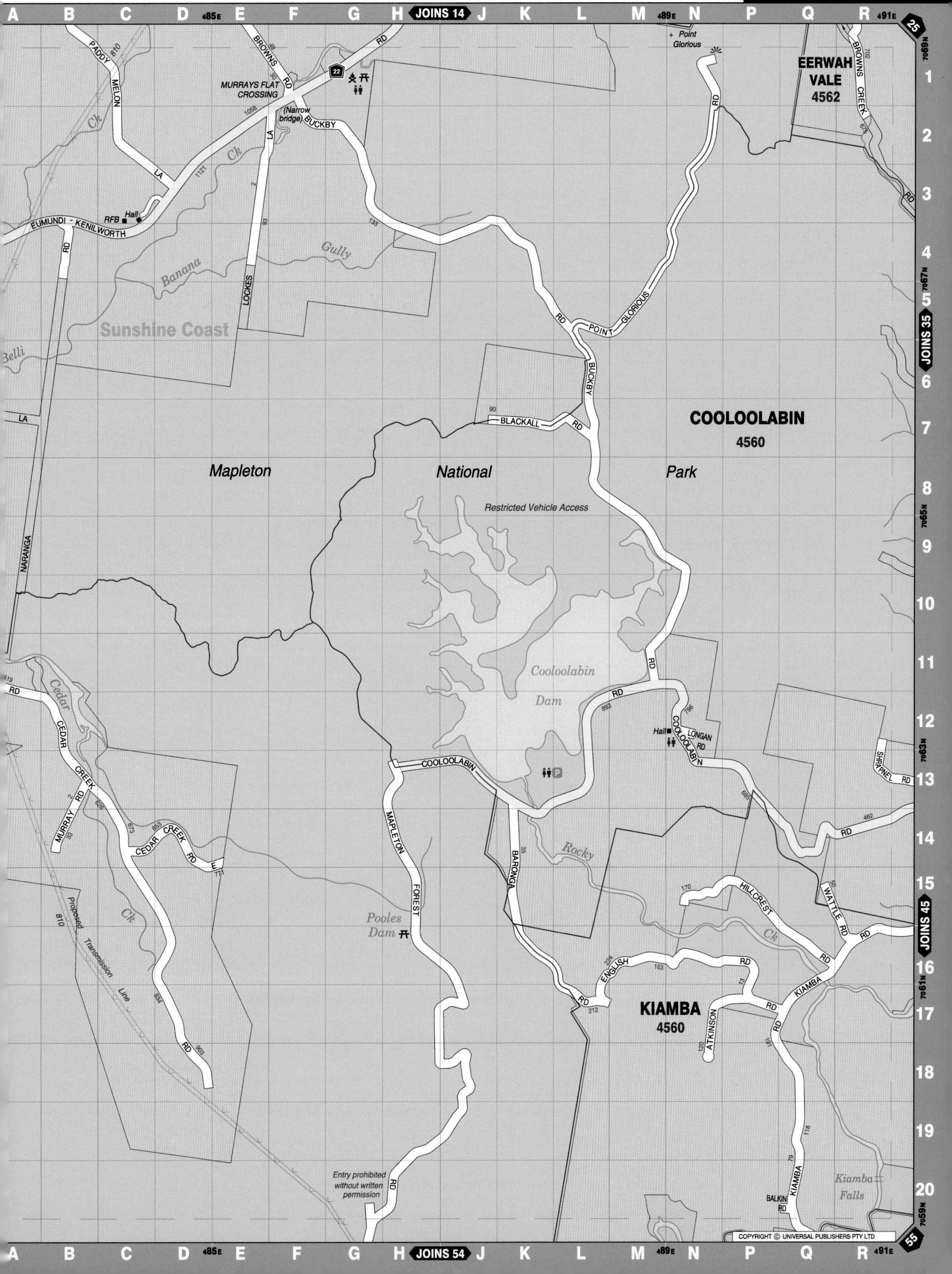

A B C D 485E E F G H **JOINS 14** J K L M 489E N P Q R 491E

25

EERWAH VALE 4562

1

2

+ Point Glorious

3

PADDY MELON Ck 810

BROWNS RD

MURRAYS FLAT CROSSING

22

(Narrow bridge) BUCKBY LA

BROWNS CREEK

4

EUMUNDI - KENILWORTH RD

RFB ■ Hall

LOCKES LA

Banana Gully

5

JOINS 35

Belli

Sunshine Coast

Mapleton

BLACKALL RD

POINT GLORIOUS RD

BUCKBY RD

COOLOOLABIN 4560

6

7

LA

NARANGA

National

Restricted Vehicle Access

Park

8

9

10

Cooloolabin Dam

RD

11

Cedar RD

CEDAR CREEK

Cooloolabin Dam

RD

Hall

LONGAN RD

COOLOOLABIN

SHRAPNEL RD

12

MURRAY RD

CEDAR CREEK RD

COOLOOLABIN RD

RD

13

Ck

Proposed Transmission Line

MAPLETON FOREST RD

BARONGA

Rocky

RD

14

HILLCREST RD

WATTLE RD

15

JOINS 45

Pooles Dam

Ck

Kiamba

16

ENGLISH RD

KIAMBA

RD

17

RD

ATKINSON

KIAMBA 4560

KIAMBA RD

18

19

Entry prohibited without written permission

RD

KIAMBA RD

BALKIN RD

Kiamba Falls

20

55

A B C D 485E E F G H **JOINS 54** J K L M 489E N P Q R 491E

MAP 35

1 KILOMETRE EQUALS 4 GRID SQUARES

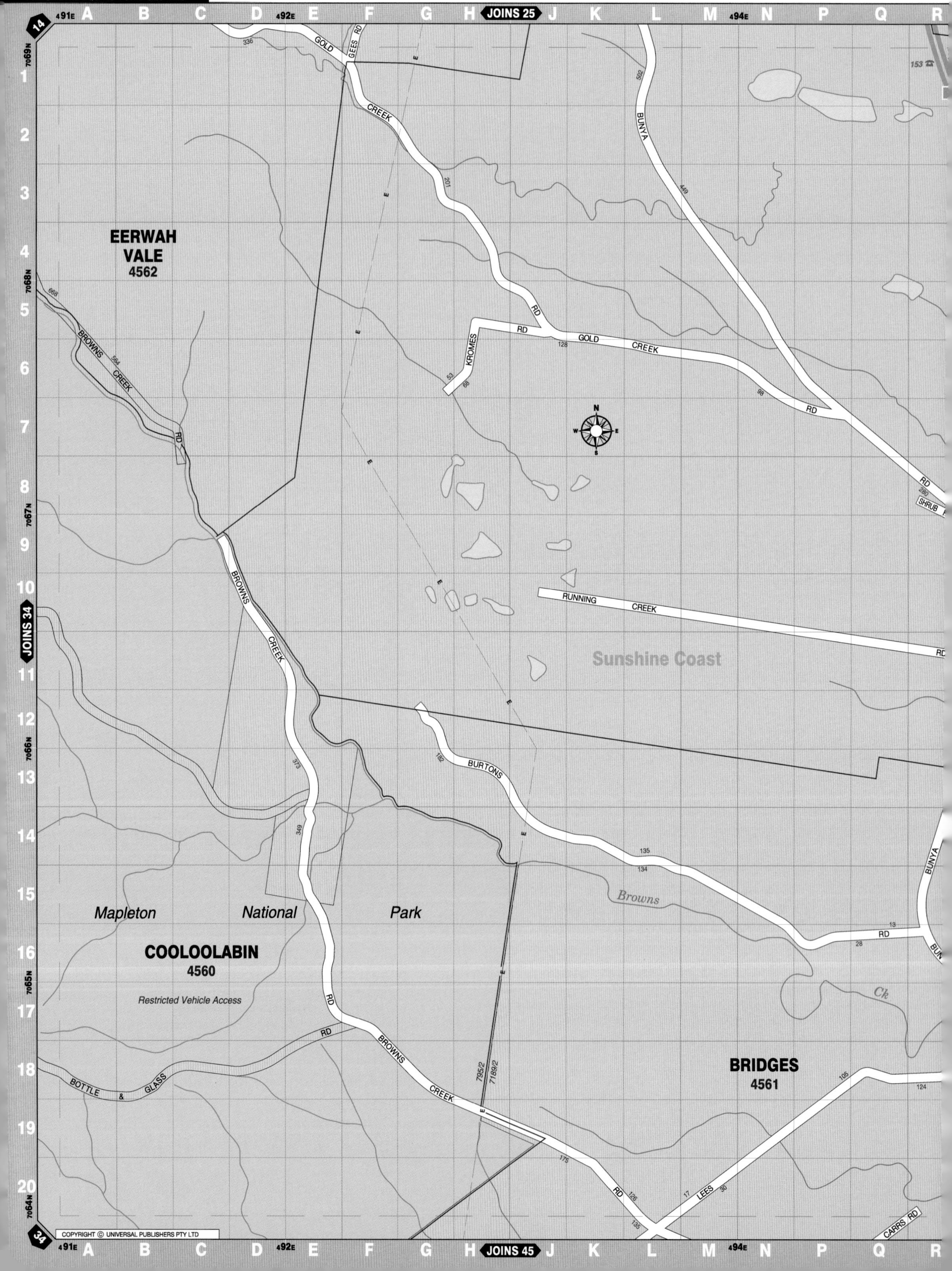

JOINS 25
JOINS 34
JOINS 45
14
34
491E
492E
494E
7069N
7068N
7067N
7066N
7065N
7064N
A B C D E F G H J K L M N P Q R
1 2 3 4 5 6 7 8 9 10 11 12 13 14 15 16 17 18 19 20
EERWAH
VALE
4562
COOLOOLABIN
4560
BRIDGES
4561
Mapleton National Park
Restricted Vehicle Access
Sunshine Coast
GOLD CREEK RD
GEES RD
BUNYA RD
KROMES RD
BROWNS CREEK RD
RUNNING CREEK RD
BURTONS RD
BOTTLE & GLASS RD
LEES RD
CARRS RD
SHRUB
Browns Ck
795/2
7189/2
153
336
502
449
201
128
98
53
68
668
564
280
373
349
182
135
134
13
28
105
124
175
126
135
17
30
COPYRIGHT © UNIVERSAL PUBLISHERS PTY LTD

MAP 36
1 KILOMETRE EQUALS 4 GRID SQUARES

JOINS 26

27

EUMUNDI
4562

Forest Reserve
Restricted Vehicle Access

NORTH ARM
4561

North Arm
Forest Reserve

Restricted Vehicle Access

NORTH ARM

MAROOCHY

PATHARA

SEIB RD

WEGNER RD

NORTH ARM

BRUCE

HAFLINGER RD

HIDDEN VALLEY

NORTH ARM - YANDINA CREEK RD

NORTH ARM - YANDINA CREEK RD

ALLANDALE

YANDINA CREEK
4561

JOINS 37

NORTH ARM - YANDINA CREEK

NAK RD

North
Arm
Park

RFB

Hall

M1

BRUCE HWY

North Arm
Pmy

FAIRHILL RD

Davison Range
Shooting Complex

WARDROP RD

DORANS

VALDORA RD

CELESTIAL CT

NINDERRY SLOPES RD

KRAUSE RD

DAVISON RD

WOMBAT

KANGA CT

BERNHARDT PL

COACH VIEW

HONEYDEW

ELOUERA PL

SKYBOLT

ROTH LA

FAIRHILL

FAIRHILL

KARNU

VALDORA
4561

RIVER

CANDLE NUT CT

Fairhill Ent
Fairhill
Botanic Gardens

QLD COACH

NINDERRY
4561

EILINGA

CLARINDA RD

EUCALYPTUS CR

WEDGETAIL CT

BEN WILLIAMS

OUTLOOK

DR

DR

M1

JENSEN

RD

RD

JOINS 46

47

COPYRIGHT © UNIVERSAL PUBLISHERS PTY LTD

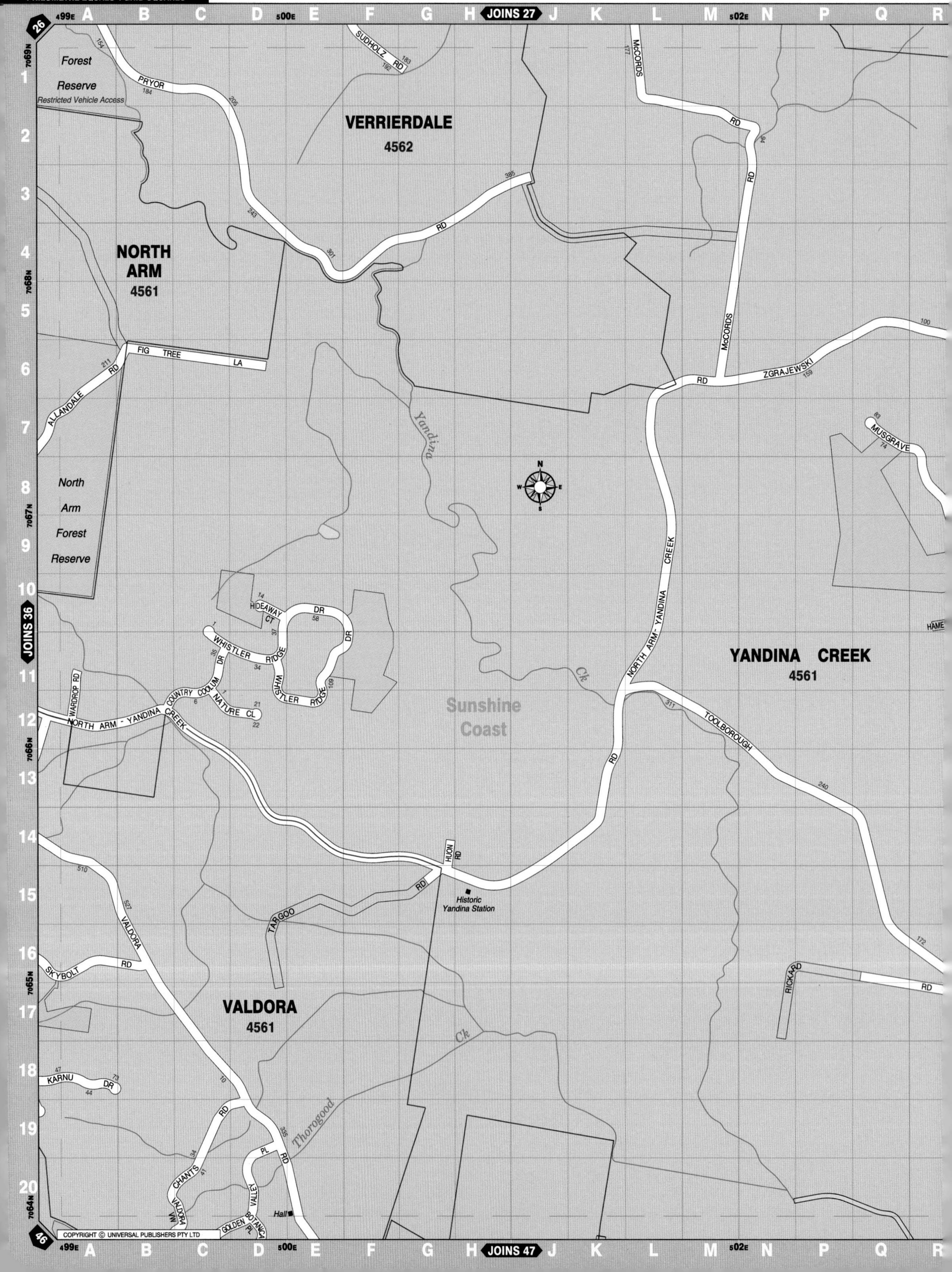

MAP 37
1 KILOMETRE EQUALS 4 GRID SQUARES

JOINS 27

26

VERRIERDALE
4562

NORTH
ARM
4561

Forest
Reserve
Restricted Vehicle Access

PRYOR

SUDHOLZ RD

RD

FIG TREE LA

ALLANDALE

RD

North

Arm

Forest

Reserve

JOINS 36

McCORDS

RD

McCORDS RD

ZGRAJEWSKI

MUSGRAVE

N
W E
S

HIDEAWAY
CT

DR

WHISTLER RIDGE DR

WHISTLER RIDGE

COOLUM NATURE CL

COUNTRY

WARDROP RD

NORTH ARM - YANDINA CREEK

NORTH ARM - YANDINA

CREEK

RD

YANDINA CREEK
4561

Sunshine
Coast

Ck

TOOLBOROUGH

RD

HLOW RD

RD

Historic
Yandina Station

VALDORA

VALDORA
4561

SKYBOLT RD

TARGOO

RICKARD

RD

KARNU DR

Ck

Thorogood

CHANTS

VALDORA

BOTANICA PL

GOLDEN

RD

Hall

JOINS 47

MAP 38
1 KILOMETRE EQUALS 4 GRID SQUARES

JOINS 28

JOINS 48

JOINS 39

VERRIERDALE
4562

PEREGIAN SPRINGS
4573

Peregian Springs Golf Club

COOLUM BEACH
4573

Coolum MX

Suncoast Model Aero Centre

BLAST

Aqua Park Coolum

Arcoona Road

Bushland

Conservation

Reserve

Industrial

Estate

Corbould Road
Bushland
Conservation
Reserve

Coolum Beach Christian College

Coolum Waste Landfill Centre

DOONAN RD

BRIDGE RD

ARCOONA DR

AUBURN CT

CANIA PL

CARNARVON CT

QUANDA RD

QUANDA RD

RESEARCH ST

RESEARCH ST

LSAGHT

JUNCTION

ACCESS

VENTURE CL

DACMAR RD

DACMAR RD

FOCAL AV

QUANDA DR

LINK CR

LINK CR

LOMANDRA PL

CORBOULD RD

YANDINA COOLUM RD

SUNSHINE MOTORWAY

THE AVENUE

PEACHTREE

MAP 39
1 KILOMETRE EQUALS 4 GRID SQUARES

JOINS 29

JOINS 38

JOINS 49

PEREGIAN SPRINGS
4573

COOLUM BEACH
4573

Noosa National Park

Noosa National Park

Mt Peregian
(Emu Mt)
+ 71.5m

Coolum High

Noosa

National

Park

Sunshine Coast

Noosa
National Park

CORAL

Coolum
Rugby Peregian
Netball Sports
Tennis
Complex

Coolum Soccer

RSL
SEACOVE
Croquet

Sundale
Ret
Resort

Lions
Park

Peregian
Springs

Aged
Care

Havana Rd E

Stumers

Coolum Primary School

Coolum Park

St Marys Aged Care

Coolum Beach

Morgan Pk

Civic Cntr

Tickle Pk
Liberty Swing
SLSC

Wilkinson Park
Pt Perry
Lows Lookout

Cassia Wildlife Corridor

Eurungunder Hill

COPYRIGHT © UNIVERSAL PUBLISHERS PTY LTD

MAP 45
FOLLOWS
1 KILOMETRE EQUALS 4 GRID SQUARES
40

A B C D s12E E F G H JOINS 30 J K L M s14E N P Q R s15E

SEA

7069N
1
2
3
4
7068N
5
6
7
8
7067N
9
10
11
12
7066N
13
14
15
16
7065N
17
18
19
20
7064N

A B C D E F G H **JOINS 35** J K L M N P Q R

34

7064N
7063N
7062N
7061N
7060N
7059N

491E 492E 494E

Mapleton National Park

Restricted Vehicle Access

BRIDGES
4561

Yandina Transfer Station

KANES

BROWNS CREEK

CARRS

LEES RD

BRANDONS

DELTA RD

RD

COOLOOLABIN STEGGALLS

HONEYSUCKLE PL

APPLEBERRY PL

REO

COOLOOLABIN
4560

SHRAPNEL RD

COOLOOLABIN

Sunshine Coast Shooting Club

ELK RD

RD

NICHOLS RD

COOLOOLABIN

ALLAN RD

WAPPA OUTLOOK HAVEN

EMERALD PL

VISTA

HEADWATERS CT

DR

SUNSHINE DUCK PL

GROVE PL

PEAK MA CT AV

OLD GYMPIE

MONARCH SKYRING

WARNER CR

FRYAR CR

MAROOCHY

CEDAR PL

MAROOC

JOINS 34

KIAMBA

RD

(Narrow bridge)

COLEMANS RD

RD Pipers Park

MAROOCHY

ANDERSONS RD

GOBBERTS RD

Sunshine Coast

Wappa Dam

Wappa Falls

Jack Harrison Park

PUMP STATION RD

SOUTH

Maranatha Recreational Camp at Yandina

CANE RD

WAPPA

COLEMAN FARM RD

FALLS

BRACKEN—FERN

WAPPA PARK RD

WAPPA FALLS

HUTTON RD

(Narrow bridge)

795/2
7189/2

+ Mt Wappa 211m

McCombe

CREIGHTONS

GLENROWAN

KIAMBA
4560

UPPER HUTTON RD

WAPPA DAM RD

Mapleton National Park

Restricted Vehicle Access

MOUNT

Kiamba Falls

SCHULTZ RD

SMALL RD

DOOM

RD

IMAGE FLAT
4560

MC

MAP 46
1 KILOMETRE EQUALS 4 GRID SQUARES

JOINS 36

NINDERRY
4561

NINDERRY

Water Pollution Control Works

Yandina Prmy

Ginger Factory

Nutworks

INDUSTRIAL PL

MACHINERY

Industrial Estate

Yandina Historic House

Tea Tree Park

BOWDER RD

YANDINA
4561

MAROOCHY RIVER
4561

JOINS 47

Sports Complex

Tennis

Wonga Park

Sports Fields

RSL

JAMES LOW BRIDGE

Yandina Sanctuary

Private Road

CENTRAL PARK

Cemetery

INDUSTRY CT (Priv Rd)

(Narrow bridge)

FLOWERS RD

ROCKY CREEK FOREST RD

KULANGOOR
4560

PARKLANDS
4560

Parklands

Conservation Park

Restricted Vehicle Access

Rocky Ck

Kulangoor Lawn Cemetery

MAP 47
1 KILOMETRE EQUALS 4 GRID SQUARES

JOINS 37

36

499E · 500E · 502E

A B C D E F G H J K L M N P Q R

NINDERRY
4561

YANDINA CREEK
4561

VALDORA
4561

11

N
W E
S

Solar Farm

JOINS 46

GOLDEN VALLEY PL
BOTANICA
VALDORA
Hall
AKANIA PL
ATMOSPHERE
CRUMP RD
Ck
RFB
KILNER
NEVA CT
DR
RD
Galt
48 RD
RD
DYNES
THOMSON VALLEY 76
79
HUGHES PL
BROWNE RD
AURORA PL
RD
199
TINARRA
RD
WANTS
CL 71
OCEAN 215
222
VISTA 171
172
CAREE CT 25
RIVER VISTA CT
DR 155
OCEAN
DONOVAN PL
CALLISTEMON 116
CALADENIA CT
VISTA
132
BELVEDERE W
WANTS PL
CANANDO Q
WARREUER PL
NIMBIN PL 18
17
YANDINA
RD
AMANI
PL
COOLUM
Want Hill
MT COOLUM CL 81
VALDORA 38
COOLUM
APPS
ASHTONS WHARF RD
11
RD
DR 33
ROAD
YANDINA
COOLUM
MAROOCHY
Ck
Boggy
LAKE DUNETHIN
DUNETHIN ROCK
Lake Dunethin
RD
DR
PEARCE 2
STORE RD 17

MAROOCHY RIVER
4561

RIVER

57

YANDINA - BLI BLI 352
Rocky
RD
PEARCE
490
ROAD 509
DR
YANDINA - BLI BLI 590
658
RIVER STORE RD
THOMPSONS
KIRRA
180
RD
TAMIN 47
PL 32
19
PARKYN HILL PL 18
ROAD

JOINS 57

499E · 500E · 502E

A B C D E F G H J K L M N P Q R

56

7064N 7063N 7062N 7061N 7060N 7059N

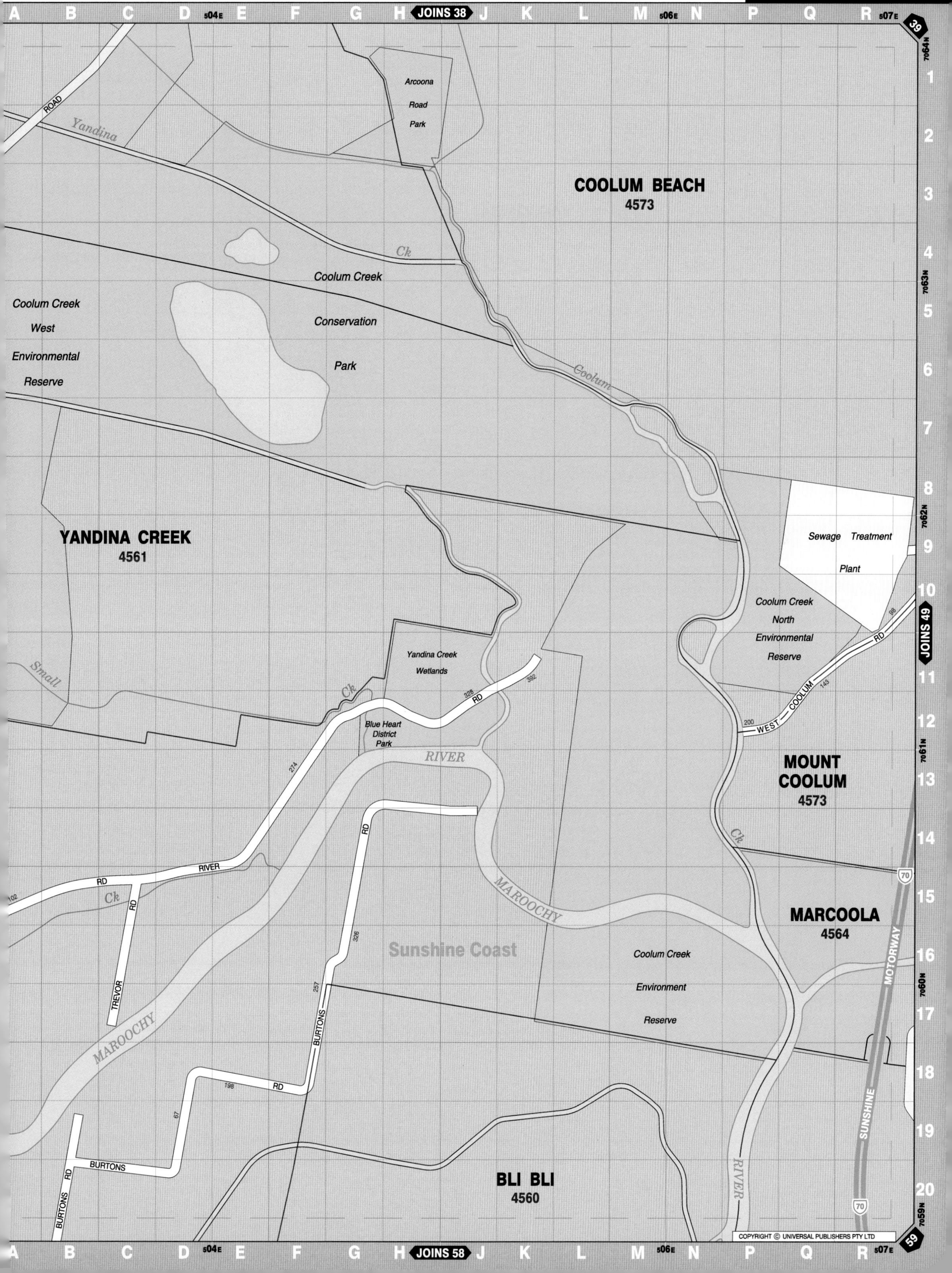

MAP 48
1 KILOMETRE EQUALS 4 GRID SQUARES

A B C D 504E E F G H **JOINS 38** J K L M 506E N P Q R 507E

39

Arcoona
Road
Park

COOLUM BEACH
4573

Ck

Coolum Creek

Conservation

Park

Coolum

Coolum Creek
West
Environmental
Reserve

YANDINA CREEK
4561

Sewage   Treatment

Plant

Coolum Creek
North
Environmental
Reserve

JOINS 49

Small

Yandina Creek
Wetlands

328
RD
392

WEST   COOLUM   RD

143

200

Ck

Blue Heart
District
Park

RIVER

274

**MOUNT
COOLUM**
4573

Ck

RD

RD

River
RD
102
Ck

MAROOCHY

MARCOOLA
4564

328

Sunshine Coast

257

Coolum Creek

Environment

Reserve

70

TREVOR

MAROOCHY

198   RD

Burtons

67

MOTORWAY

BURTONS RD

BURTONS

BLI BLI
4560

RIVER

SUNSHINE

70

59

A B C D 504E E F G H **JOINS 58** J K L M 506E N P Q R 507E

MAP 49
1 KILOMETRE EQUALS 4 GRID SQUARES

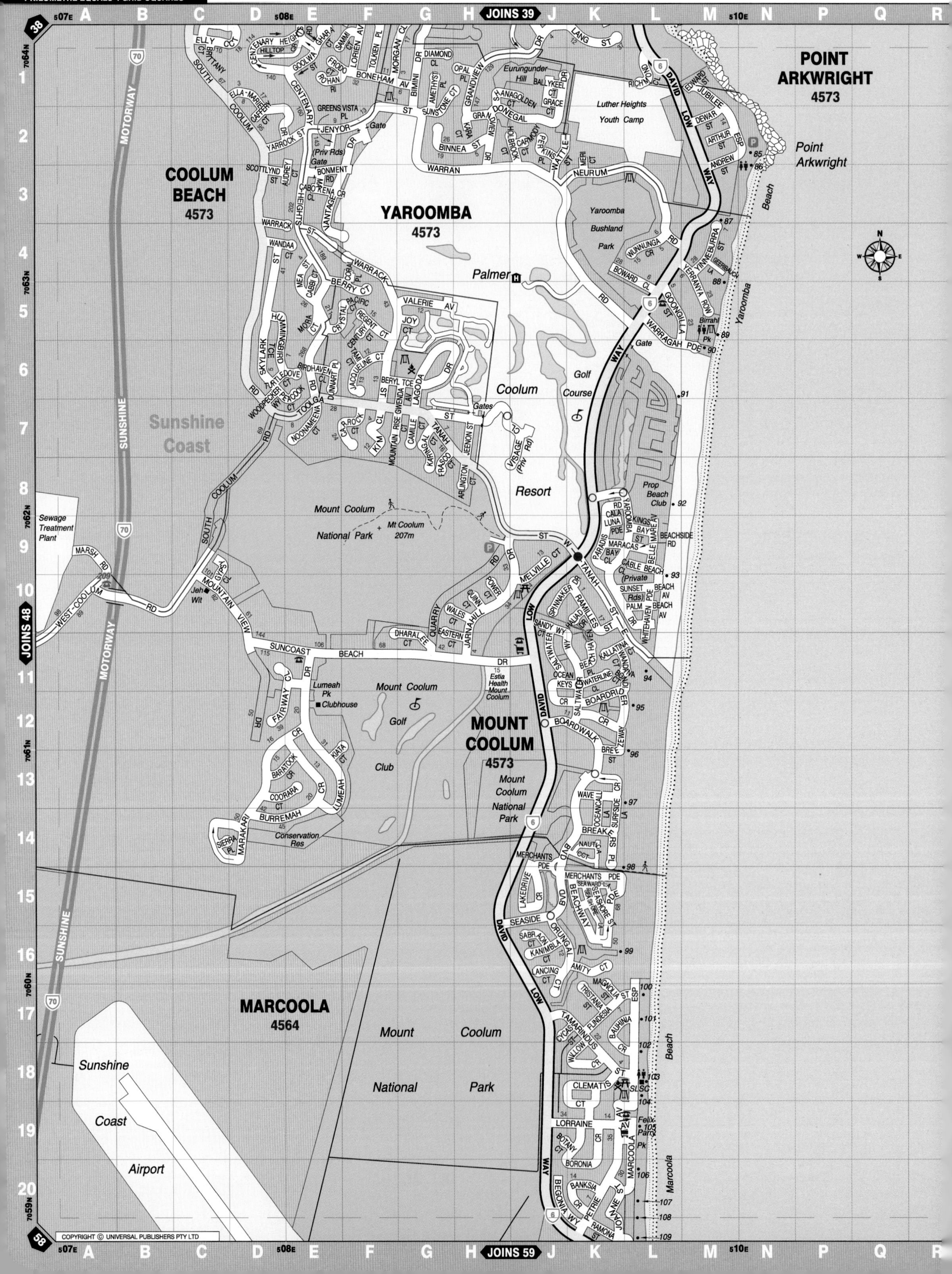

JOINS 39

POINT ARKWRIGHT 4573

Point Arkwright

COOLUM BEACH 4573

YAROOMBA 4573

Luther Heights Youth Camp

Eurungunder Hill

Palmer

Yaroomba Bushland Park

Coolum

Golf Course

Sunshine Coast

Prop Beach Club

Mount Coolum National Park

Mt Coolum 207m

Resort

Sewage Treatment Plant

JOINS 48

Mount Coolum Golf Club

Lumeah Pk — Clubhouse

MOUNT COOLUM 4573

Mount Coolum National Park

Estia Health Mount Coolum

Merchants

Conservation Res

Seaside

MARCOOLA 4564

Mount Coolum National Park

Beach

Marcoola

Sunshine Coast Airport

SLSC

Felix Parry Pk

JOINS 59

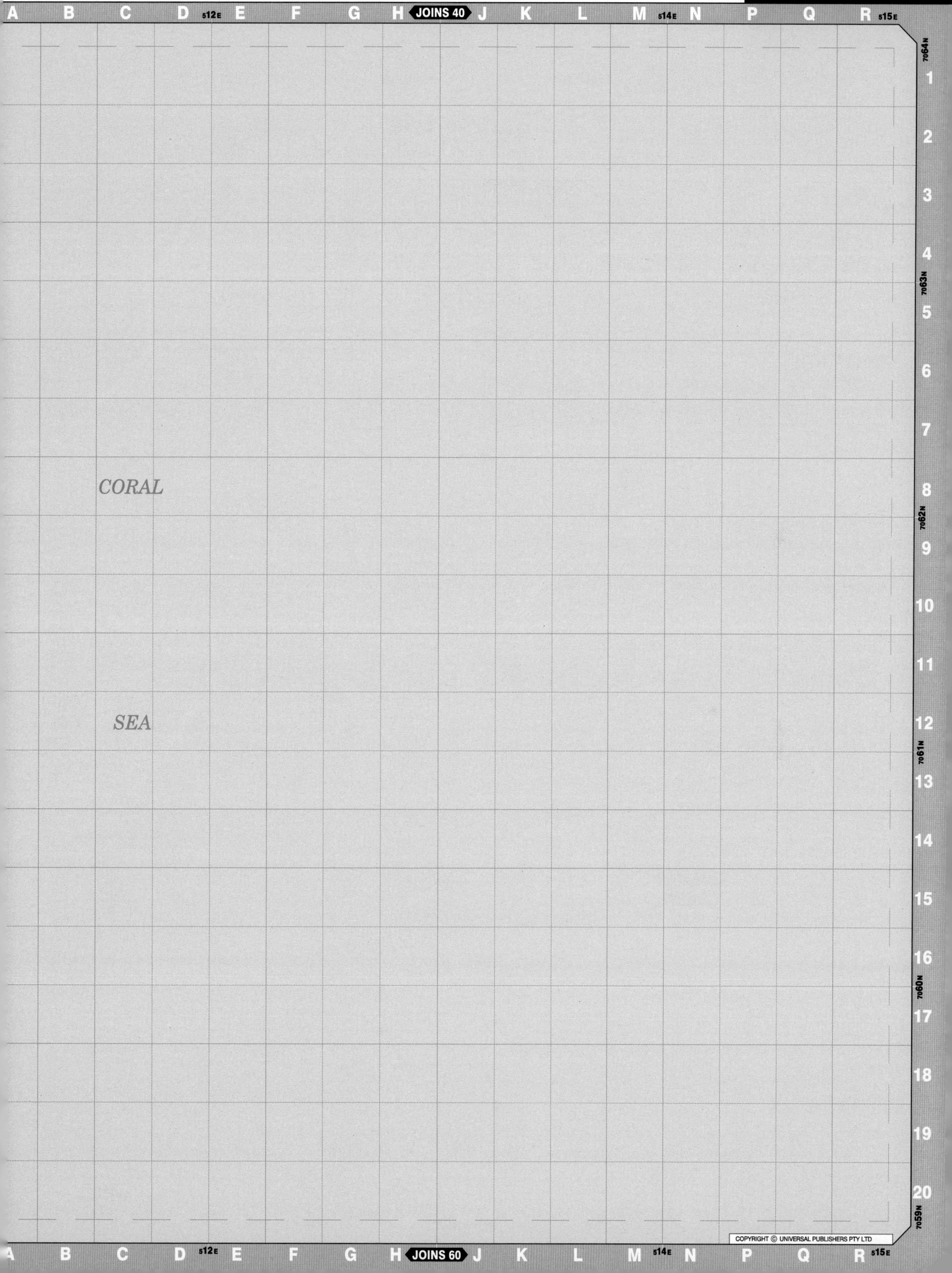

MAP 53
FOLLOWS
50
1 KILOMETRE EQUALS 4 GRID SQUARES

A B C D s12E E F G H JOINS 40 J K L M s14E N P Q R s15E

7064N
1
2
3
7063N
4
5
6
7
CORAL
7062N
8
9
10
11
12
SEA
7061N
13
14
15
16
7060N
17
18
19
20
7059N

A B C D s12E E F G H JOINS 60 J K L M s14E N P Q R s15E

JOINS 33

31

A B C D 477E E F G H J K L M 481E N P Q R

1

70 59N

Mapleton National Park

BEACON HILL RD

68

115

TELEPHONE RD

DELICIA

2

Restricted Vehicle Access

1005

973

3

COOLABINE
4574

COOLABINE

134

SUTTON RD

195

855

DELICIA

4

268

807

RD

888

5

70 57N

JOINS 31

1748

OBI

OBI

1601

Obi

Obi

COOLABINE

392

EAST-COOLABINE

RD

609

6

KENILWORTH
4574

1578

Hugh Cochrane
Lookout

423

RD

548

RD

SMYTHES RD

BRAEHEAD LA
(Pfv Rd)

7

1359

RD

495

RD

8

70 55N

State

Forest

HUNSLEY

9

HUNSLEY

Creek

CONNORS KNOB RD

10

(Narrow bridge)

RD

RD

1288

146

CUTMORE RD W

PENCIL CREEK

135

RD

35

11

70 53N

29

KIDAMAN CREEK

RD

48

(Narrow bridge)

Bonney Park

CUTMORE RD E

12

142

RD

PERRY RD

KIDAMAN

103

KIDAMAN

1049

OBI

OBI

(Narrow bridge)

Pencil

64

NAVILS FALLS CREEK RD

OBI
OBI
4574

13

CREEK

Obi

Obi

862

23

673

RD

14

421

470

STAVE RD

MANUEL HORNIBROOK BRIDGE

15

KIDAMAN
CREEK
4574

76

29

BROWNS RD

RD

561

RD

SLACKS RD

LOWER SUSES POCKET RD

Creek

16

70 51N

JOINS 32

17

Forest

Restricted Vehicle Access

580

RD

KIRBY RD

18

Reserve

19

CURRAMORE
4552

Forest Reserve

KIDAMAN CREEK

20

70 49N

Restricted Vehicle Access

THOMPSON RD

WITTA
4552

32

A B C D 477E E F G H J K L M 481E N P Q R

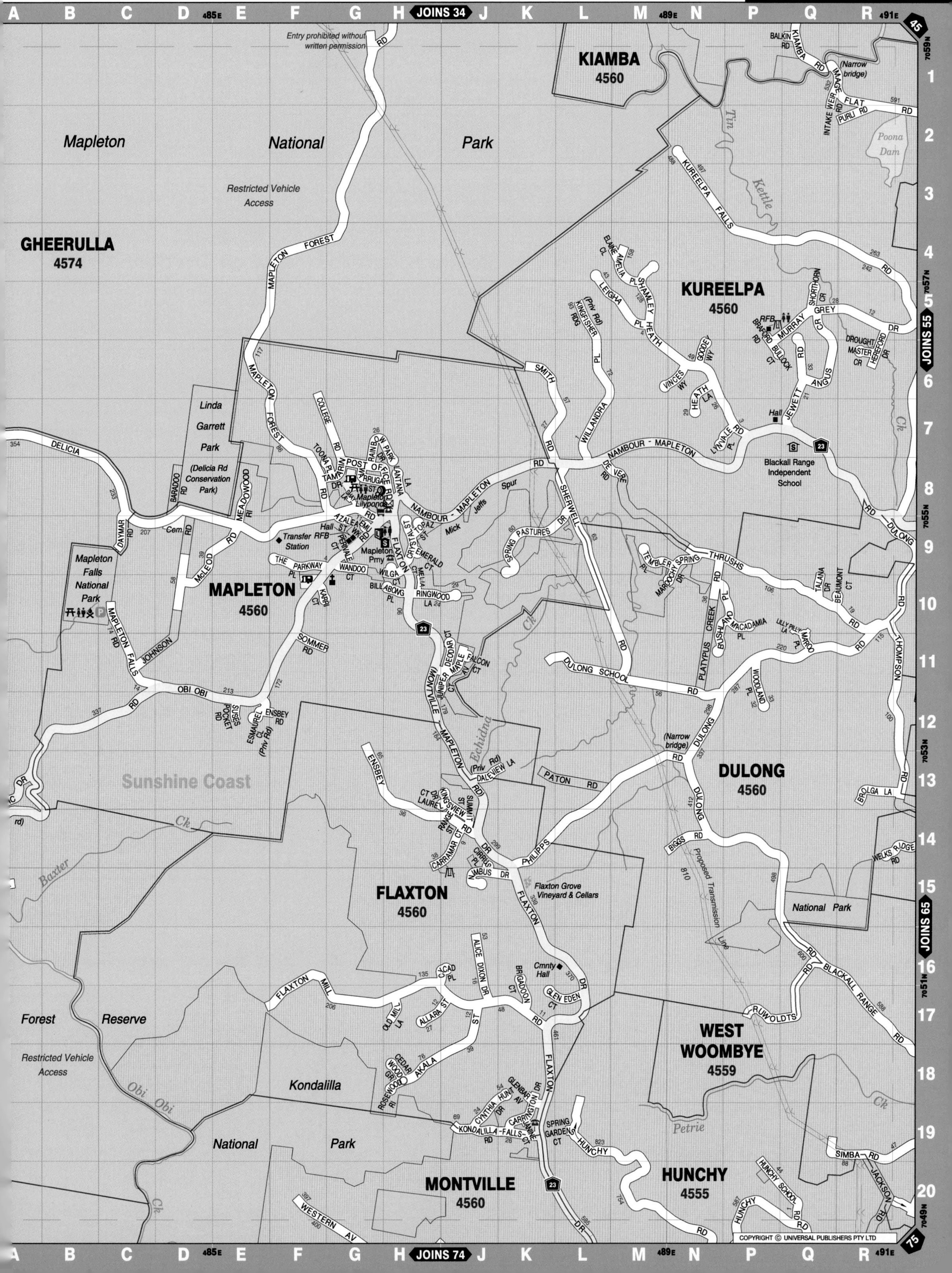

MAP 54
1 KILOMETRE EQUALS 2 GRID SQUARES

JOINS 34

JOINS 55

JOINS 65

JOINS 74

KIAMBA 4560

KUREELPA 4560

GHEERULLA 4574

Mapleton National Park

Restricted Vehicle Access

Entry prohibited without written permission

Linda Garrett Park

(Delicia Rd Conservation Park)

Mapleton Falls National Park

MAPLETON 4560

Transfer RFB Station

Mapleton Pmy

Blackall Range Independent School

DULONG 4560

FLAXTON 4560

Sunshine Coast

Flaxton Grove Vineyard & Cellars

National Park

WEST WOOMBYE 4559

Forest Reserve

Restricted Vehicle Access

Kondalilla

National Park

MONTVILLE 4560

HUNCHY 4555

Cmnty Hall

Blackall Range Independent School

MAP 55

1 KILOMETRE EQUALS 4 GRID SQUARES

JOINS 45

KIAMBA 4560

KIAMBA 4560

Mapleton

National Park

Restricted Vehicle Access

Poona Dam

Narrow bridge)

MIRAN RD

Council Quarry

KUREELPA 4560

SHARP RD

MISTY RISE

IMAGE FLAT 4560

Heidenreich Hill

Image Flat Substn

JOINS 54

MURRAY GREY DR

Tin Kettle

WALSH

Nambour Heights

HIGHWORTH 4560

Glenbrook Downs Park

Aged Care

Estia Health Nambour

Glenbrook

Walter Lanham Park CASUARI

Dulong Lookout

Kanyana Park

Sunshine Coast

NAMBOUR 4560

Reservoir

OneSchool Global

Edmund & George Biggs Pk

Burnside Pk

DULONG 4560

BURNSIDE 4560

TAFE Queensland Nambour Campus

Burnside High

Burnside Primary

PERWILLOWEN 4560

Rotary Garden Village (Rod Voller Hostel)

Nambour Special School

MAP 56
1 KILOMETRE EQUALS 4 GRID SQUARES

JOINS 46

KULANGOOR
4560

MAROOCHY
RIVER
4561

PARKLANDS
4560

Parklands State Forest

Restricted Vehicle Access

Commonwealth
of
Australia

Commonwealth
of
Australia

Ferntree
Creek
National
Park

Quarry

Ferntree

Nambour

Creek

Golf

Club

National

Park

Nambour
Garden Lawn
Ent Cemetery
Ent

Nambour
Waste
Landfill
Centre

BLI BLI
4560

BLI BLI

Council
Depot

Old
Nambour
Cemetery

Nambour
Crematorium

Nambour
Substn

Nambour
Selangor
Private

Nambour
Showground
and
Sportsground

Nambour
Leagues
Club

Exhibition
Open
Arena

Croquet
Lawn

Nambour
State
College

Plantation
Retirement
Resort

ROSEMOUNT
4560

Koala Park

St Josephs
Catholic
Pmy

JOINS 66

COPYRIGHT © UNIVERSAL PUBLISHERS PTY LTD

MAP 57

1 KILOMETRE EQUALS 4 GRID SQUARES

JOINS 47

46

JOINS 56

65

MAROOCHY RIVER 4561

Parklands
Conservation
Park

Restricted Vehicle Access

Reservoir

Commonwealth
of
Australia

Good Samaritan Catholic College

Halcyon Lakeside Retirement Village

Lake

Parklands Sports Complex

Environmental Park

CLEARWATER

INSPIRATION CT

GALLERY

ATKINSON RD

ATKINSON RD W

ATKINSON

FRANCIS

CYGNUS PL

LYRA CT

TRAINSTOP CT

PRENTIS

THOMPSONS

HIGHLANDS

TIMBERLAND CL

HILL

FOREST HILL DR

CONSTELLATION WY

KIRRA

CALLOOMA

KIRRA

SKIEL

EAST VIEW

BLACK SWAN

SPARROW ST

DARTER TCE

CORELLA

MINERVA

HALCYON WY

KINGFISHER

JACANA

GREBE

EGRET PL

BUTCHER BIRD

LITTLE BITTERN PL

CURRAWONG

HONEYEATER

PARDALOTE

WATTLEBIRD CT

KINGFISHER

AGNES

ARIEL

LAKE VIEW PL

PARKLAKES

CAMELOT CT

SCHOOL BOAT

RIVERSTONE PL

BIRDWING

DEEPWATER

GECKO

FEATHERTAIL

TREEFROG DR

COCKATOO

BOTTLE BRUSH

RINGTAIL

FLOODED GUM AV

LILLY

CONWAY

SYLVANIA CL

CLARENCE ST

TARSHAM ST

GINGER

BELL

SHALE CT

CAMP FLAT RD

WHITECROSS

CAMP FLAT RD

BLI BLI

PIONEER

ROAD

BLI BLI

BENNETT

WILM

Reservoir

Petrie Ck

ROSEMOUNT 4560

PETRIE CREEK

SUGAR VIEW LA

SEYMOUR

WOODCHESTER CL

CELESTINE

PETRIE CREEK

Petrie

UPPER ROSEMOUNT RD

KOALA HILL DR

COOLWATER PL

CLEARVIEW

UPPER ROSEMOUNT

EVERTON PL

PAYNTERS

LEMON GROVE

PAYNTERS CREEK RD

PAYNTERS CREEK

ROSEMOUNT LA

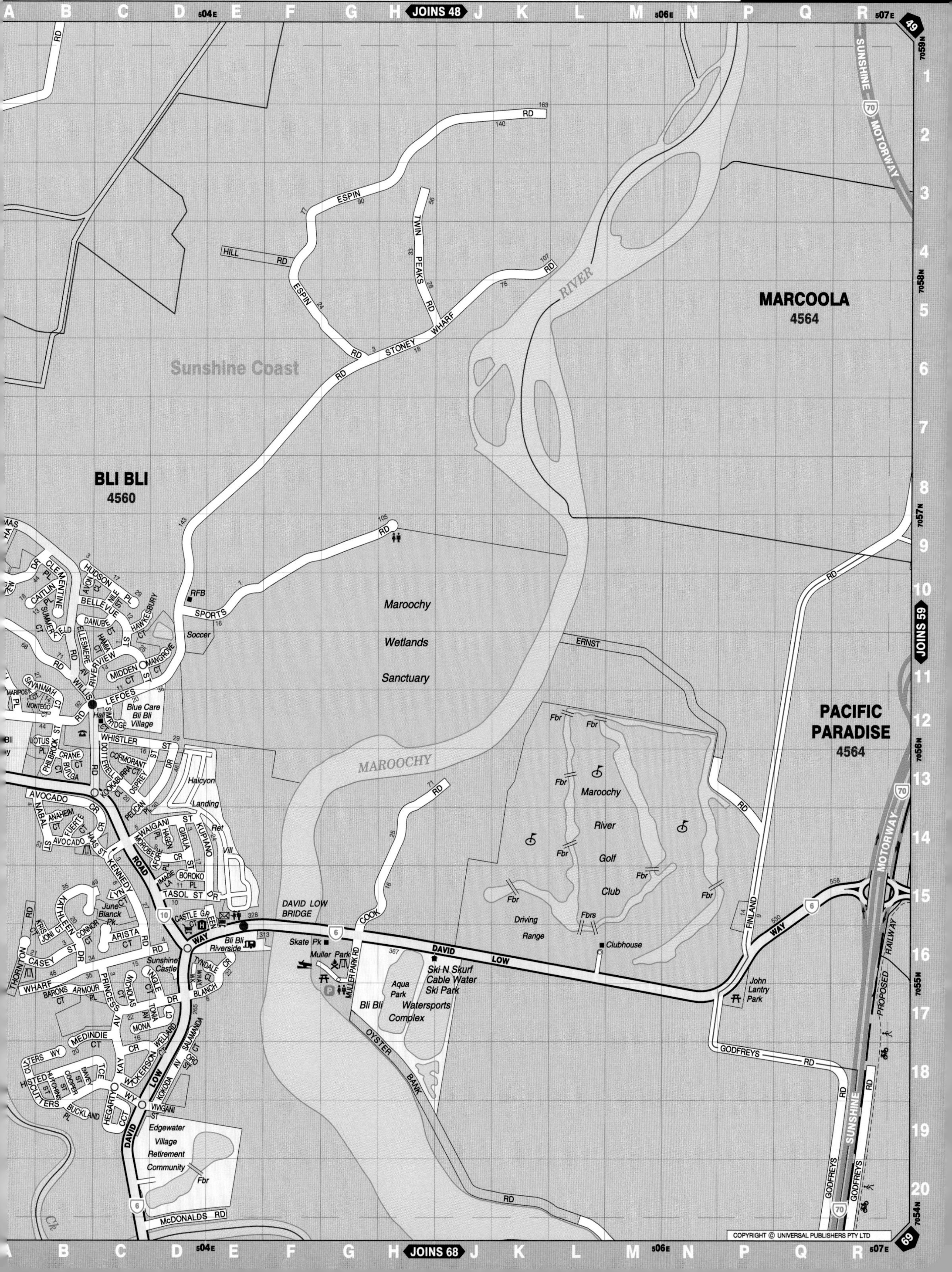

MAP 58

1 KILOMETRE EQUALS 4 GRID SQUARES

A B C D 5 04 E F G H J K L M 5 06 E N P Q R 5 07 E

49
7059N
1
2
3
4 7058N
5
6
7
8 7057N
9
10
JOINS 59
11
12
13 7056N
14
15
16 7055N
17
18
19
20 7054N
59

RD 140
163

ESPIN 90
77

TWIN PEAKS RD 56
33

HILL RD
ESPIN 24 RD 3 STONEY 18 WHARF RD 78 107 RD

RIVER

MARCOOLA
4564

Sunshine Coast

105 RD
RD
SPORTS 16 1
RFB
Soccer

BLI BLI
4560

Maroochy

Wetlands

Sanctuary

ERNST

RD 9

PACIFIC PARADISE
4564

CLEMENTINE
HUDSON PL
CAITLIN
BELLEVUE
DANUBE
SUMMER
ELLESMERE
RIVERVIEW
HAMA
MIDDEN
MANGROVE
SAVANNAH
MARIPOSA
MONTEGO
LEFOES
WILLIS
Blue Care
Bli Bli
Village
LOTUS
PHILBROCK
CRANE
BULGA
WHISTLER ST
CORMORANT
DOTTERELBURRA
OSPREY DR
MOOKABURRA
PELICAN

Halcyon
Landing

MAROOCHY

AVOCADO
NABAL
ANAHEIM
FUERTE
HAAS
AVOCADO
ROAD
KENNEDY
WAIGANI
MOROBE
JACORE
IMAGE
HAGEN
GIRUA
BOROKO
KIAPANO
TASOL ST
Ret
Vill

RD 71

June
Blanck
Pk
CASTLE GARDEN
LYN
ARISTA
CT
WAY

RD 82

DAVID LOW
BRIDGE

COOK

Fbr Fbr
Fbr
Maroochy
River
Golf
Club
Driving
Range
Fbr
Fbr
Fbrs
Fbr
Clubhouse

FINLAND
RD
WAY
558
530

KATHLEEN
KRISTAN
JONI
CONNORS
CASEY
THORNTON
WHARF
BARONS
PRINCESS
ARMOUR
NICHOLAS
ANGLE
MONA
Sunshine
Castle
TYNDALE
BLANCH
313
328
Skate Pk
Muller Park
Aqua
Park
Bli Bli
Watersports
Complex
Ski N Skurf
Cable Water
Ski Park
367

DAVID LOW

John
Lantry
Park

MEDINDIE
ICE
WCKERSON
WELLARD
SALIMANDA
MULLER PARK RD
OYSTER BANK

HISTED
COUTERS
BUCKLAND
HEGARTY
KOKODA
VIVIGANI
DAVID LOW WY

Edgewater
Village
Retirement
Community
Fbr

GODFREYS RD

A B C D 5 04 E F G H J K L M 5 06 E N P Q R 5 07 E

McDONALDS RD

RD

SUNSHINE MOTORWAY
PROPOSED RAILWAY
GODFREYS RD

69

MAP 59
1 KILOMETRE EQUALS 4 GRID SQUARES

JOINS 49

48

59

MARCOOLA
4564

Mount Coolum National Park

Sunshine Coast Airport

Sunshine Coast

SUNSHINE

MOTORWAY

PROPOSED RAILWAY

Mount Coolum National Park

Sunshine Coast

Water Pollution Control Works

PACIFIC PARADISE
4564

Aviation Rescue & Fire Fighting

Control Tower

Terminal

Gate

The Menzies @ Pacific Paradise

Pacific Paradise Primary

North Shore Village

Mudjimba Multisports Complex

Gate

NORTH SHORE CONNECTION

DAVID LOW RD

MUDJIMBA BEACH

COOLIBAH ST
SYCAMORE ST
CURRAWONG ST
SASSIFRAS ST
PANDANUS ST
CUPANIA ST
SUNDEW ST
COTTONWOOD ST

SLSC

Cmnty Cntr

Mudjimba Beach

MUDJIMBA
4564

Maroochy River Conservation Park

North Shore Soccer Club

School Site

Twin Waters

Golf

Club

TWIN WATERS
4564

Living Gems Pacific Paradise

Settlers Pk

Clubhouse

Aged Care

Apex Camp Mudjimba

Living Choice

Twin Waters Ret Vill

BROLGA AV	6
CRANE CL	2
EGRET AV	3
HERRON AV	5
IBIS CCT	1
JABIRU AV	4

Novotel Twin Waters Resort

Lagoon

Twin Waters Beach

Discovery Beach

Marcoola Beach

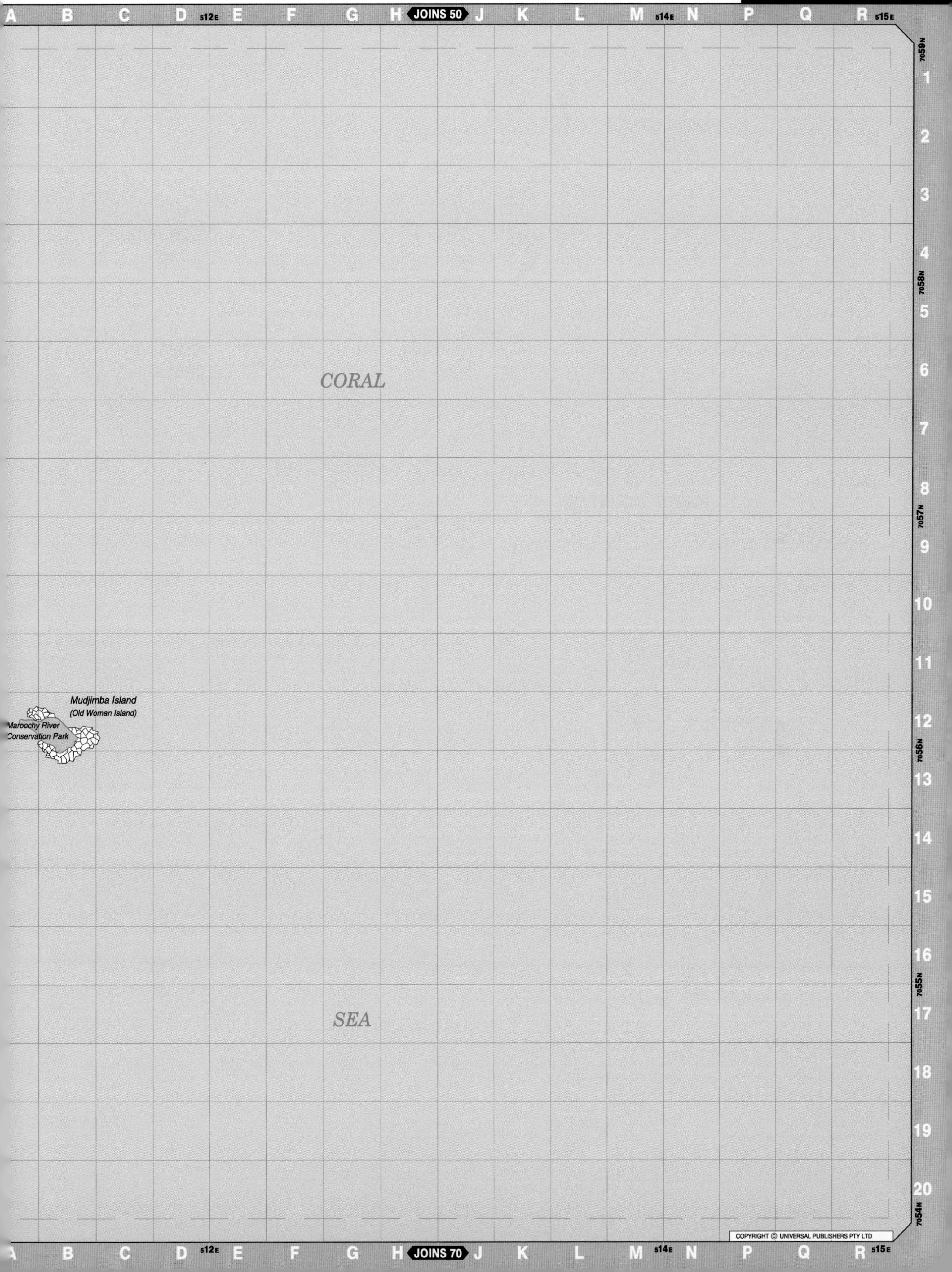

MAP 65
FOLLOWS
60
1 KILOMETRE EQUALS 4 GRID SQUARES

CORAL

Mudjimba Island
(Old Woman Island)

Maroochy River
Conservation Park

SEA

JOINS 55

PERWILLOWEN
4560

PERWILLOWEN RD
PERWILLOWEN
BRIGGS RD
PERWINKLE LA
Coes Ck

CHARLTON CT
ROBERTSON
BURNSIDE
HERITAGE WY
BUCHANAN CT
GRIMES
FERNLEA ST
GLENSIDE
RIDGEWOOD
WINDSOR
Sundale Rotary Garden Village (Rod Voller Hostel)
Nambour Special School
MCKINNON
DALZEL
WHITE OAK PL
EUCALYPTUS PL
GUM TREE PL
POINCIANA PL
ALTITUDE
PINNAC
CLEO
ELEVATE
PUTORCO LA
DUNMAR
VALLEY VIEW
St Johns Cath College
SILVERWOOD PL
WARABI PL
KINGS
JUDITH ST
GLENYS
HALL CT
BEGA ST
DANDENONG
NORA CT
SUE ST
BALOO

BURNSIDE
4560

Coes

COES CREEK
4560

YARRAWAH
KUNDART
NAUN CT
CAPROO RD
MUNDARA
BERRINGAR CT
RENDILLE LA
KIAMA ST
CHILTERN CT

Department of Agriculture & Fisheries Maroochy Research Facility

TOWEN VIEW CT
MAYERS
SIMONS RD
TOWEN MOUNT RD
+ Towen Mtn 309m
THISTLEDO LA (Pvt)

WEKS RIDGE (Unsealed rd)
BROLGA LA
CARRUTHERS RD
THOMPSON

TOWEN MOUNTAIN
4560

COES CREEK RD
MENARY RD
JADE ST
MUNDOO ST
KERRS
IDLE PARK
BREEZE
MOUNTAIN WY
RAINBOW
CL

N
W   E
S

WEST WOOMBYE
4559

CARRUTHERS RD
BAGNALL RD
CARRUTHERS RD

WHITE CEDAR PL
MENARY BRIDGE
BLACKALL
REIDS
MULLER

Ck
Petrie

Sunshine Coast

BLACKALL RANGE
SHEKINAH CT
BLACKALL RANGE RD
HAMILTON RD
KNOB
PARSONS

Petrie

KALANG DR
ILUKA ST
SIMBA RD
GLENFERN RD
JACKSON RD

CHRISTENSENS
PARSONS KNOB
MCKEES
RD S

HUNCHY
4555

PALMWOODS
4555

RATCLIFFE

JOINS 54

MAP 66
1 KILOMETRE EQUALS 4 GRID SQUARES

NAMBOUR
4560

ROSEMOUNT
4560

4559
DIDDILLIBAH

WOOMBYE
4559

MAP 67
1 KILOMETRE EQUALS 4 GRID SQUARES
JOINS 57
56

ROSEMOUNT
4560

DIDDILLIBAH
4559

KIELS
MOUNTAIN
4559

Sunshine Coast

+ Kiels Mtn
151m

Kaalba Court
Natural Amenity
Res

WOOMBYE
4559

FOREST
GLEN
4556

Glenfinnan
Bushland
Reserve

Big Pineapple
Redevelopment
Site

TreeTop
Challenge

Wildlife
Headquarters

NAMBOUR CONNECTION

Montessori
International
College

PAYNTERS CREEK

Paynter

DIDDILLIBAH

BRUCE HWY

M1

Cmnty
Hall
Cem
RFB

Creek

East Eudlo

Eudlo

MAROOCHYDORE RD

OLD MAROOCHYDORE RD

B by Halcyon
Retirement
Village

Scenic
Reserve

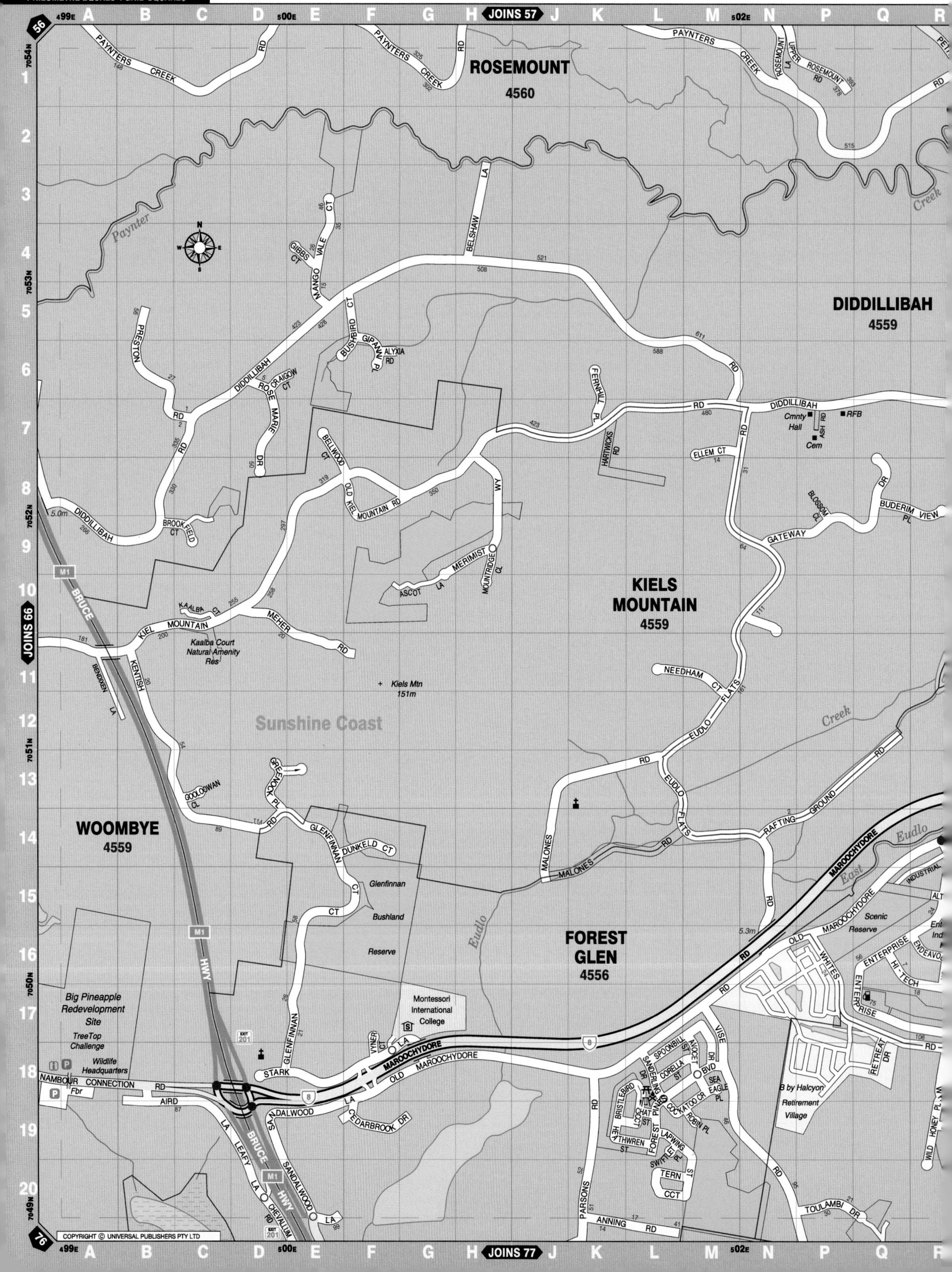

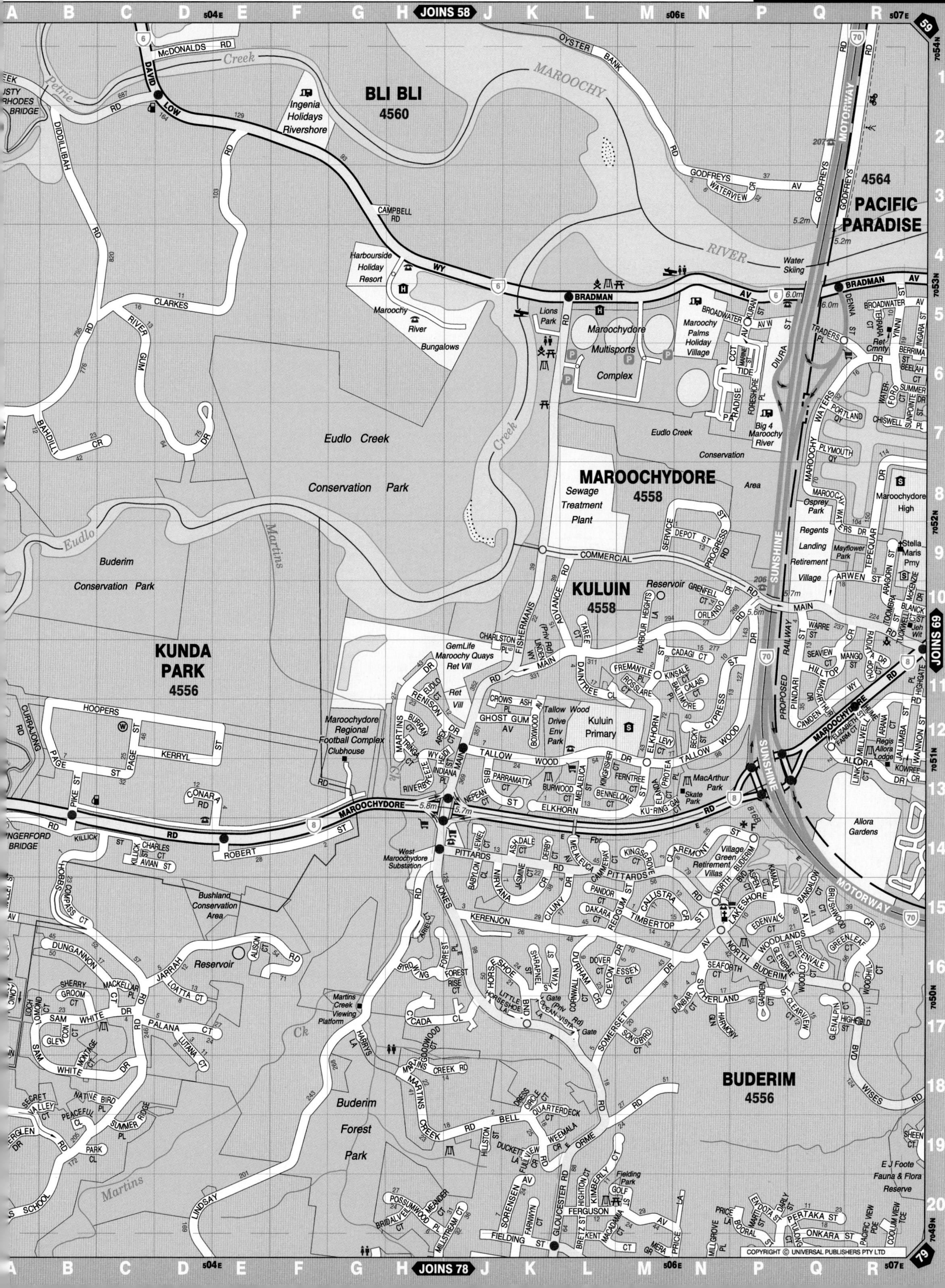

MAP 68
1 KILOMETRE EQUALS 4 GRID SQUARES

JOINS 58
JOINS 69
JOINS 78

BLI BLI
4560

PACIFIC PARADISE
4564

MAROOCHYDORE
4558

KULUIN
4558

KUNDA PARK
4556

BUDERIM
4556

Eudlo Creek Conservation Park

Buderim Conservation Park

Buderim Forest Park

Bushland Conservation Area

Martins Creek Viewing Platform

Maroochydore Regional Football Complex Clubhouse

Maroochydore Multisports Complex

Sewage Treatment Plant

Maroochy River

Lions Park

Ingenia Holidays Rivershore

Harbourside Holiday Resort

Maroochy River Bungalows

Big 4 Maroochy River

Eudlo Creek Conservation Area

Maroochy Palms Holiday Village

Kuluin Primary

Tallow Wood Drive Env Park

MacArthur Park

Skate Park

Village Green Retirement Villas

Allora Gardens

Maroochydore High

Stella Maris Pmy

Regents Landing Retirement Village

Mayflower Park

Osprey Park

GemLife Maroochy Quays Ret Vill

Reservoir

E J Foote Fauna & Flora Reserve

Fielding Park

MAROOCHY RIVER

MAP 69
1 KILOMETRE EQUALS 4 GRID SQUARES

JOINS 59

PACIFIC PARADISE 4564

TWIN WATERS 4564

Novotel Twin Waters Resort

Lagoon

Maroochy River Conservation Park

MAROOCHY RIVER

Main

Channel Island

Maroochy River Conservation Park

Goat Island

South Channel

Pincushion Island

Sunshine Coast

Sailing Club

Chambers Island

BRADMAN AVENUE BRIDGE

Picnic Pt

Maroochydore High

Sunshine Home

PRIMARY SCHOOL

Maroochydore Primary

Sunshine Plaza

Cotton Tree Park

Cotton Tree

THE ESPLANADE

Kon-Tiki Business Centre

Cinema

SunCentral Development

MAROOCHYDORE 4558

Bunnings

Spotlight

Aged Care

PROPOSED

SUNSHINE

Sportsfield

Council Depot

QT

Zone Maroochydore

Thompson Park

Subsrn

BUDERIM 4556

PALMYRA

Immanuel Lutheran College

Immanuel Gardens Ret Vill

Buderim Gardens Retirement Village

ALEXANDRA HEADLAND 4572

Alexandra Park Conference Centre

Alex Beach

Bushland Park

Alex Forest

MOTORWAY

Aged Care

Elizabeth Daniels Park

E J Foote Fauna & Flora Reserve

AWINYA LA 1
BURRUM LA 3
COOMBOO LA 4
FRASER AV 5
HERVEY CH 7
ROUNDBUSH CCT 6
YIDNEY ST 2

JOINS 79

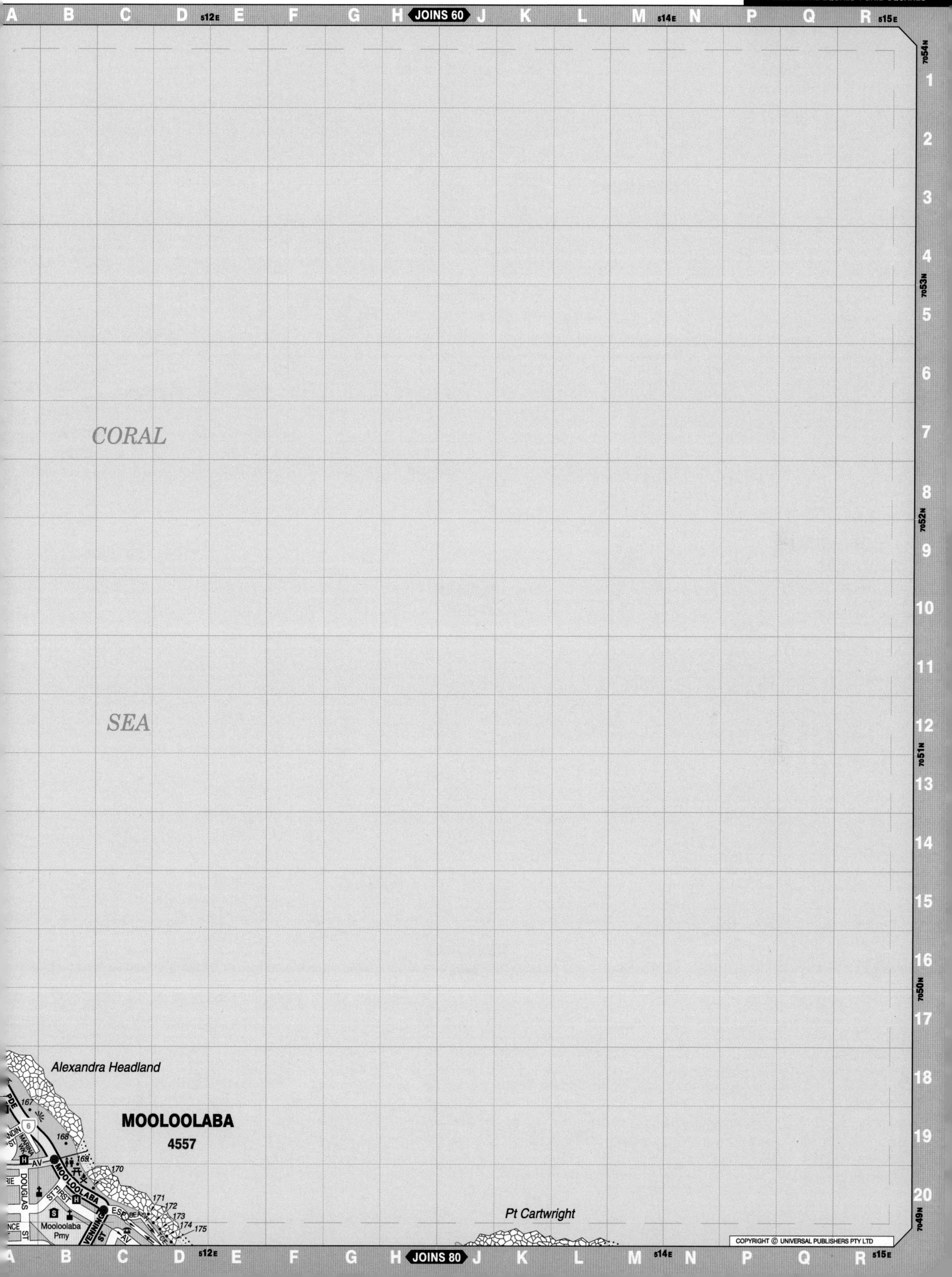

MAP 73
FOLLOWS
70
1 KILOMETRE EQUALS 4 GRID SQUARES

A B C D s12E E F G H JOINS 60 J K L M s14E N P Q R s15E

7054N

1

2

3

4

7053N

5

6

7

CORAL

8

7052N

9

10

11

SEA

12

7051N

13

14

15

16

7050N

17

Alexandra Headland

18

MOOLOOLABA

4557

19

Pt Cartwright

20

7049N

A B C D s12E E F G H JOINS 80 J K L M s14E N P Q R s15E

JOINS 53

Restricted Vehicle Access

Forest Reserve

CURRAMORE
4552

CURRAMORE RD

THOMPSON

CURRAMORE

EKERT LA

GRANITE RD

EKERT RD

COOKES RD

UPPER CEDAR CREEK

HUMPHRIES RD

BYTHEWAY RD

Obi Lookout

Nothling La

SCHULTZ RD

ROSE GUM LA

ANSELL

SOMM

MEASBERG RD

WITTABERG RD

GEMELLE CT

MEAGAN CT

STERNBERG RD

RAVENSBERG DR

TEUTOBERG LDABERGS WY

CURRAMORE

COOKE RD

FREEMAN

ATTUNGA CT

WITTA
4552

Sportsground

Witta (Teutob)
Old Wit Cmn

CHURCH (Priv Rd) RD

BERGANNS

MALENY

MARGARET ST

BAKERS RD

DEVILS ELBOW LA

KENILWORTH

MALENY RD

CONONDALE
4552

22

RESERVE RD

Green Park

ELAMAN CREEK RD

ELAMAN
CREEK
4552

Elaman Ck

GRUNDON RD

KENILWORTH

MALENY

MINCHENTONS CROSSING

Minchenton Gully

KENILWORTH

GUMLAND
KOALA CT
PARKLAND CT

MIDDLETON RD

Fleiter Hill

COX RD

WITTA

COX

WATSON

OXENHAM LA

POCKET

CORKS

RIDLEY

TROON LA

KELS LA

HARPER CREEK

Harper Ck

ENGLE RD

REESVILLE
4552

REESVILLE RD

WATSON LA

HASSALL LA (Priv Rd)

MEADOW RD

FLESSER RD

Clark Ck

Clark

ARCADIA LA (Priv Rd)

SYDNEY LA (Priv Rd)

CLIMER LA

REESVILLE RD

LAWRENCE PL

Howell Knob Lookout

HOWELL KNOB LOOKOUT RD

22

Alcorn

KINGS RD

Arley Ck

RUDDLE RD

Obi Obi Ck

LIMIT OF MAPS

JOINS 32

MAP 74

1 KILOMETRE EQUALS 2 GRID SQUARES

JOINS 54

JOINS 94

JOINS 75

JOINS 85

HUNCHY 4555

MONTVILLE 4560

NORTH MALENY 4552

MALENY 4552

EUDLO 4554

DIAMOND VALLEY 4553

BALMORAL RIDGE 4552

BALD KNOB 4552

Kondalilla

Forest Reserve

National Park

Obi Obi

The Narrows

Conservation Area

Lake Baroon

Sunshine Coast

Conservation Area

Conservation Area

Elston Falls

Pobblebonk

Crawford & Foster Lookout

Flame Hill Vineyard

Russell Family Pk

Montville Pmy

Razorback

Memorial

Hall

Gerrards Lookout

Dilkusha Nature Refuge

Balmoral Lookout

Chenrezig Institute

Sportsground

Ananda Marga River School

Causeway

Roen-Mar Pathway

Maleny Soldiers Mem Hosp

Showground

Maleny Pmy

Maleny Golf Club

Blue Care Ben Bryce

Park Village & Erowal Residential Aged Care

Maleny High

Walker + Hill

Maleny Cheese

Restricted Vehicle Access

CARINYA CL 3
CHERRY ST 5
FAIRVIEW CT 9
FLAME ST 6
MAJUBA CL 4
MORVEN PL 8
PARKGLEN PL 10
PINEWOOD CCT 1
SUNNYSIDE CT 2
WONGABEL ST 7

ASPEN CT 2
CINNAMON ST 5
CLOUDWALK DR 1
EBONY CT 7
GREENHILLS ESP 4
PEPPER BERRY DR 6
SNOWWOOD AV 3

COPYRIGHT © UNIVERSAL PUBLISHERS PTY LTD

MAP 75
1 KILOMETRE EQUALS 4 GRID SQUARES

JOINS 65

HUNCHY
4555

RATCLIFFE

HUNCHY

347
283
411
372
330
230

795/1
7189/1

RD

OLINGTON LA
ANNWAL LA
15

(Narrow bridge)
28

HARDINGS RD

HUNCHY
144
119
198
96

OLD
MERINDA AV
138
122
BOWLING GREEN
75
87

CORNELIUS RD
19
74
38

Federal Park
PRIM

(Narrow bridge)
9

BLACKBUTT RD
60

BUSH TREE CT
RIDGE VISTA

LINGAF

RA

76

PALMWOODS

RD

PETERS
PINOLLOWS
CIGNAL
PAYNE
CORNELEIGH

ROBERTS
TYTHERLEIGH
100

S

Palmwoods Primary

KENSINGTON ST

MONTVILLE
Palmwoods
150
161

PALMWOODS SCHOOL
COACHE
OLD ORCHARD

Sunshine Coast

Creek

SHURVELL RD
810
140
119
349

BARSON RD
185
579

GemLIfe Lifestyle Resort

LANDERSHUTE RD

TANGERINE PL
Kuskopf PK
PETIG
KINDAL
CROWSNEST
RAIN
PICCA PL

32

MONTVILLE
4560

PALMWOODS
MONTVILLE RD

COUNTRY RD
80
98

MACDONALD
110
77
41

RD

216

251
286
305

Stonebridge Gardens

RIFLE RANGE
LANDERSHUTE

CITRUS
82
103
28

RD
70

REMINGTON SHUTE RD
14
517

RD
438
373

156

LANDERSHUTE
185

Palmwoods Substation

777 - 778
Proposed Transmission Line

KIRBY

Paynter

RD
23
86

ROYS
229

L RD
38

RD

UPPER LANDERSHUTE
294

LANDERS SHOOT
4555

286

RD
310

CITRUS RD

EUDLO SCHOOL
156

LOWER LANDERSHUTE
190
181
149

EVE LA
97

SKORPIL LA

SUNRIDGE
100
109

56

RD
156

EUDLO
4554

Proposed Transmission Line
808

RD
410
379

RD
322

745/4 & 746/2 E

UPPER
566
500

LANDERSHUTE
429

HOUGHTONS RD

HIGHLANDS RD
229
189

JOINS 85

JOINS 74

MAP 76
1 KILOMETRE EQUALS 4 GRID SQUARES

JOINS 66

WOOMBYE
4559

The Oasis
Golf & Tennis
Palmwoods

G Rae Oval
Soccer
AFL
Briggs
Park

Palmwoods
Garden
Village

Woombye
Cemetery

WINSTON

Kolora Park

Palmwoods
Railway

PALMWOODS
4555

Eudlo

Creek

National

Park

CHEVALLUM
4555

CHEVALLUM

CARLYLE RD

BAMBOO RD

McGILCHRIST RD

JOINS 77

Eudlo

Proposed Transmission Line
777 - 778

SLAUGHTER YARD

ILKLEY
4554

MAP 77
1 KILOMETRE EQUALS 4 GRID SQUARES

A B C D E F G H J K L M N P Q R

66 499E 500E **JOINS 67** 502E

WOOMBYE
4559

FOREST
GLEN
4556

The Oasis
Golf & Tennis
Palmwoods

PALMWOODS
4555

Clubhouse
WINSTON RD

Eudlo

Sunshine Coast
Grammar

FOREST
CT

VILLAGE CENTRE
WY

Greenwood Forest Glen
Ret. Village

FOREST VIEW
CT

MONS

MONS
4556

Owen

Ck

CHEVALLUM
4555

KEMBLA
CT

Forest Glen
Resort

LIANA
PL

SAWREYS

TWIN
RIDGES

TYLER RD

TELCO RD

HERITAGE PL

SAWREY

EMPIRE CR
Toll
PALMETTO ST
GIBBINS WY
EMPIRE CR
KIKUYU

HWY
RD

ARMSTRONG CT

Sunshine Coast

FERNY GLEN RD

HIDEAWAY
PL

BOWERBIRD
PL

MOUNTAIN TOP
CT

Chevallum
Primary

MONARCH

EXIT
200

TOURIST

FERNY GLEN RD

25

GALLAGHERS

RAINFOREST PL

KITNEY
CL

BRUCE

MAIN CREEK RD

DR

SARAH
CT

CHEVALLUM
SCHOOL
LISA

GLENN VISTA PL

ILKLEY

Main

RADBOURNE

LAWRENCES UPS
MAIN CREEK

TOPVIEW
KIRSTY

DR

BOUGHENS RD

LUCIDA PL

FOLEYS

PALM CREEK

Tanawha Valley
Golf &
Tennis

Gate

ELISABETH VALLEY PL

ILKLEY
4554

Maroochy Regional

OLSEN RD
ILKLEY RD
JACK FROST CT

Bushland

Proposed Transmission Line
777 - 778

Botanic Garden

Mountain

A B C D E F G H J K L M N P Q R

86 499E 500E **JOINS 87** 502E

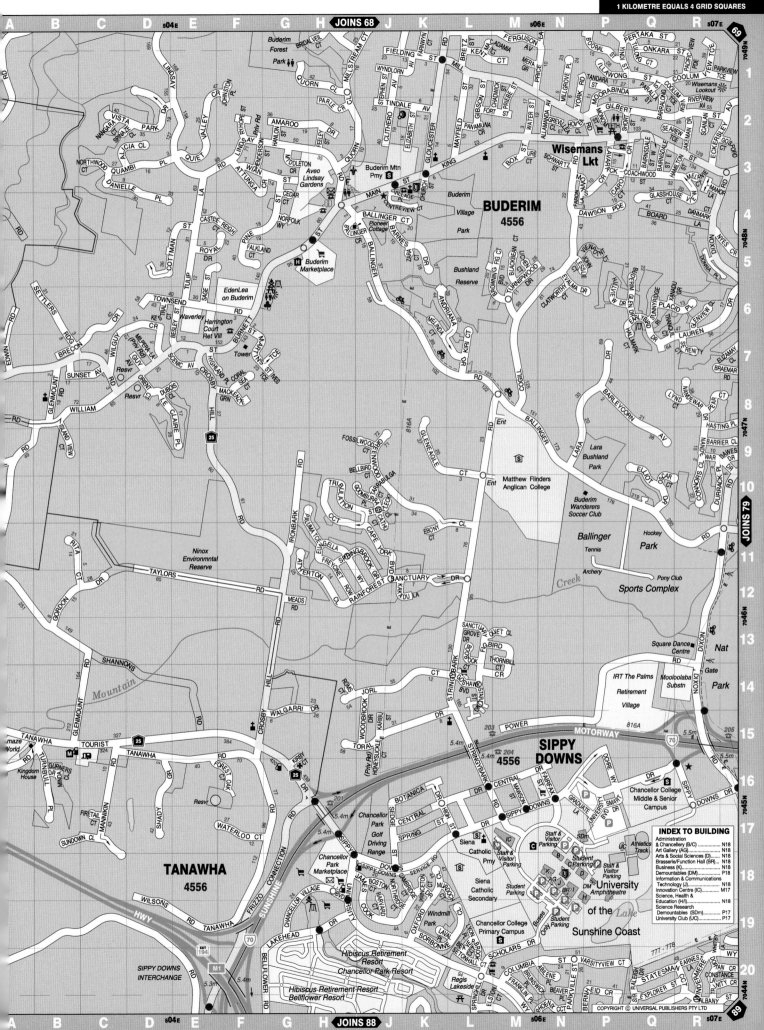

MAP 78

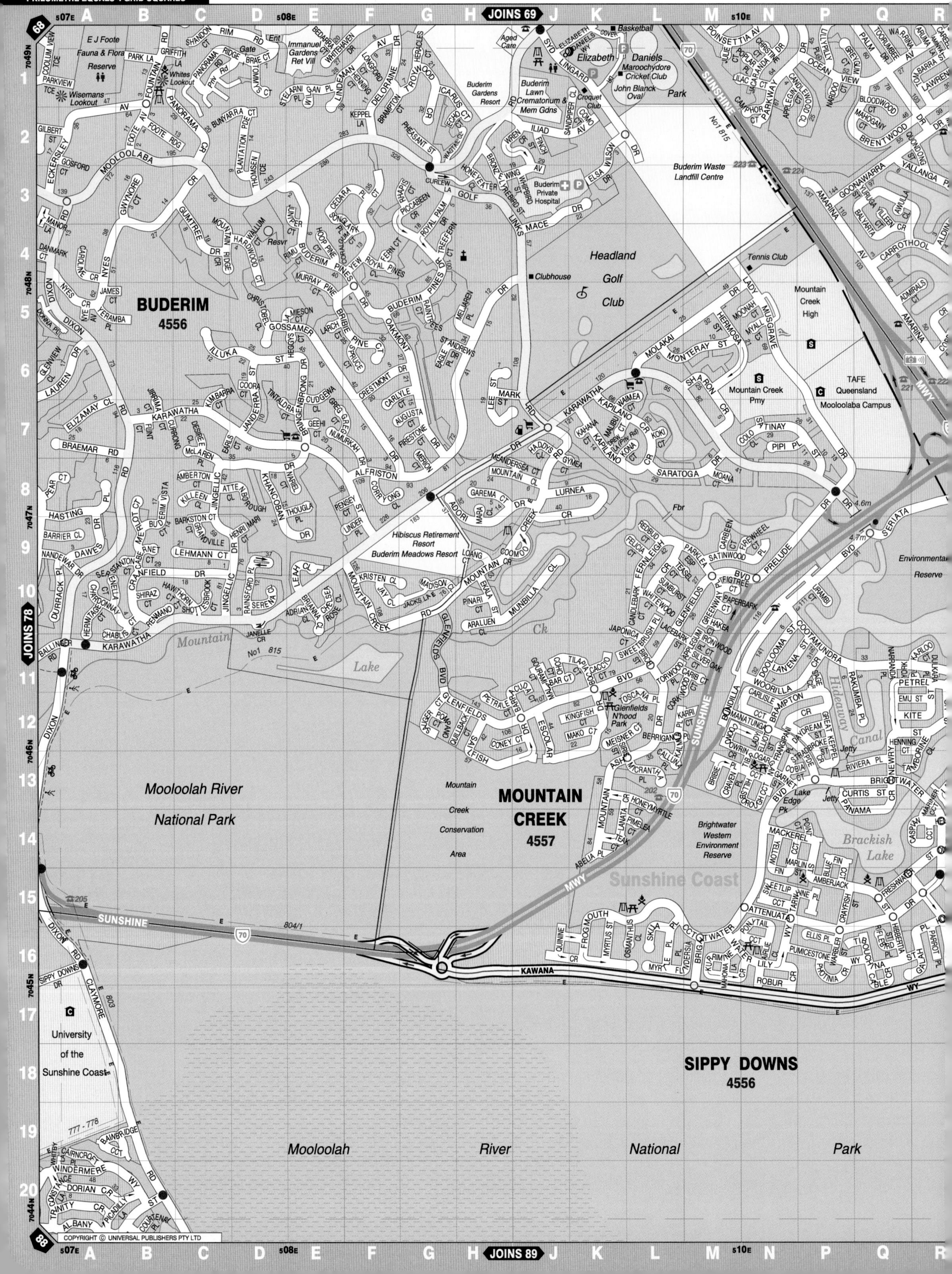

MAP 79
1 KILOMETRE EQUALS 4 GRID SQUARES

JOINS 69

JOINS 89

JOINS 78

BUDERIM
4556

MOUNTAIN CREEK
4557

SIPPY DOWNS
4556

Mooloolah River

National Park

Mountain Creek Conservation Area

Headland Golf Club

University of the Sunshine Coast

Mooloolah River National Park

Brackish Lake

Hideaway Canal

Brightwater Western Environment Reserve

Environmental Reserve

Sunshine Coast

SUNSHINE MWY

KAWANA

Buderim Private Hospital

Buderim Gardens Resort

Buderim Lawn Crematorium & Mem Gdns

John Blanck Oval

Maroochydore Cricket Club

Mountain Creek High

TAFE Queensland Mooloolaba Campus

Buderim Waste Landfill Centre

A B C D E F G **JOINS 75** J K L M N P Q R

74
491E 492E 494E

EUDLO
4554

7044N
7043N
7042N
JOINS 74
7041N
7040N
7039N

GERRARD

ALBERT WOOD RD

GLENEITH PL

HIGHLANDS

HIGHLANDS RD

SULLIVANS RD

RAMBERTS

UPPER RAMBERT RD
JOHNSON RD

BROOKS

MOOLOOLAH

LOGWO

BUSHLARK

MOSSY BANK
(4 Wheel drive only)

BINYA RD

MOSSY BANK

PERRINS

Coonoona
Nature
Refuge
(Private)

CLIMNER

NEILL RD

NEILL ST

Sunshine Coast

745/4 & 746/2

Environmental

Park

RAINTREE CL

RAINFOREST

MOOLOOLA

RIVER

HARRIS

RISSO RD

EATON ST

SHADY LA

DIAMOND

VALLEY

RATCLIFFE

RATCLIFFE

ENSBEY RD

DIAMOND
VALLEY
4553

ANDERSEN

BALD
KNOB
4552

JILLIAN

RD

(Narrow bridge)

(Unsealed road)

BRANDENBURG

94
491E 492E 494E **JOINS 95**

MAP 86
1 KILOMETRE EQUALS 4 GRID SQUARES

JOINS 76

ILKLEY
4554

MOOLOOLAH VALLEY
4553

GLENVIEW
4553

Eudlo

RFB
Hall
Eudlo Pmy

(Narrow bridge)

(Narrow bridge)

ANZAC RD
ILKLEY
McGILCHRIST
CORLIS AV
EUDLO SCHOOL RD
ROSEBED ST
RD
MOOLOOLAH RD
COGDEN
THE PINCH
Tunnel
NOBLES LA
ROBINSONS RD
ILKLEY RD
SLAUGHTER YARD
SARA PL
NOBLES RD
WILSON RD
HUTCHINSONS RD
ILKLEY RD

OLD GYMPIE
UPPER TOLSON
Gate RD
EAGLE VIEW LA
BIRDSONG
BILBY PL
PLATYPUS CT
EUDLO DR
PALMWOODS-MOOLOOLAH RD
KNOX DR
SMITH DR
NEILL RD

DIAMOND VALLEY DR
TAYLOR CT
SAMUEL PL
FERN GULLY
Reservoir
VIEWLAND DR
FAIRVIEW RIDGE
THE RIVERS
Mooloolah Primary
Mooloolah Gardens Retirement Resort
Hall
BRAY RD
PAGET
HATTEN
KING ST
JONES ST
ERIC CT
LORNAL CT
KA RANNE DR
SUZEN WAY
CHRISTINE CT
RIDGE CT
TREETOP CT
JELEN DR
MOOLOOLAH RD
BLOODWOOD CL
SCRIBBLY GUM
SOUTH
SUGAR GUM CT
COOLIBAH
RIVER GUM
LILLYPILLY
SOUTH RIVER Park
TW HAMILTON BRIDGE
CONNECTION RD
BENJARA LA
Maria Higgs Conservation Park
Mooloolah Rec Res
Mooloolah
TUNNEL RIDGE RD
VALLEY VIEW
WOODLANDS CT
CASSIA CL
BRENDA
NICOLLE
COACH HOUSE CT
KINGSTON CT
OLD GYMPIE RD
Dent Pk
HAMILTON CL
FORSYTH PL
GLENVIEW RD
TOLSON CR
GULFOYLE CR

MOOLOOLAH RIVER
SOUTH MOOLOOLAH

(Narrow bridge)
3.7m
Low bridge clearance 3.7m

JOINS 96

COPYRIGHT © UNIVERSAL PUBLISHERS PTY LTD

JOINS 87

77
97

MAP 87
1 KILOMETRE EQUALS 4 GRID SQUARES

JOINS 77

Ck

Maroochy Regional
Bushland
Botanic Garden

777-778
Proposed Transmission Line

WILSON

RD

247

232

169

320

N
W · E
S

266

Mountain

TANAWHA
4556

ILKLEY
4554

ILKLEY

441

382

128

12
39
WILSON

356
SIPPY CREEK
328

Sippy

Ck

RD

259

RD

378

RD

413

HUTCHINSONS

65

SIPPY CREEK

506

DEREE

479

RD

RD

124

LINK

73

ROCKTON CT

APPLEBY CT

RD

Mt Sippy
180m +

MISSING

JOINS 86

UPPER TOLSON RD

RD

MISSING

102

LINK

129

GLENVIEW
4553

MISSING LINK

RD

RD

TOLSON

EVANS GROVE

35

38

10

9

624

629

70

ISAMBERT

DUNNE

DE

RD

55

16

CLINTON CT

GLENVIEW

HAZEL

CHAMBERS CT

PL

598

516

LEEDING

FIRETAIL PL

WHIPBIRD

ST IVES AV

246

244

12

236

RD

209

EVERGREEN

MOOLOOLAH

LAVENDER

40

30

12

CL

RD

260

MARIA CT

278

HIDEAWAY LA

DR

42

MOOLOOLAH
VALLEY
4553

BRENDA CT

NICOLLE CT

4

3

481

ROSEMARY AV

420

405

RD

Glenview
S Primary

356

367

GLENVIEW

326

287

STEVENS

89

68

RIVER

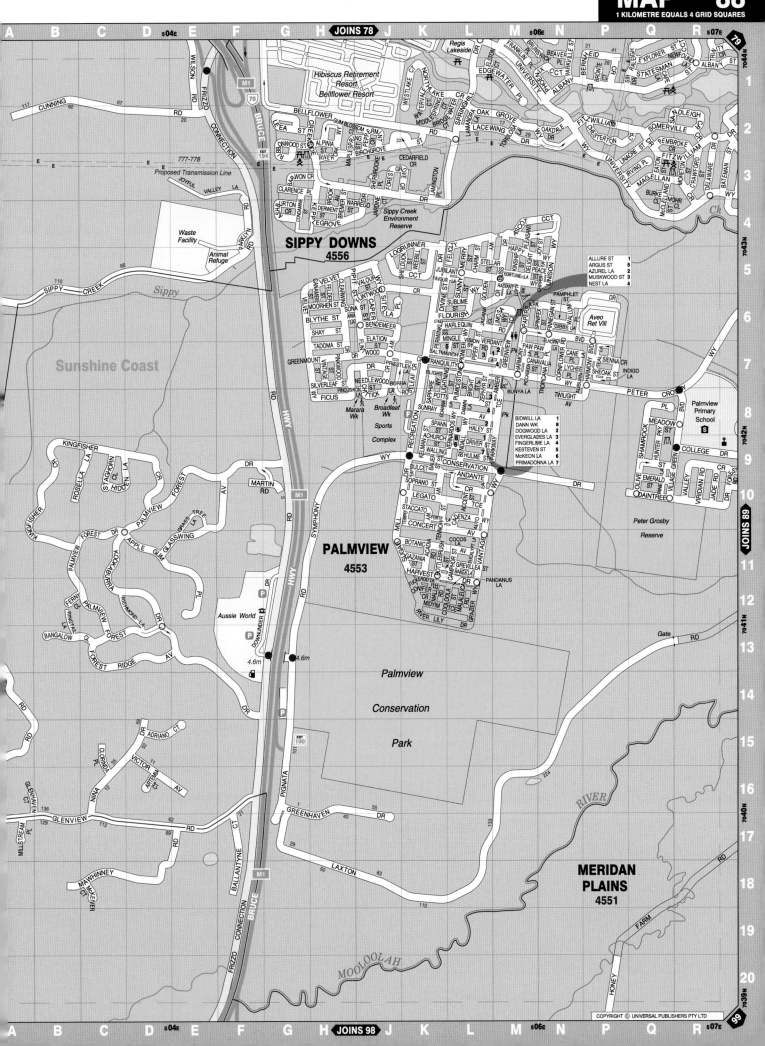

MAP 88
1 KILOMETRE EQUALS 4 GRID SQUARES

SIPPY DOWNS
4556

PALMVIEW
4553

PALMVIEW
Conservation
Park

MERIDAN
PLAINS
4551

Sunshine Coast

Palview Primary School

Peter Grosby Reserve

ALLURE ST 1
ARGUS ST 5
AZUREL LA 2
MUSKWOOD ST 3
NEST LA 4

BIDWILL LA 1
DANN WK 8
DOGWOOD LA 2
EVERGLADES LA 3
FINGERLIME LA 4
KESTEVEN ST 5
McKEON LA 6
PRIMADONNA LA 7

JOINS 78
JOINS 98

COPYRIGHT © UNIVERSAL PUBLISHERS PTY LTD

MAP 89
1 KILOMETRE EQUALS 4 GRID SQUARES

JOINS 79

JOINS 78

JOINS 88

JOINS 98

JOINS 99

Mooloolah River National Park

SIPPY DOWNS
4556

Lower Mooloolah River

Environmental Reserve

Sippy

Creek

Peter Crosby

MOOLOOLAH

PALMVIEW
4553

Palmview Primary School

Palmview Special School

College Dr

Valley Cr

Jade Rd

Daintree

Glover

Basil Pl

Ivy Rd

Sage

Forest Rd

River

Gate

Sunshine Coast

MOOLOOLAH

Laxton

Westaway Rd

Rainforest Rd

Reservoirs Av

803

Reservoir

MERIDAN PLAINS
4551

Meridan Plains Conservation Park

Meridan Fields Sportsground

Honey Farm

Westaway Rd

Meridan Dr

Pacific Lutheran College

IRT Woodlands

Lemonwood St

Kurrajong

Satinash

Macaranga

Stavewood

Rapanea

Wilkiea

Tuckeroo

Leacys Bushland Conservation Reserve

Currimund

PROPOSED RAILWAY

CALOUNDRA - MOOLOOLABA

Bancrofts Redgum Environment Reserve

Halcyon Parks Caloundra

5.8m

Sunjewel Environme

SUNJEWEL BVD

Keswick St

Shaw St

Capricorn

Magnetic

Harvey

Canning

Braidon Av

Maclean Dr

Creekwood

LIMIT OF MAPS

Grid references (top): A B C 469E D E F G 471E K L 473E M N P Q 475E 73

Conondale
(Narrow bridge)
AHERNS

(Narrow bridge)
BEAUSANG LA

REESVILLE
4552

Ck MARY

Ck

LA

Sunshine Coast

(Narrow bridge)

CONONDALE
4552

RD KILCOY
Roads
Private

POLICEMAN SPUR

Geraghty Creek
RD

Visitors
Area

787

RIVER

RD

Crystal Waters

(Narrow bridge)
RD
AHERNS

Geraghty Ck

Permiculture

KENNEDY

941

Village

Roads

Scrub

118
Kilcoy
BROKEN BRIDGE
Private

JIMNA
BELLTHORPE

Somerset

(Private
CORBETTS RD
LA
WINDRED
Priv

SANDY
CREEK
4570

CONONDALE

BROKEN BRIDGE

RD

only
suitable
10

Bellthorpe

Broken

Bridge

RD

JOINS 93

Road

Forest

Reserve

PLUMB

Bellthorpe
West
RD

WEST

RANGE

WILLETT
RD

RD

BOOROOBIN
4552

BELLTHORPE

Moreton Bay

RD
170

BRANDONS
RD

GOODLA RD
BEACON RD

BELLTHORPE WEST

BELLTHORPE
4514

WILLETT

CONONDALE

RANGE

RD
GAP
CAMPBELL

RD

Camp

RD

RD

345
BELLTHORPE WEST

Ck

BRANDONS
RD

RFB

KEIR
RD

Cmnty Hall
Bellthorpe
Environmental
Park

RD
BELLTHORPE RANGE

BELLTHORPE RANGE
297

Mary
Ck
Smokers
Ck

Branch
Ck

Bellthorpe   *Forest*   *Reserve*
Restricted   Vehicle   Access

B33

Grid references (bottom): A B C 469E D E F G JOINS BRISBANE 32 K L 473E M N P Q 475E

LIMIT OF MAPS

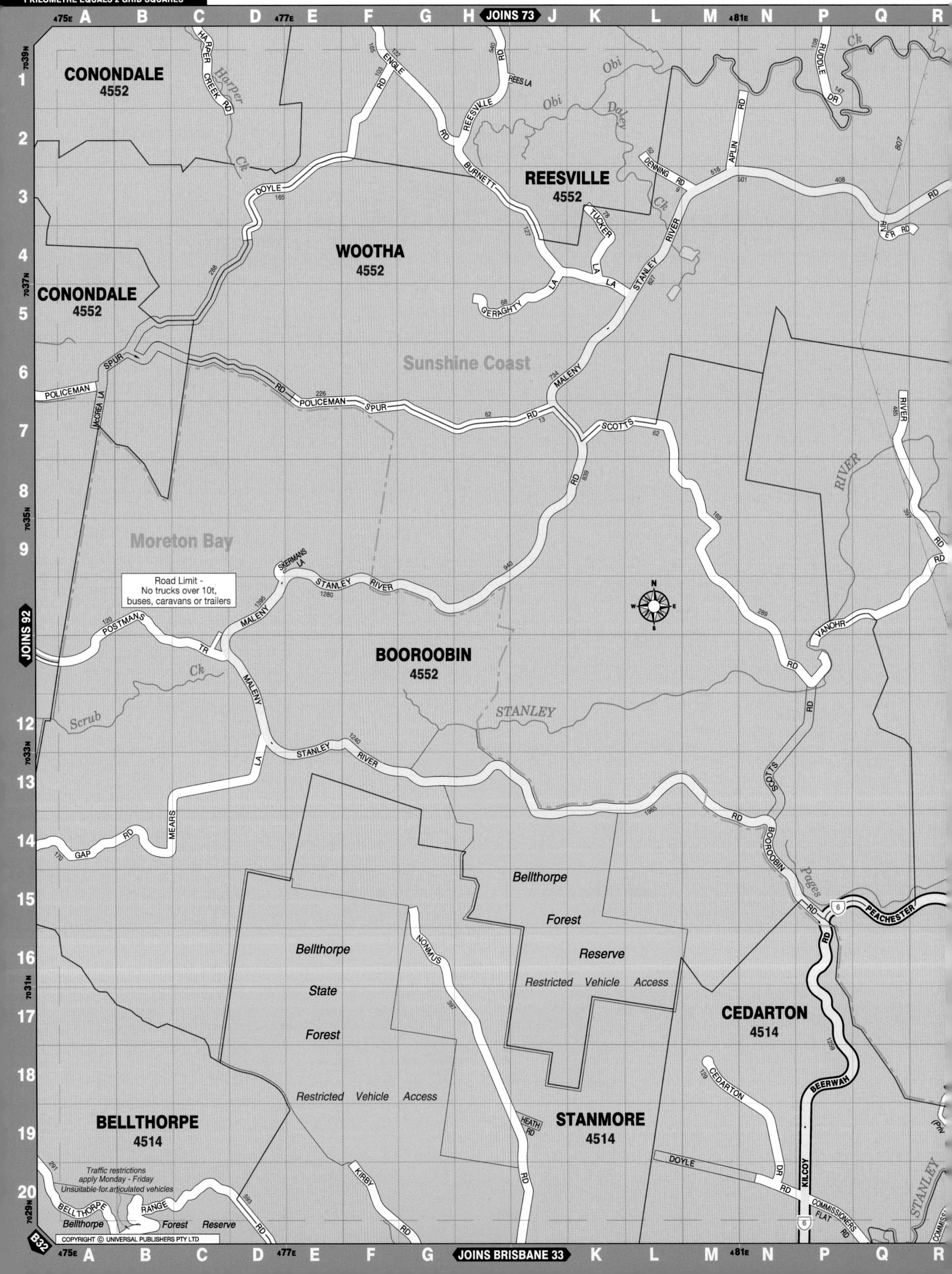

MAP 93
1 KILOMETRE EQUALS 2 GRID SQUARES

JOINS 73

CONONDALE
4552

CONONDALE
4552

REESVILLE
4552

WOOTHA
4552

Sunshine Coast

Moreton Bay

Road Limit -
No trucks over 10t,
buses, caravans or trailers

BOOROOBIN
4552

STANLEY

Bellthorpe

Forest

Bellthorpe

Reserve

State

Restricted   Vehicle   Access

Forest

CEDARTON
4514

Restricted   Vehicle   Access

BELLTHORPE
4514

STANMORE
4514

Bellthorpe   Forest   Reserve

JOINS 92

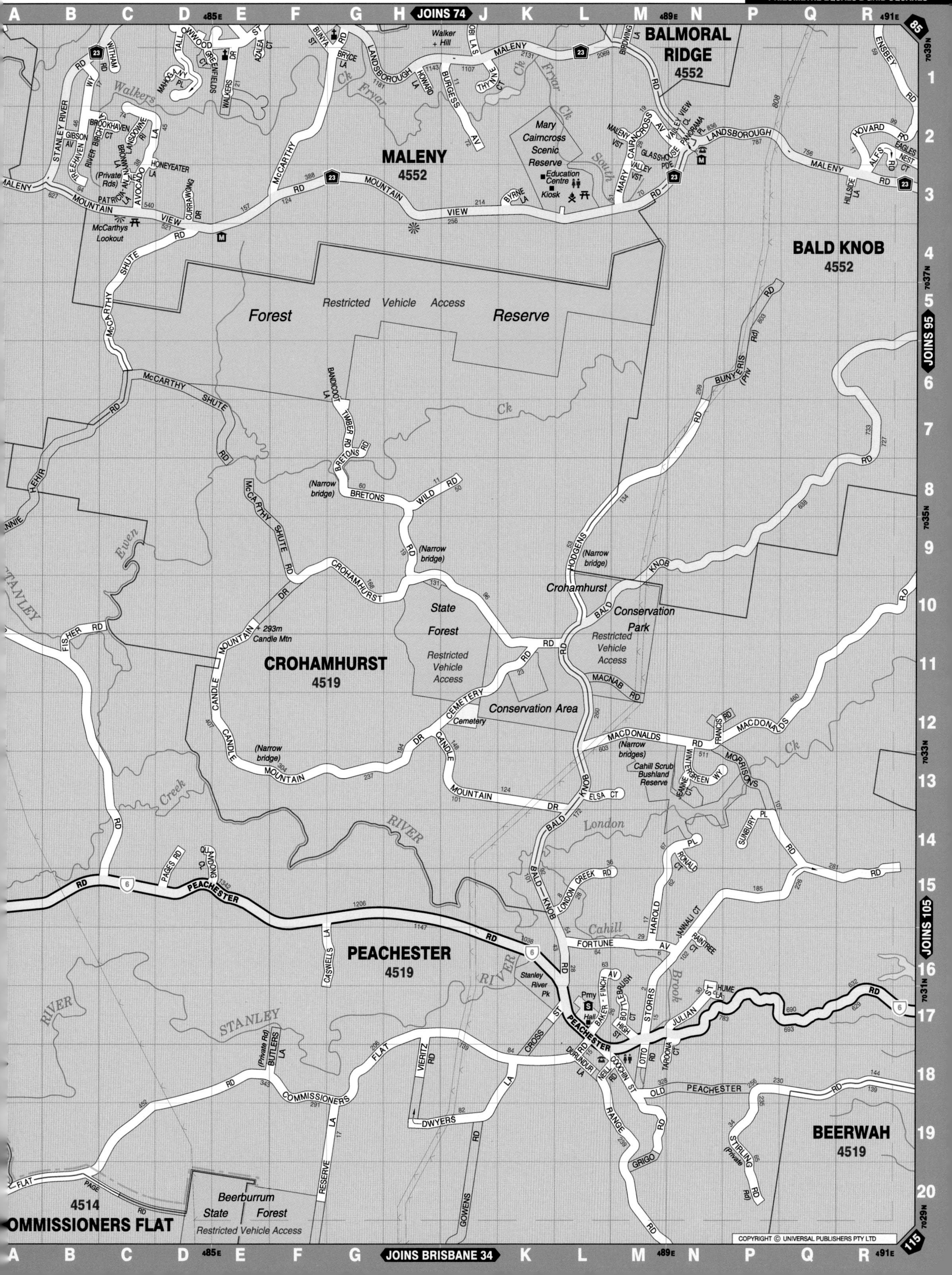

MAP 94
1 KILOMETRE EQUALS 2 GRID SQUARES

JOINS 74

JOINS BRISBANE 34

JOINS 95

JOINS 105

JOINS 115

BALMORAL RIDGE 4552

MALENY 4552

BALD KNOB 4552

CROHAMHURST 4519

PEACHESTER 4519

BEERWAH 4519

COMMISSIONERS FLAT 4514

Forest Reserve — Restricted Vehicle Access

State Forest — Restricted Vehicle Access

Crohamhurst Conservation Park — Restricted Vehicle Access

Conservation Area

Cemetery

Cahill Scrub Bushland Reserve

Mary Cairncross Scenic Reserve — Education Centre — Kiosk

McCarthys Lookout

Candle Mtn 293m

(Narrow bridge)

Stanley River Pk

Beerburrum State Forest — Restricted Vehicle Access

Walker + Hill

MALENY MOUNTAIN VIEW RD
McCARTHY SHUTE RD
CROHAMHURST DR
CANDLE MOUNTAIN RD
BALD KNOB RD
LANDSBOROUGH
PEACHESTER RD
COMMISSIONERS LA
MACNAB RD
MACDONALDS RD
MORRISONS RD
BUNYERIS RD
HODGENS RD
WILD RD
BRETONS RD
BANDICOOT TIMBER RD
FISHER RD
STANLEY RIVER RD
OLD PEACHESTER RD

COPYRIGHT © UNIVERSAL PUBLISHERS PTY LTD

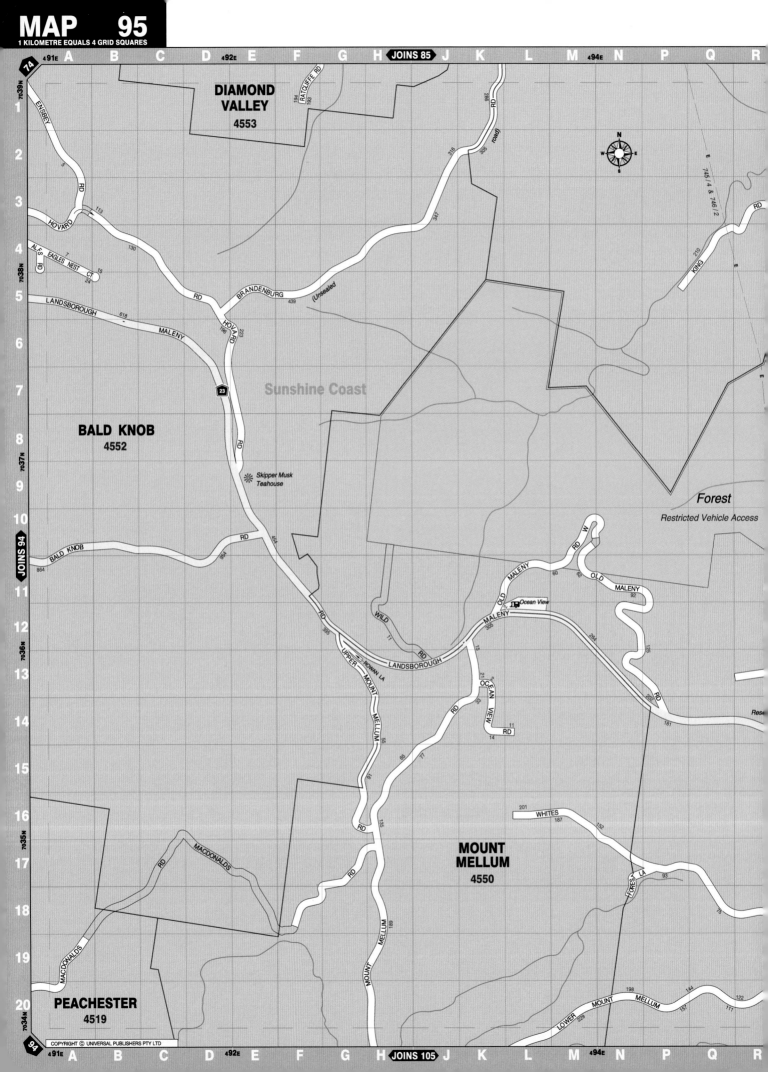

MAP 95
1 KILOMETRE EQUALS 4 GRID SQUARES

JOINS 85

74

DIAMOND VALLEY
4553

BALD KNOB
4552

Sunshine Coast

Skipper Musk Teahouse

JOINS 94

Forest
Restricted Vehicle Access

Ocean View

MOUNT MELLUM
4550

WHITES

PEACHESTER
4519

94

JOINS 105

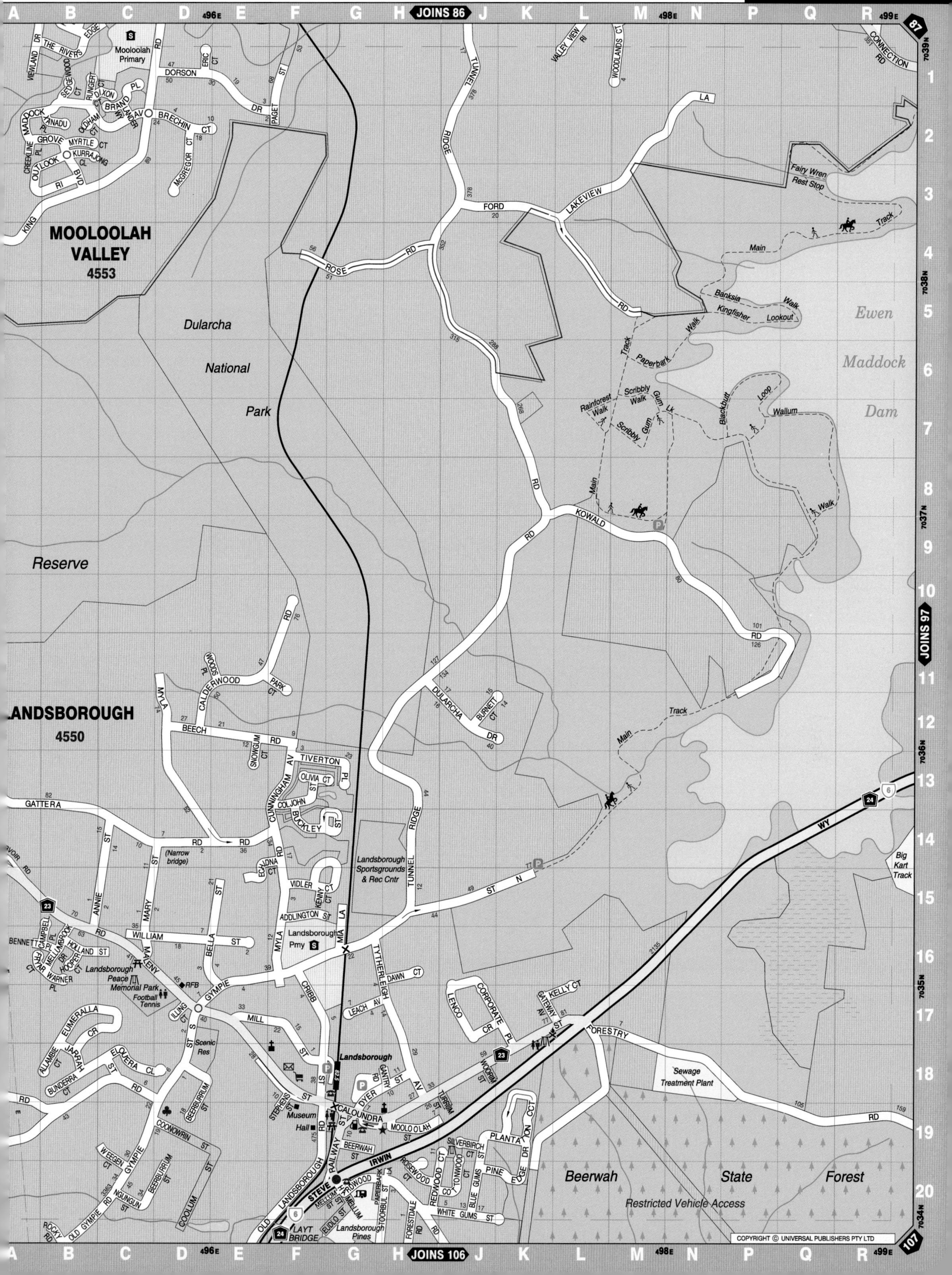

MAP 96
1 KILOMETRE EQUALS 4 GRID SQUARES

JOINS 86

87

MOOLOOLAH VALLEY
4553

LANDSBOROUGH
4550

Dularcha

National

Park

Reserve

Ewen

Maddock

Dam

Fairy Wren Rest Stop

Main

Banksia

Kingfisher Lookout

Walk

Paperbark

Rainforest Walk

Scribbly Walk

Gum Lk

Scribbly

Gum

Blackbutt

Loop

Wallum

Walk

Mooloolah Primary

Main

KOWALD

RD

Track

Dularcha DR

Burnett CT

Main

Track

Landsborough Sportsgrounds & Rec Cntr

Landsborough Pmy

Landsborough Peace Memorial Park

Football
Tennis

RFB

Scenic Res

Museum Hall

Landsborough

Beerwah

Landsborough Pines

LAYT BRIDGE

STEVE

Big Kart Track

Sewage Treatment Plant

Beerwah   *State*   *Forest*

Restricted Vehicle Access

JOINS 97

JOINS 106

COPYRIGHT © UNIVERSAL PUBLISHERS PTY LTD

107

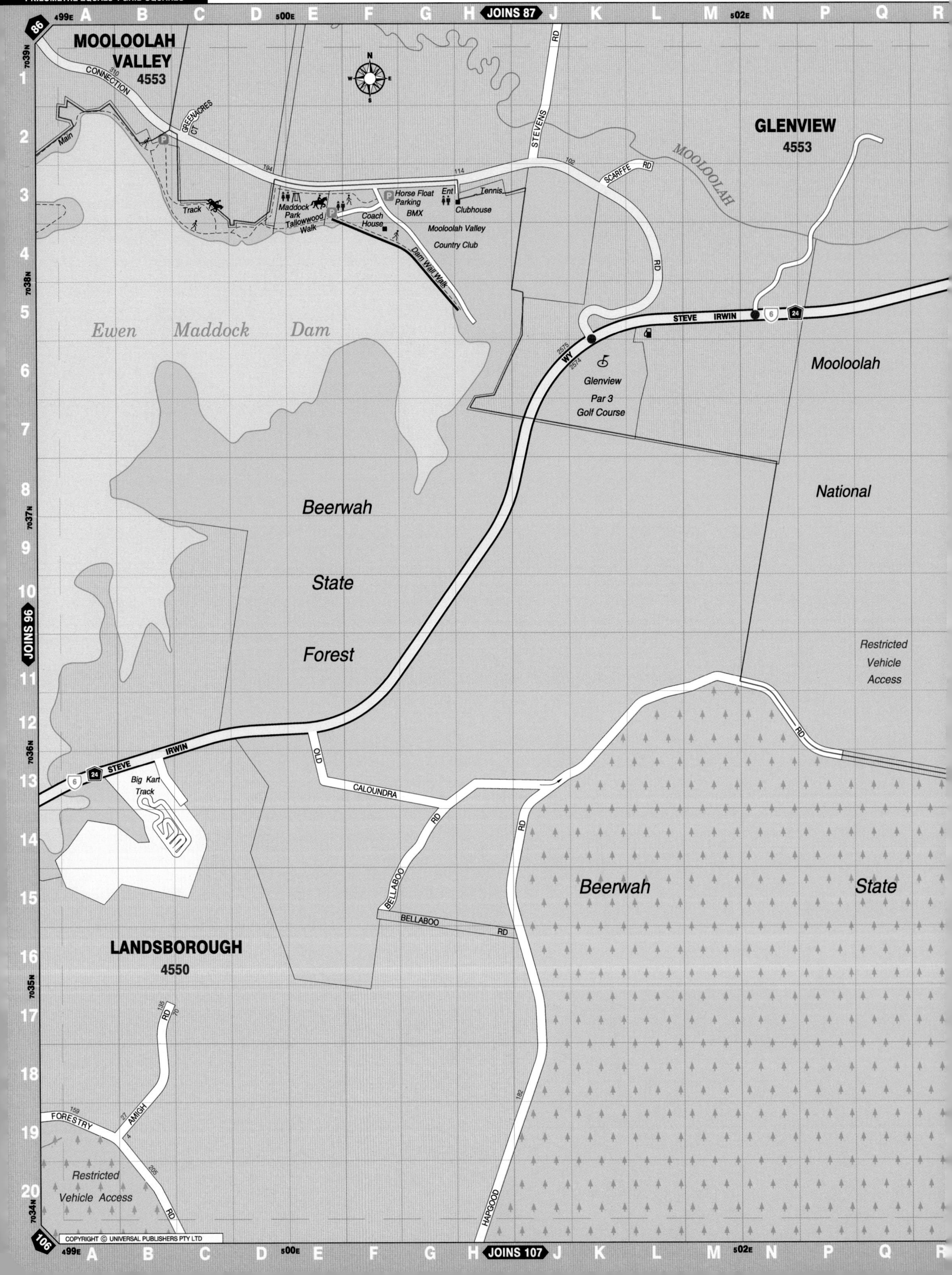

MAP 97
1 KILOMETRE EQUALS 4 GRID SQUARES

JOINS 87

86

MOOLOOLAH VALLEY
4553

CONNECTION

GREENACRES CT

Main

P

194

310

Track

Maddock Park
Tallowwood Walk

Coach House

Horse Float Parking
BMX

Ent
Clubhouse

Tennis

114

102

STEVENS RD

SCARFFE RD

MOOLOOLAH

GLENVIEW
4553

Mooloolah Valley
Country Club

Dam Wall Walk

Ewen   Maddock   Dam

STEVE   IRWIN

6 24

RD

WY

2578

2574

Glenview
Par 3
Golf Course

Mooloolah

National

Beerwah

State

Forest

Restricted
Vehicle
Access

RD

STEVE   IRWIN

6 24

Big Kart
Track

USSC

OLD

CALOUNDRA

RD

BELLABOO

BELLABOO   RD

RD

Beerwah

State

LANDSBOROUGH
4550

135
70
RD

AMIGH
27
4

FORESTRY
159

208
RD

189

HAPGOOD

Restricted
Vehicle Access

106

JOINS 107

JOINS 96

499E   500E   502E

7o39N   7o38N   7o37N   7o36N   7o35N   7o34N

MAP 98
1 KILOMETRE EQUALS 4 GRID SQUARES

MERIDAN PLAINS 4551

Caloundra

Conservation

Park

CORBOULD PARK 4551

Mooloolah

River

National

Park

NIRIMBA 4551

BARINGA 4551

Forest

River

Park

Sunshine Coast

MAP 99
1 KILOMETRE EQUALS 4 GRID SQUARES

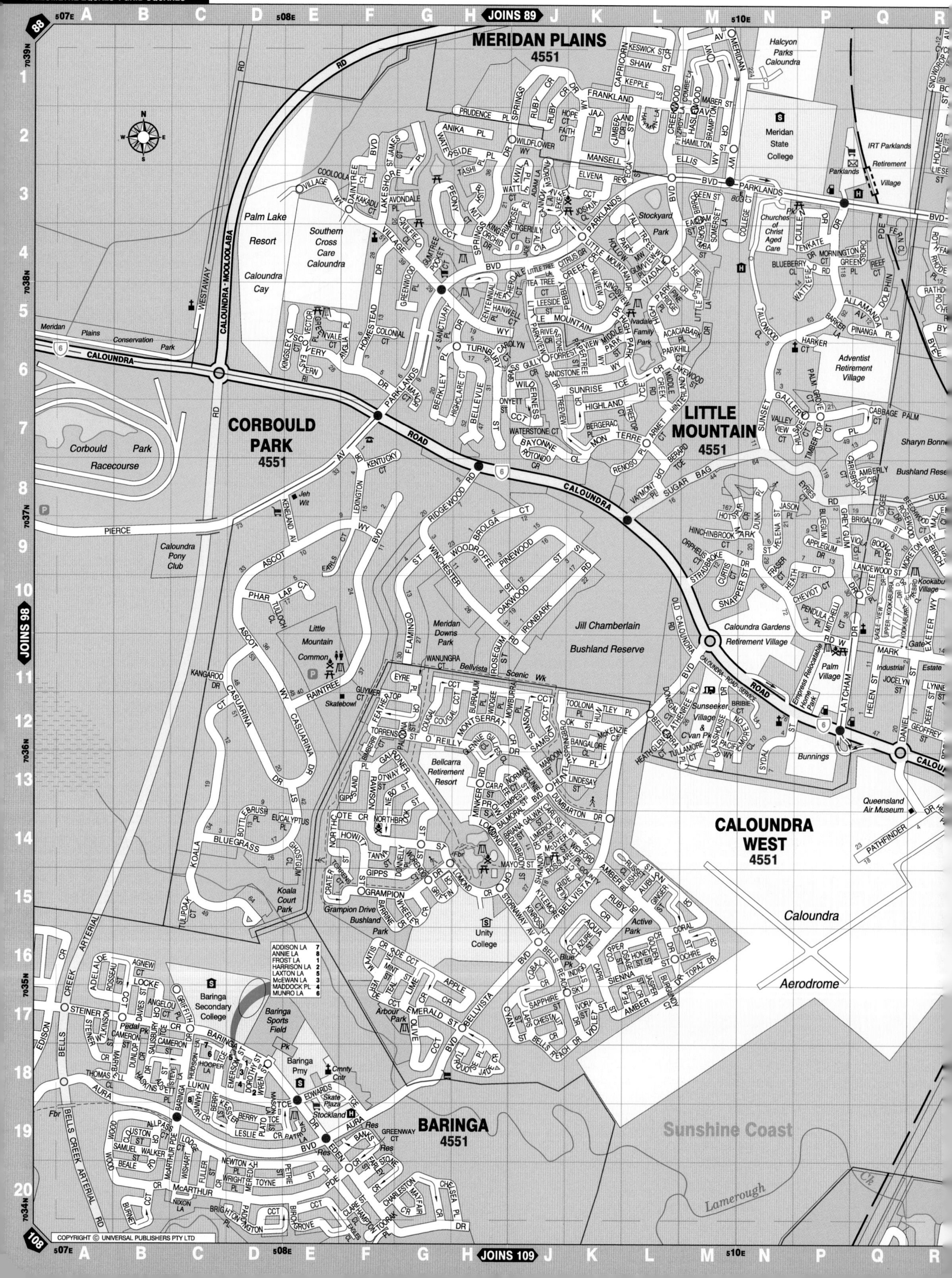

JOINS 89

MERIDAN PLAINS
4551

CORBOULD PARK
4551

LITTLE MOUNTAIN
4551

CALOUNDRA WEST
4551

BARINGA
4551

Palm Lake Resort

Southern Cross Care Caloundra Cay

Corbould Park Racecourse

Caloundra Pony Club

Little Mountain Common

Meridan Downs Park

Jill Chamberlain Bushland Reserve

Bellcarra Retirement Resort

Koala Court Park

Grampion Drive Bushland Park

Unity College

Baringa Secondary College

Baringa Sports Field

Baringa Prmy

Queensland Air Museum

Caloundra Aerodrome

Caloundra Gardens Retirement Village

Adventist Retirement Village

Meridan State College

IRT Parklands Retirement Village

Halcyon Parks Caloundra

Churches of Christ Aged Care

Sunshine Coast

Lamerough

ADDISON LA 7
ANNIE LA 8
FROST LA 1
HARRISON LA 2
LAXTON LA 5
McEWAN LA 3
MADDOCK PL 4
MUNRO LA 6

MAP 105
FOLLOWS
100
1 KILOMETRE EQUALS 4 GRID SQUARES

JOINS 90

CURRIMUNDI 4551

BATTERY HILL 4551

AROONA 4551

Currimundi Lake Ret Villas

Currimundi Recreation Camp & Centre

Currimundi Primary

Currimundi Markets

Ramsay Clinic Caloundra

Water Treatment Plant

PROPOSED RAILWAY

Caloundra Golf Club

Clubhouse

MOFFAT BEACH 4551

DICKY BEACH 4551

Bunbubah

CORAL

SEA

Sunshine Coast

Moffat Head

George Watson Park

SHELLY BEACH 4551

Caloundra Community Youth Hall

Treatment Works

Ben Bennett Botanical Park

Caloundra High

Caloundra Primary

Caloundra Central

Cemetery

CALOUNDRA 4551

Blue Care Kirimi Vill Waroona Gardens Aminya Residential Aged Care Caloundra

Christian College

Caloundra Hospital

Crematorium

Council Depot

Rotary Park

Soccer

Russell Barker Memorial Park

Caloundra Indoor Stadium

Caloundra Australian Rules FC

GOLDEN BEACH 4551

Village Life Caloundra Ret Cmnty

Caloundra Sailing Club

Coast Guard

Caloundra Rugby League FC

Golden Beach Primary

The Events Centre

Art Gall

KINGS BEACH 4551

Deepwater Pt

Caloundra Hd
(Wickham Pt)

Moreton Bay

Marine Park

Bribie Island National Park

BRIBIE ISLAND NORTH 4507

Pumicestone Channel

JOINS 110

COPYRIGHT © UNIVERSAL PUBLISHERS PTY LTD

A B C D E F G H **JOINS 95** J K L M N P Q R

491E 492E 494E

94

7o34N

7o33N

7o32N

7o31N

7o30N

7o29N

B34

PEACHESTER
4519

MOUNT MELLUM
4550

Mount
Mellum
+ 406m

PEACHESTER
4519

BEERWAH
4519

JOINS 94

Conservation Area

AGNEW

MOUNT MELLUM RD

LOWER MOUNT MELLUM RD

PAPER

MOUNT MELLUM

RD

OLD GYMPIE

CLARKES

ALFS

PINCH

Waldrons

PEACHESTER

OLD PEACHESTER

RD

RD

PEACHESTER

Gully

NOTTINGHAM CT

Beerwah Substn

WALTON

RD

OLD GYMPIE

PINE CAMP

RD

OLD GYMPIE RD

WALTON BRIDGE

Coochin Ck

Coochin Ck

OLD GYMPIE

PALMERSTON

FIG TREE DR

CULGOA CT

TOWER

Settlement Park

Beerwah Primary

McKenzie Aged Care
Glasshouse Views

Resource Recovery Cntr

KILCOY - BEER

PINEVIEW DR

IRONWOOD

GREBER

SPEARGRASS CT

FEATHE

MARBLE

PINE

BARBARA ST

CHANTILLY

MANGROV

JAMES CT

BELTON CT

LLOYD ST

GEORDY

ROXTON CT

ROBERTS

COOLAMON

BELIND

Little Rocky

Rocky

A B C D E F G H **JOINS 115** J K L M N P Q R

491E 492E 494E

MAP 106
1 KILOMETRE EQUALS 4 GRID SQUARES

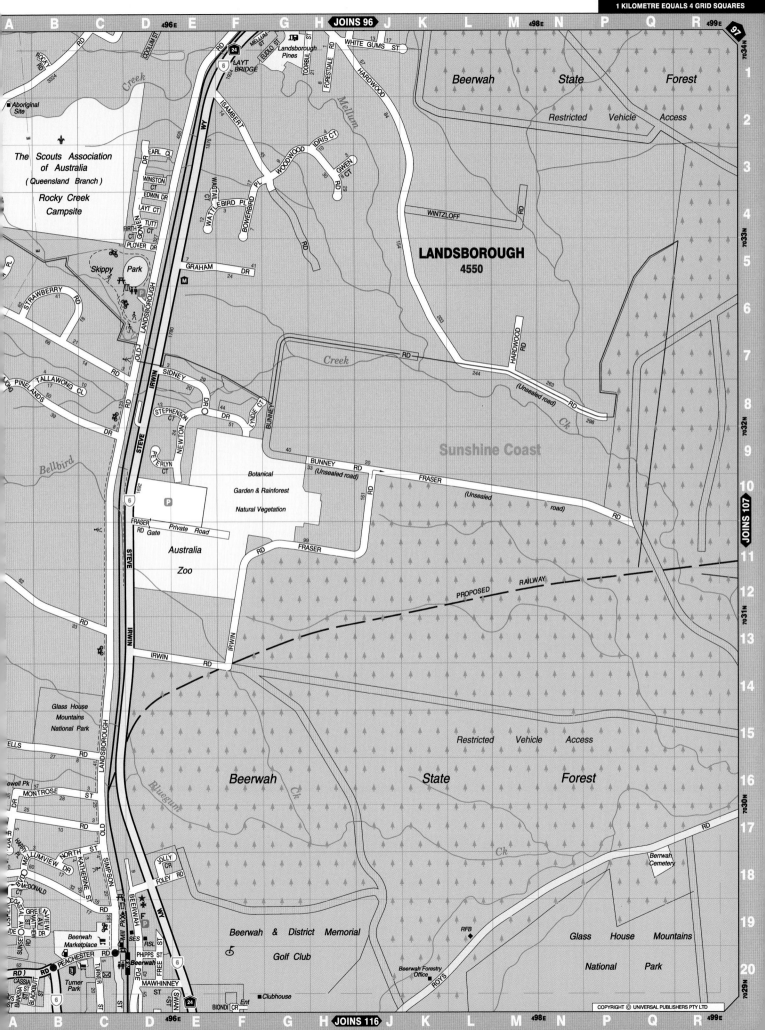

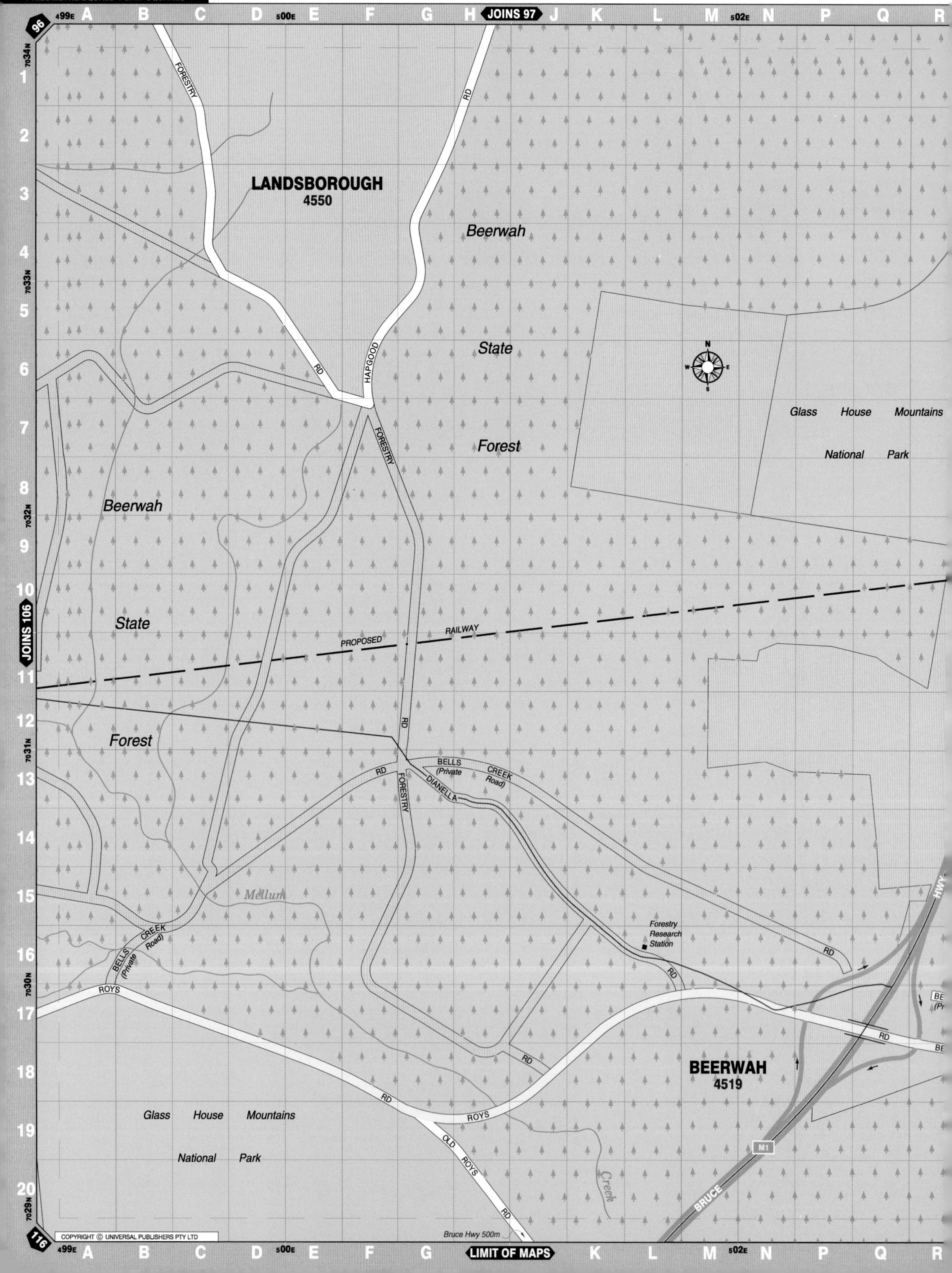

MAP 107
1 KILOMETRE EQUALS 4 GRID SQUARES

LANDSBOROUGH
4550

Beerwah

State

Forest

Beerwah

State

Forest

Mellum

Glass House Mountains

National Park

Beerwah

Glass House Mountains

National Park

PROPOSED RAILWAY

FORESTRY

HAPGOOD

RD

FORESTRY

RD

FORESTRY

RD

DIANELLA

BELLS
(Private
Road)

CREEK

BELLS
(Private Road)

CREEK

ROYS

RD

ROYS

RD

OLD ROYS RD

Creek

Forestry
Research
Station

BEERWAH
4519

BRUCE

HWY

RD

BE
(Pr

RD

BE

M1

JOINS 97

JOINS 106

JOINS 96

JOINS 116

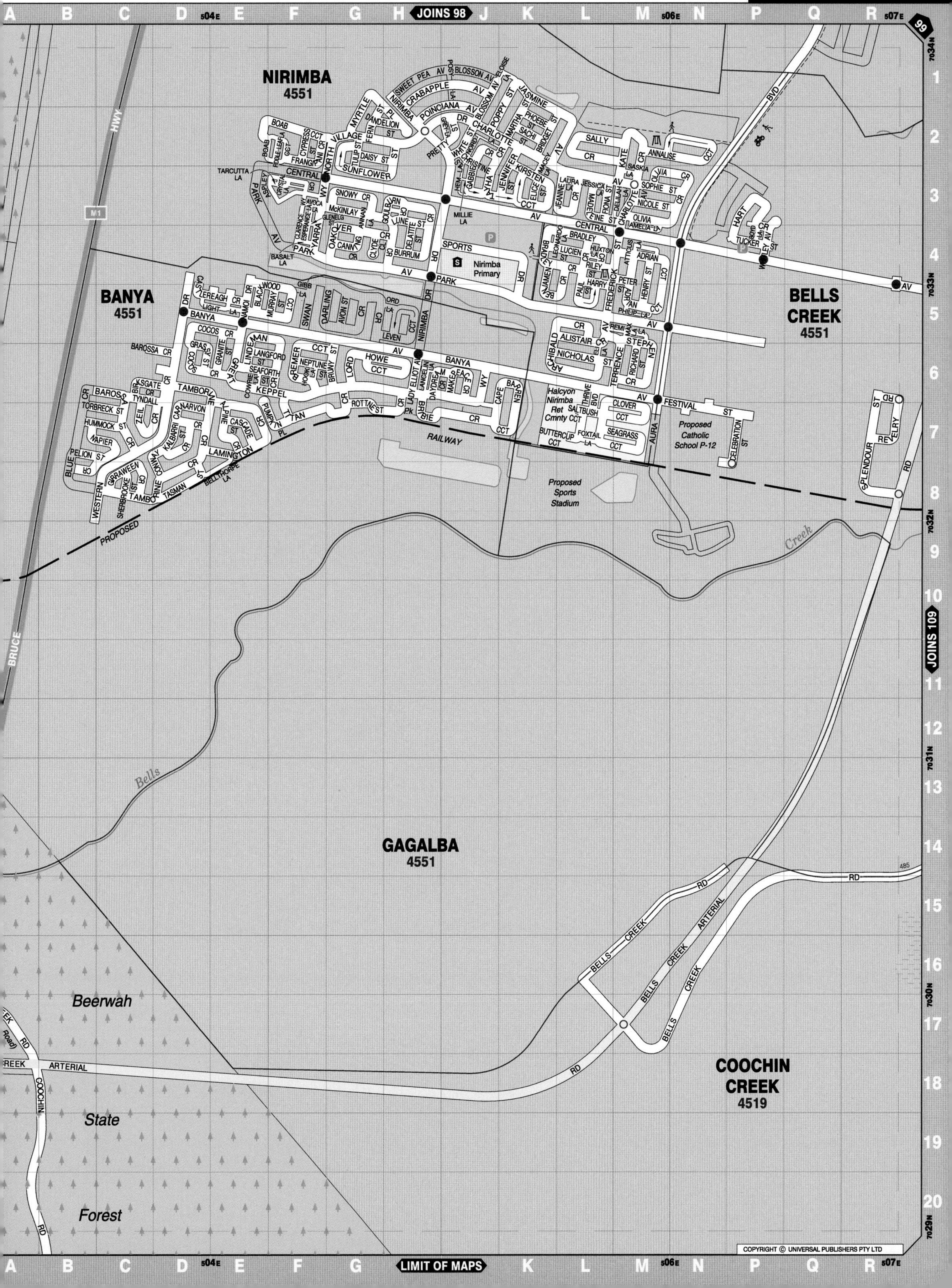

MAP 108

1 KILOMETRE EQUALS 4 GRID SQUARES

JOINS 98

JOINS 99

NIRIMBA
4551

BANYA
4551

BELLS CREEK
4551

GAGALBA
4551

COOCHIN CREEK
4519

Beerwah

State

Forest

Nirimba Primary

Proposed Catholic School P-12

Proposed Sports Stadium

Proposed Sports Stadium

RAILWAY

Bells Creek

Bells Creek

BRUCE HWY

M1

LIMIT OF MAPS

JOINS 109

COPYRIGHT © UNIVERSAL PUBLISHERS PTY LTD

504E 506E 507E

7o34N 7o33N 7o32N 7o31N 7o30N 7o29N

MAP 109
1 KILOMETRE EQUALS 4 GRID SQUARES

JOINS 99

98

JOINS 108

BARINGA
4551

CALOUNDRA WEST
4551

Dog Park

Lamerough Creek West Environment Reserve

Caloundra City School

Pelican

Waters

Golf

Club

Aged Care

Clubhouse

PELICAN WATERS
4551

BELLS CREEK
4551

Sunshine Coast

Bells

Bells Creek

Pelican Waters Shopping Village

Marina

COOCHIN CREEK
4519

Creek

Scribbly Gum Pk

Chris Handy Pk

Judy Henzell Park

Central Pk

PROPOSED RAILWAY

JOINS 99

LIMIT OF MAPS

MAP 115
FOLLOWS
110
1 KILOMETRE EQUALS 4 GRID SQUARES

A B C D s12E E F G H **JOINS 100** J K L M s14E N P Q R s15E

7o34N

1

2

3

GOLDEN BEACH
4551

CORAL

4

5

6

TS Onslow
Naval Reserve
Cadets

Magellan

7

8

Woorim
Park

*Caloundra
Power Boat
Club*

Moreton   *Bay*

9

320

Military
Jetty

10

321

BRIBIE ISLAND
NORTH
4507

Marine   *Park*

11

12

13

14

Bribie

15

16

Island

SEA

17

Bribie

18

National

19

Island

20

Park

Golden Beach
Primary

Gemini Resort
319

William
Landsborough
Mem
Pk

Valentine
Park

Keith
Hill Pk

St
Marys
Aged
Care
Park

Porter
Park

7o33N

7o32N

7o31N

7o30N

7o29N

Pumicestone

Channel

308
309
310
311
312
Fraser
Pk
313
314
315
316
317
318

JOINS 105

JOINS 125

JOINS BRISBANE 34

Glass House Mountains National Park

Sunshine Coast

GLASS HOUSE MOUNTAINS

4518

Glass House Mountains National Park (Ngungun Section)

Glass House Mountains National Park

PEACHESTER (KILCOY

BEERWAH RD)

Coochin

Sandy

Settlement Park

Resource Recovery Cntr

Resvr

Murphys

Fullertons

Yeates

Pikes

Sargeants

Watson Rd

Palmer Rd

Gympie Old

Larapinta Dr

Lindeman

MAP 125 FOLLOWS
116
1 KILOMETRE EQUALS 4 GRID SQUARES

A B C D E 496E F G H **JOINS 106** J K L M 498E N P Q R 499E

70 29N 1

BEERWAH
4519

Turner Park

KILCOY - BEERWAH

TURNER ST
CASSIA
BANKS
CUS
BLACKBUTT
Glasshouse Christian College
MAWHINNEY ST
SIMPSON
ROBERTS
BEERWAH
STEVE IRWIN
SWAN ST
LAUREL
PDE
MORONEY
BION
PL
CR
Ent
Clubhouse
Beerwah & District Memorial Golf Club
Ped Upass
SPORTSGROUND
RD
6
Sportsground
Beerwah High
Beerwah State Forest
Glass House Mountains National Park
RD
24
ROYS
WY
CREEK
CASUARINA ST
HARVEST ST
Jeh Wit
MAWSON
BURYS
CR
CABRERA
CR
KELLO RD
SANTA ANA CT
AUSTINE CT
IRWIN
DR
SAPPHIRE CT
COCHIN HILLS
RD DR
TOBACCO
SUNLAND CT
TWIN PEAKS
STEVE
MAHOGANY CT
HOLT RD
BARRY RD
SMITH LA
WOOD RD
RD
BACK CREEK
ROVERA RD
BELL
HARLEY ST
AMY DR
WY
SAND RD
COOK RD
RD
WILBUR CT
GARRADS
KINGS
YOUNGS
PDE
ROBERTS ST RD
KINGS RD
PSTOCK
HEM ST
LITTLES RD
JEFFREYS
IRWIN
BISHOP ST
TURNER
BRUCE
RYAN ST
COULON
STEVE
PDE
GARDNER RD
BURGESS RD
CO-OP
RWA DR
VISTA
NA CL
Cmnty Cntr
COONOWRIN
PITT
PAGE ST
TRILBY
MCINTYRE
DISCOVERY
Glass House Mountains
Sports Complex
Glasshouse Mountains Sports Club
ENDEAVOUR
WHITBY ST
PETERS
BRICALLI RD
BARK DR
SCOTTS RD
WHITING RD
PLANTATION RD
RIVERS RD
PECAN RD
LINK RD
KINGS RD
Beerburrum East State Forest
Restricted Vehicle Access
BASSETTS RD
KINGS
RD
SPANNER RD
LINK RD

LIMIT OF MAPS
No Through Road

Bray Bridge (Narrow bridge)
Coonowrin Ck
Coochin Creek
Creek

COPYRIGHT © UNIVERSAL PUBLISHERS PTY LTD

A B C D 496E E F G H **JOINS 126** J K L M 498E N P Q R 499E

B34

Glass House Mountains Nat Pk

JOINS 115

Coonowrin

N
W E
S

The Australian Teamsters Hall of Fame & Spirit of Cobb & Co

MOUNT BEERWAH RD

McCRICKS RD

COONOWRIN

COONOWRIN RD

PIETZ LA

FULLERTONS

RD

PEAK VIEW PL
PINEAPPLE PL
NGUN
DUNNOTTAR CR
ALBYN
COONOWRIN
POOLE
OUTLOOK
MOUNTAINVIEW
KABIANA PL
HILLSIDE
CRESTWOOD RD
CRESTHAVEN CT
RIDGEMOUNT PL
PARKVIEW
BULIC CT
DR
PINNACLES DR
SUMMIT CL

Glass H Mount Prim

Coonowrin Creek

Sunsine Coast

Glass House

Mountains

National Park

Tibrogargan 364m

Tibberoowuccum 220m

JOINS BRISBANE 34

GLASS HOUSE WOODFORD RD

Conservation Area

OLD GYMPIE RD

MARSHS RD

ORCHARD DR

BARRS RD

Beerburrum West State Forest

745/2 & 746/2 RD

Tibrogargan

Restricted Vehicle Access

Creek

CAVES

OLD GYMPIE RD

BEERBURRUM WOODFORD RD

B36

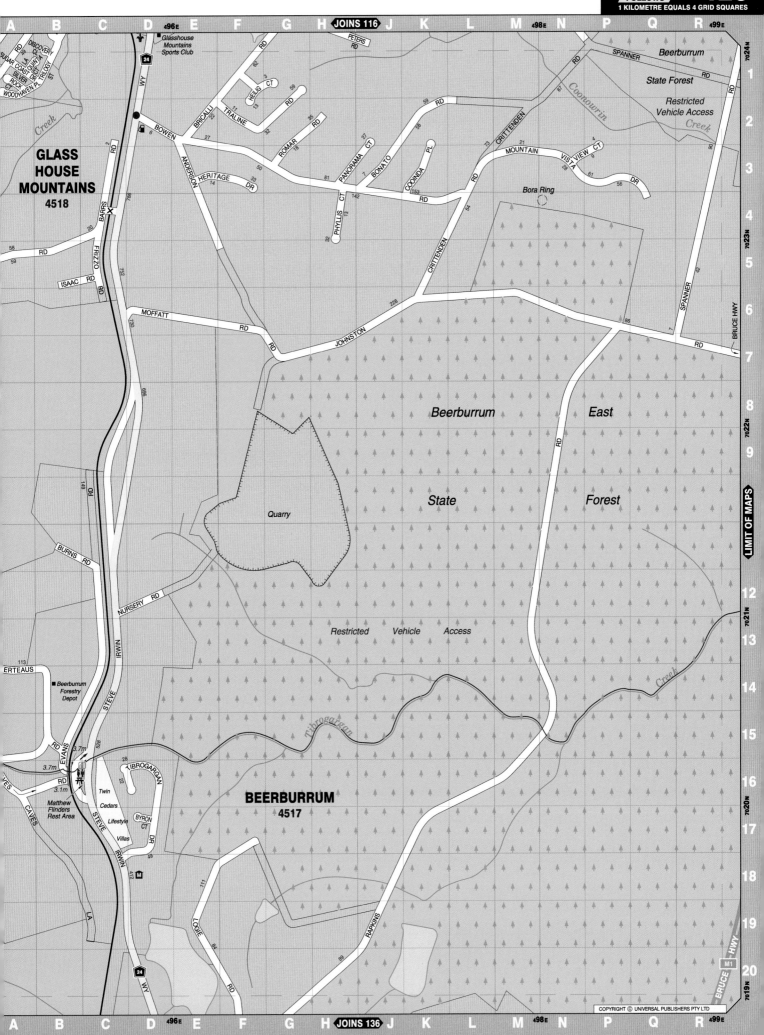

MAP 135 FOLLOWS

126

1 KILOMETRE EQUALS 4 GRID SQUARES

GLASS HOUSE MOUNTAINS
4518

Glasshouse Mountains Sports Club

Beerburrum State Forest

Restricted Vehicle Access

Bora Ring

Beerburrum East

State Forest

Quarry

Restricted Vehicle Access

Beerburrum Forestry Depot

Matthew Flinders Rest Area

Twin Cedars Lifestyle Villas

BEERBURRUM
4517

LIMIT OF MAPS

COPYRIGHT © UNIVERSAL PUBLISHERS PTY LTD

B34

JOINS 125

Beerburrum RD

WOODFORD

745/2 & 746/2

OLD GYMPIE

Beerburrum

Mt Beerburrum

Ck

Beerburrum

EATON

RD

EATON

BECKETT RD

JOINS BRISBANE 36

Rose

Beerburrum   West   State   Forest

ELIMBAH

4516

Ck

Rose

Restricted   Vehicle   Access

Rose

OLD GYMPIE

TWIN VIEW

McDOUGALL

McDOUGALL

RD

RD

RD

RD

McDOUGALL

CARAWATHA

BEERBURRUM

ROSE CREEK RD

60

Moreton Bay

B36

491E   492E   494E

7019N 7018N 7017N 7016N 7015N 7014N

MAP 136
1 KILOMETRE EQUALS 4 GRID SQUARES

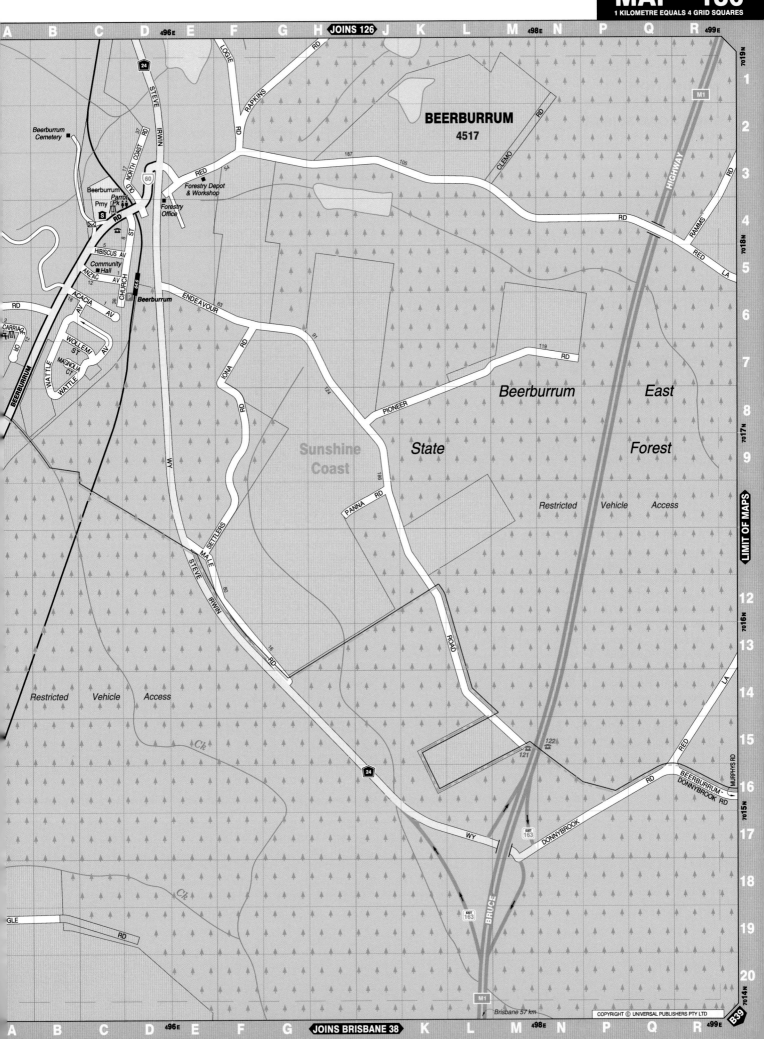

BRIBIE ISLAND

LOCATION
66km north of Brisbane

POPULATION
Approx 21 500

RACQ ROAD SERVICE
Ph: 13 1111

VISITOR INFORMATION

Bribie Island Visitor Information Centre
Benabrow Av, Bellara
Ph: (07) 3408 9026
www.visitmoretonbayregion.com.au

This long and thin sand island is linked at its southern end to the Australian mainland. It is connected by a bridge that lies across the protected waters of Pumicestone Channel. The northern tip of Bribie Island lies close to the Sunshine Coast city of Caloundra. Residential and holiday development is restricted to the southern part of the island. Around eighty per cent of the island is comprised of national park and forest, including Bribie Island National Park and Buckleys Hole Conservation Park, making bushwalking a popular pastime. This also ensures that most of the island's northern end remains in its natural state and provides a sanctuary for the flora and fauna of the island.

ACCOMMODATION GUIDE

Bellara Caravan Park **2 D2**
Bellara Caravan Park **2 D2**
Bongaree Caravan Park **2 H8**
Bribie Island Caravan Park **2 D12**
Bribie Island Hotel **2 C2**
Bribie Waterways Accommodation & Conference Centre **2 G5**
Fairways Golf & Beach Retreat **2 D18**
Sandstone Point Holiday Resort **2 A7**

FACILITIES & ATTRACTIONS GUIDE

Apex Park **2 H11**
Bluey Piva Park **2 E13**
Bongaree Bowls Club **2 J12**
Bongaree Post Office **2 H11**
Brennan Park **2 G11**
Bribie Island Bowls Club **2 H9**
Bribie Island Community Arts Centre **1 M11**
Bribie Island Golf Club **2 D18**
Bribie Island Memorial Gardens **2 A15**
Bribie Island Post Office **2 G1**
Bribie Island Retreat & Recreation Centre **2 D11**
Bribie Island RSL & Citizens Memorial Club **2 K13**
Bribie Island Seaside Museum **2 H11**
Bribie Island Shopping Centre **2 G1**
Bribie Island Surf Life Saving Club **2 F13**
Buckleys Hole Conservation Park **2 N16**
Col Fisher Park **1 D7**
Cook Park **1 K5**
Cosmos Park **1 G11**
Crest Park **1 H17**
Dampier Park **1 K8**
Edwin Schrag Memorial Park **2 F14**
Ernest Sendall Memorial Park **2 L5**
Fire Station **2 F1**
Library **2 H10**
Lions Park **2 C2**
Melsa Park **2 J12**
Miniature Steam Trains **2 J12**
Oxley Park **1 K6**
Pacific Harbour Golf & Country Club **1 K4**
Pirate Park **1 F17**
Police Station **2 F2**
Quota Park **2 F5**
Rotary Park **2 C8**
Solander Lake Bowls Club **1 G10**
Sunset Park **1 E14**
Swimming Pool **2 L8**
Visitor Information Centre Bribie Island **2 F2**
Woorim Post Office **2 D13**
ZZ11UU

Street	Map	Grid

Acacia St   1   J15
Albatross Ct   1   F4
Allamanda Dr   2   G4
Alpinia Av   1   J10
Alstonia Ct   2   N6
Ampere Ct   2   F1
Anchor Ct   1   J9
Angelica Ct   1   J1
Anjanette St   2   D10
Aquila Cct   1   L13
Arcadia Av   2   D14
Arinya Av   1   L17
Avon Av   1   J10
Azalea Dr   2   G4
Banda Av
   Bellara   1   J18
   Bellara   2   C1
Banks St   1   D7
Banksia St   1   K15
Banya La   2   K11
Banya St   2   J11
Barklya Cr   2   L6
Bass Ct   1   F8
Baza Pl   1   L12
Beagle Av   1   B9
Bearberry St   1   K1
Beaufort Cct   1   H13
Bellara St   1   G15
Benabrow Av
   Bellara   2   E2
   Bongaree   2   E2
Benalong St   2   F17
Bestman Av   2   G6
Bibimuyla St   2   C2
Blaik St   2   E13
Blueberry St   1   H2
Bongaree Av   2   J2
Bonham St   2   K11
Boronia Dr   1   G15
Botany Cr   1   E9
Bow Ct   1   G8
Bowsprit Cr   1   H5
Box St   2   D15
Boyd St   2   E13
Bracken St   2   C13
Brake St   2   J13
Bribie Bridge   2   B4
Brigantine Pl   1   G6
Broadbill St   1   E5
Brookes Cr   2   C14
Broom St   2   E16
Burrawong Av   2   G2
Calena Cl   1   G2
Callitris St   1   K15
Calm Ct   2   M3
Caltowie Av   1   H11
Camellia Dr   2   G3
Campbell St   2   K11
Capstan Ct   1   J9
Captain Cook Dr   1   D9
Caraway Cr   1   K1
Carl Ct   1   E8
Carp Wy   1   K2
Cassia Av   1   H10
Castaway Ct   1   F11
Casuarina St   1   H15
Catamaran Ct   1   J6
Charles St   1   A2
Charlotte Av   2   F4
Cicada St   2   E16
Clayton St   2   D14
Clement St   2   C9
Clipper St   2   H6
Club Pl   2   C15
Clubrush Ct   1   K2
Cobea Ct   2   M3
Cod Cct   2   M2
Commodore Pl   1   G8
Coolgarra Av   2   J3
Cormorant St   2   J5
Corymbia Wy   1   K2
Cosmos Av
   Banksia Beach   1   H11
   Banksia Beach   1   M12

Cotterill Av   2   H8
Crane St   2   K5
Crouch Av   2   G4
Crystal Av   2   L2
Cumming St   2   L11
Curlew St   2   E16
Currong Cr   1   M17
Currong La   1   M17
Cutter Ct   1   G10
Cypress Av   2   D13
Cypress La   2   D12
Dandar Av   1   J17
Daniel Pl   1   E9
Dianella Cr   1   G2
Dianthus Av   1   H9
Dolphin Dr   2   G5
Doomba Dr   2   J5
Dugong Cr   1   H7
Dunebean Dr   1   H3
Dux Dr   2   K1
Eagle Ct   1   D9
Eagles Landing   1   L12
Eden Cr   2   D16
Eel Pl   2   J2
Eighth Av   2   B9
Elanus Ct   1   L13
Elcata Av   1   H17
Elizabeth Batts Ct   1   D7
Elkhorn Av   1   H17
Emu Wk   2   H5
Endeavour Dr   1   E7
Esplanade   1   B5
Ethel St   1   A2
Eucalypt St
   Bellara   1   J17
   Bellara   2   D1
Fairway Av   2   C14
Fairweather St   2   D16
Falco Ct   1   L13
Faraday St
   Bellara   1   M18
   Bellara   2   F1
Fathom Ct   1   H8
Fauna La   2   K5
Fearn Av   2   E3
Ferguson Av   2   D3
Fifth Av
   Bongaree   2   H8
   Woorim   2   D10
First Av
   Bongaree   2   H10
   Bongaree   2   J10
Flamingo Dr   1   H2
Flinders St   2   N11
Foley St   2   J10
Ford St   1   L13
Fortune Av   2   H2
Foster St   2   J11
Fourth Av
Bongaree   2   J9
Woorim   2   D11
Foxtail Cr   1   K2
Frederick St   1   H8
Freshwater Dr   1   J3
Fulmar Cr   1   E12
Gahnia Ct   1   N13
Gannet St   2   E15
Genoa Pl   1   H6
Gidya Av   2   F2
Goby St
   Bongaree   2   M1
   Woorim   2   M1
Golf Dr   2   D17
Goodwin Dr
   Bellara   2   F2
   Bongaree   2   F2
Green St   1   E10
Gregory St   2   L14
Grevillia St   1   H15
Gull St   2   E16
Hall Av   2   H7
Harbour Prm   1   G13
Harmony Av   2   M2
Haven Ct   2   J3

Hawaii Cr   1   H11
Hazell Av   1   H9
Headsail Dr   1   J5
Heathland St   1   K4
Heron St   2   E17
Herring St   2   K2
Hibbertia Pl   1   M13
Hibiscus Ct   2   H3
Hill St   2   L11
Hodges St   1   D7
Honeymyrtle St   1   K2
Horace St   1   A3
Hornsby Rd
   Bellara   1   N18
   Bellara   2   G1
   Bongaree   1   N18
   Bongaree   2   G1
   Woorim   1   L5
Hovea St   1   M16
Hoya Cr   2   K4
Hunter St   2   N10
Hutchinson St   2   D14
Illawarra Av   1   K16
Illoura Av   1   J17
Indra Av   2   D2
Iris Ct   2   G3
Island Pde   1   F8
Jabiru La   1   G16
Jabiru St   1   F15
Jacana Av   2   D13
Jacaranda Dr   2   G5
Jasmin Dr   2   K4
Kakadu Cct   1   E12
Kalmia Ct   2   K5
Kamala St   1   K1
Kangaroo Av   2   H7
Karee Dr   1   K17
Keala Ct   1   J11
Kekua Ct   1   H11
Kendall St   2   M15
Kennedia Ct   1   J2
Kingfisher Dr   2   H6
Kitt Av   1   J10
Koopa St   2   H6
Larool Av   1   J16
Larool La   1   J16
Lawn St   2   K3
Lee Av   2   G3
Leeward Pl   1   G12
Lilac Ct   2   L4
Links Ct   2   D18
Livistona Pl   1   N13
Longland Ct   2   C10
Lowry St   2   E16
Lungfish Cct   2   K2
Lyre Bird La   2   J7
Mcdonald St   2   K13
Mcdowall St   2   L14
Magdalena Pl   1   E8
Mainbrace Ct   1   F7
Malva Ct   2   M3
Marbrin Cl
   Bellara   1   J18
   Bellara   2   C1
Marina Bvd
   Banksia Beach   1   E14
   Bellara   1   M15
Marine Pde
   Bellara   1   H18
   Bellara   2   B1
Marlin Ct   1   G5
Marron Wy   2   L2
Marton Pl   1   E11
Masthead Ct   1   H8
Melia St   2   M3
Melrose Av
   Bellara   1   K18
   Bellara   2   D1
Midyim Ct   1   N14
Minnow Av   1   J10
Mirimar St   2   J5
Mirree Av   1   K17
Morinda St   1   K1
Morris St   2   M10

Murrawong St   1   L17
Murray St   2   E14
Nannawarra Av   1   J16
Neenuk St   2   E3
Nicholson Cl
   Bellara   1   J18
   Bellara   2   C1
Norman St   2   M11
Norrland Ct   1   E7
North Pt   1   J13
North St   2   B7
Nulu La   2   K11
Nulu St   2   K11
Nungo Av   1   K18
Oleander Dr   2   K4
Oorooba Av   1   H16
Orara Av   1   H10
Orchid St   1   J15
Oriole Cl   1   E13
Ottiwell St   2   E15
Oxley Wy   2   D14
Pacific Dr   1   G8
Palm Av   2   E3
Pandanus St   1   G15
Pandara Av   1   K16
Paradise Pde   2   J7
Partridge St   2   K6
Parwan Av   1   L17
Pectoral Pl   1   L15
Pelican St   1   G15
Pembroke Pl   1   E10
Penguin St   2   H6
Pheasant Av   1   H9
Phoenix Av   2   G2
Pimpala Cr   2   K3
Pine St   2   D15
Plymouth St   1   E11
Port Dr   1   G9
Protea Dr   2   N3
Pumicestone St   1   F15
Quail St   1   F14
Quarterdeck Dr   1   G5
Queen St
   Bongaree   2   H10
   Bongaree   2   H9
Raptor Pde   1   K12
Redfin Wy   2   M2
Reef St   1   G10
Renton La   2   J13
Rickman Pde   2   D10
Rivercherry Av   1   G2
Robusta Ct   1   J2
Roggen St   2   F4
Rose Ct   2   G4
Rosella St   2   F3
Sanctuary Ct   1   K2
Schooner Ct   1   K6
Seabreeze Av   1   F13
Seacrest Ct   1   F14
Seaeagle Pl   1   L12
Seafarer Pl   1   J11
Seahorse Ct   1   F5
Seaside Dr   1   E14
Second Av   2   H10
Serrata Cl   1   G1
Seventh Av   2   C9
Shearwater Cr   1   G13
Sixth Av   2   B9
Skiff Ct   1   G10
Skysail Ct   1   G7
Solander Esp   1   D8
South Esp   2   H12
Spowers St   2   K13
Stewart St   1   J17
Sturt Ct   2   M11
Sun Ct   1   E11
Sunderland Dr
   Banksia Beach   1   E10
   Bellara   1   N17
   Bellara   2   G1
Sunset Av   2   F3
Sunshine Av   2   D13
Swallow St   1   E6
Swordfish Pl   1   F5

Sylvan Beach Esp
   Bellara   1   F15
   Bellara   2   C2
Tamala Ct   2   N5
Tarooki St   1   G16
Tasman Ct   1   F7
Taylor St   2   M10
Teal Bvd   1   E13
Tern St   2   E17
The Boulevarde
   Bongaree   2   J13
   Bongaree   2   K14
The Landing   1   M15
The Peninsula   1   L14
The Promontory   1   J13
The Quay   1   H13
Third Av   2   J9
Thornely Cl
   Bellara   1   J18
   Bellara   2   C1
Tilia Ct   2   K6
Timari Av   1   H16
Toorbul La   2   J11
Toorbul St   2   H11
Toowa St   1   A5
Topsail Cct   1   J7
Tradewinds Dr   1   G11
Tranquillity Cr   2   L3
Triller Wy   1   F12
Trimaran Ct   1   J5
Tripcony St   1   G15
Troy St   2   D16
Tully St   2   L14
Turnstone Cl   1   E12
Vanillalily Cl   1   H4
Venus St   1   E10
Verdoni St
   Bellara   1   M18
   Bellara   2   F1
Victory Rd   2   H2
Village Av   2   J3
Violet Ct   2   K5
Voyagers Dr
   Banksia Beach   1   F6
   Banksia Beach   1   F7
Walker Ct   1   D8
Wallimbi Av   1   L17
Warana Av   2   D2
Warrigal St   1   G17
Waters Edg   1   F13
Watson St   2   N10
Wattle Av   2   F4
Webster St   2   K12
Weddel Ct   2   G3
Welsby Pde   2   F5
Welsby Bridge   2   F5
Westie Pl   2   B8
Whitby Ct   1   D8
Whitehaven Pl   1   K15
White Patch Esp   1   D6
Winch Ct   1   K7
Windward Pl   1   G12
Wingbet Ct   1   K12
Winnett St   2   D14
Winston Dr   2   E3
Wirraway St   2   K6
Wise St   2   E3
Wistaria St   1   L15
Woods Ct   2   C9
Yardarm Ct   1   G6
Yeenda Av   1   J16
Yellowfin Pl   1   F4
Yorkshire Dr   1   F11

MAP 1 BRIBIE ISLAND

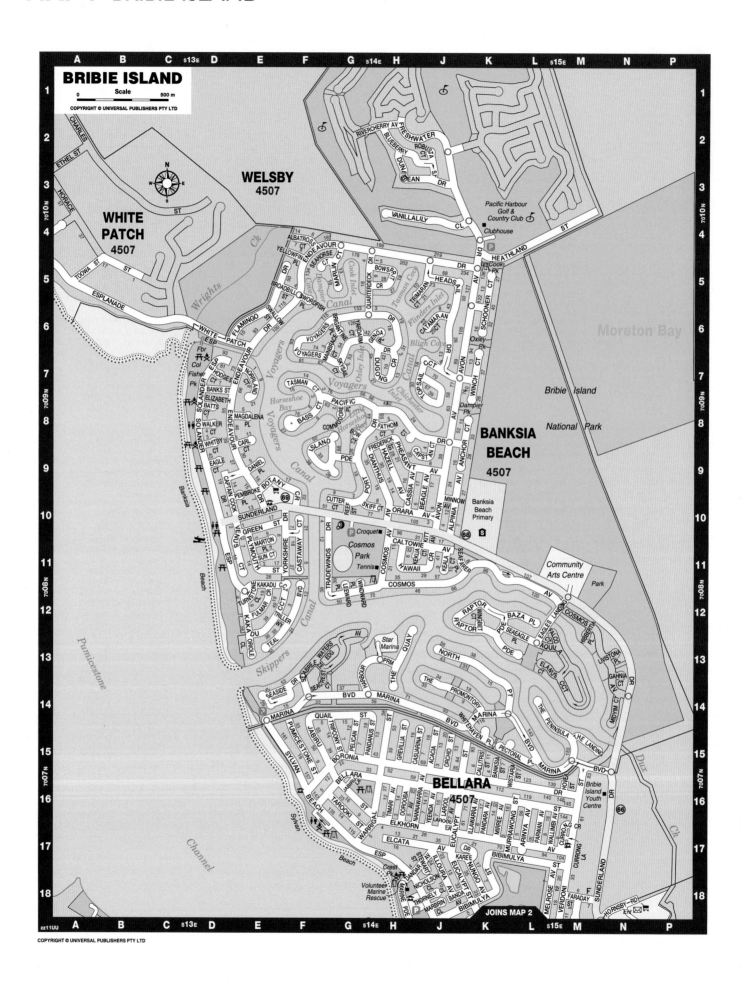

BRIBIE ISLAND

Scale 0 — 500 m

COPYRIGHT © UNIVERSAL PUBLISHERS PTY LTD

WELSBY 4507

WHITE PATCH 4507

BANKSIA BEACH 4507

Bribie Island National Park

Moreton Bay

BELLARA 4507

Pumicestone Channel

JOINS MAP 2

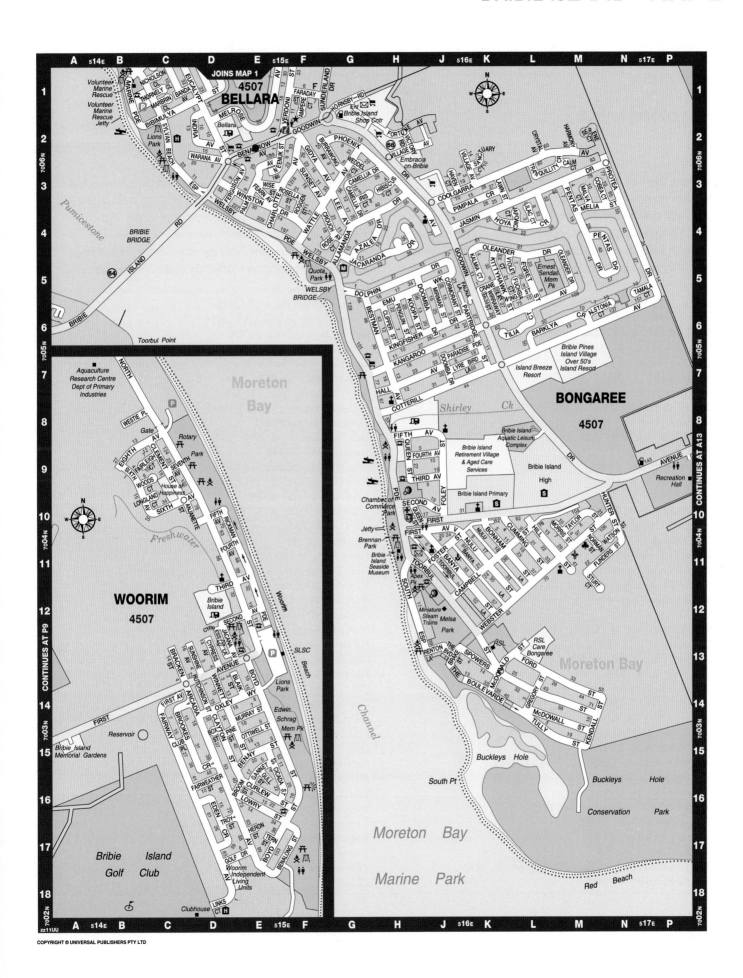

GYMPIE

LOCATION
On the Bruce Hwy
172km north of Brisbane
POPULATION
22 500
RACQ ROAD SERVICE
Ph: 13 1111

VISITOR INFORMATION
Gympie Region Visitor Information Centre –
Lake Alford
Bruce Hwy,
Monkland
Ph: 1800 444 222
www.visitgympieregion.com.au

Gympie is the hub of the Cooloola region. It has beautiful parks and gardens, historical attractions and art galleries and unique craft shops. In contrast with most country towns, Gympie's main street – Mary Street – is narrow and winding. It offers a unique character and charm that makes a detour off the highway well worthwhile. It seems that in the rush for gold, there was no time to plan; hence, buildings were erected along the route of a winding bullock track. Much of Gympie's history is preserved at the Gympie Gold Mining & Historical Museum at Monkland. The museum is a complex made up of a number of buildings, each concentrating on a different aspect of the past.

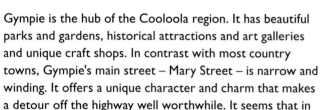

ACCOMMODATION GUIDE
Australian Hotel   **2   C16**
Calvary Gympie Views   **1   L15**
Empire Hotel   **1   M15**
Fox Glenn Motor Inn   **4   G9**
Great Eastern Motor Inn   **4   J10**
Gympie Muster Inn   **1   L16**
Nationwide Motel   **1   J11**
Royal Hotel   **1   M15**
Shady Rest Motel   **1   K14**
Victory Motel   **2   H8**

FACILITIES & ATTRACTIONS GUIDE
Adrian McClintock Park   **3   G3**
Albert Bowls Club   **1   N18**
Albert Park   **1   M17**
Andrew Fisher Memorial Park   **2   E14**
Aquatic Recreation Centre   **2   F14**
Archery Park   **1   J14**
Art Gallery   **1   M14**
Attie Sullivan Park   **4   C7**
Centenary Park   **2   B8**
Centenary Scout Hut   **1   N9**
Civic Centre   **2   B15**
Cooloola Community Private Hospital   **1   P13**
Council Office   **1   M15**
Coventry Park   **3   L14**
Deep Creek Gold Fossicking Area   **4   G5**
Don McKay Park   **3   J13**
Federation Centres Goldfields Plaza   **1   N15**
Fire Station   **2   B16**
Gunabul Homestead Golf Course   **3   K3**
Gympie & District RSL Club   **1   M15**
Gympie Bowls Club   **3   E2**
Gympie Cemetery   **1   K7**
Gympie Central   **4   B3**
Gympie Gold Mining & Historical Museum   **4   J9**
Gympie Hospital   **1   M13**

Gympie Market Place   **1   M15**
Gympie Pines Golf Club   **1   H10**
Gympie Racecourse   **3   G4**
Gympie Region Visitor Information Centre-Lake Alford   **4   J10**
Gympie Region Visitor Information Centre-Puma
   Roadhouse   **4   P18**
Gympie Showground   **3   G4**
Gympie Swimming Pool   **1   M16**
Gympie Tenpin   **4   H2**
Jack Stokes Park   **4   J7**
Jaycees Park   **3   H6**
John McMullen Complex   **4   M16**
Kidd Bridge Park   **1   M17**
Lake Alford Park   **4   J9**
Leprechaun Park   **2   C18**
Library   **2   A15**
Lion Park   **4   J9**
Madill Park   **4   B7**
Marc Dower Park   **3   D3**
Mary Valley Rattler   **2   E13**
Memorial Park   **1   N16**
Monkland Crematorium   **4   K9**
Municipal Reserve   **1   H13**
MV Brady Oval   **2   G18**
Nelson Reserve   **1   M16**
North Park Estate Park   **2   C7**
Old Gympie Railway Station   **2   D13**
One Mile Recreation Area   **4   F2**
Police Station   **1   M14**
Post Office   **2   A16**
Queens Park   **1   J14**
Railway Station   **2   H2**
Ramsey Park   **3   K3**
Sid Carter Oval   **4   F3**
Sovereign Cinema Complex   **1   M14**
Stephen Learoyd Memorial Park   **4   B17**
The Billy Phillips Park   **2   D11**
Thurecht Park   **1   M10**
Woodworks Museum   **1   E4**
ZZ5UE

STREETS

Acacia Cir 3 N10
Ada St 2 B14
Adams St 1 H10
Agapanthus Pl 3 G12
Albatross Ct 1 H5
Albert Rd 4 G6
Albert St 4 H7
Alenola St 1 M9
Alexander Pl 4 C1
Alfred St 1 L14
Alice St 2 B14
Alisha Pl 3 M6
Allen La 4 F4
Alma St 2 B15
Alpha Rd
  Jones Hill 3 L17
  Southside 3 L17
Amalie Pl 2 F10
Amber Ct 1 H11
Amy St 2 C14
Andrea Av 3 H4
Andrew St 2 E12
Ann St 2 E17
Aparima Ct 2 K13
Apollonian Va 2 C16
Araluen Tce 4 G7
Archer Ct 3 L10
Ascot Rd 2 P10
Ashford Rd 2 G17
Ashgrove Wy 1 K3
Aspen Ct 1 J3
Austin La 1 H10
Australia Dr 3 G11
Baker St 2 E17
Balmoral Cr
  Southside 3 P11
  Southside 4 A11
Banksia Dr
  Gympie 1 M11
  Gympie 1 N10
Banks Pocket Rd
  Araluen 2 E2
  Gympie 2 F6
Barrie Rd 2 C3
Barter St 1 L15
Barton Rd 2 H9
Bass Lewis Dr 4 M10
Batchelor Rd 2 G14
Bath Tce
  Gympie 2 F9
  Victory Heights 2 F9
Beaconsfield St 1 N17
Begonia Cl 1 M11
Bellflower Pl 1 M11
Benbullen Ct 2 J17
Bennett St 2 D15
Benson Rd
  Araluen 1 D2
  Chatsworth 1 D2
Bent La 2 D15
Bent St 2 D15
Beresford Cr 2 C9
Berrie St 2 C13
Bethany Ct 4 C10
Bethany La 4 H11
Bickle Rd 2 N3
Bielby Ct 2 J16
Billabong Ct 3 D18
Birdie Cr 1 H5
Bird Song Ct 3 F12
Bishop Ct 3 L9
Blake St 4 C4
Bligh St 2 A17
Bluebell Ct 3 G13
Bolcaro Rd 2 M14
Bond Dr 3 K14
Bone La 4 D4
Bonnick Rd 1 J6
Bon-Vista Rd 1 E1
Bort Rd 2 K17
Bottlebrush Pl 1 M11

Bowlers Dr 3 E2
Bracefell St 3 L10
Brewery Rd 1 G13
Brianna Ct 2 B1
Brickfield St 3 K12
Brickfields Cr 3 L12
Bridge St 4 E6
Bright St 2 D12
Brisbane Rd
  Gympie 4 F3
  Monkland 4 F3
  Monkland 4 K9
Broomlands Rd 4 J18
Browns Rd 2 K8
Bruce Hwy
  East Deep Creek 4 P1
  Glanmire 4 K12
  Gympie 4 A1
  Monkland 2 N12
  Monkland 4 E7
  Two Mile 1 D2
  Veteran 2 J1
  Victory Heights 2 N12
Buchanan St 2 E13
Buckley Dr
  Glanmire 4 K14
  Monkland 4 K14
Buggy Ct 1 H6
Bunya Pine Ct 2 H11
Burchill La 4 G7
Bushland Dr
  Southside 1 C17
  Southside 3 D1
Butler St 2 E8
Byron St 4 G2
Caddie Ct 1 H5
Caledonian Hill 2 B16
Callistemon Ct 3 L10
Calton Cir
  Gympie 1 P17
  Gympie 2 A17
Calton Hill 2 B16
Calton Tce 1 N16
Cambridge Cct 4 B10
Cameron Rd 3 B9
Campbell La 4 E6
Camphor Laurel Ct 1 K10
Campus Cl 1 M8
Carana Av 4 A18
Carbeen Ct 4 D10
Cardinal Cct 3 M18
Carey St 1 N17
Carrington Av 2 D11
Cartwright Rd
  Gympie 1 L8
  Gympie 1 N8
Cassia Ct 1 K9
Castlereagh Ct 3 E3
Cedar Ct 1 K9
Centenary Cl 1 M8
Centro Wy 4 C3
Chairmans Cl 3 P14
Chalk Cl 1 M8
Champagne La 3 M12
Channon St 1 L15
Chapple La 2 C14
Chapple St 2 D14
Chatsworth Rd
  Araluen 1 C2
  Chatsworth 1 C2
  Gympie 1 H10
  Two Mile 1 C2
Church St 1 P17
Clarke La 2 H14
Clematis St 1 K12
Club Dr 1 G7
Cockburn La 2 B17
Cogan St 2 E16
College Rd 3 D2
Colonial Ct 3 L9
Columbia St 2 E14

Commander Ct 3 N18
Compass Ct 2 B6
Conifer Ct 2 G11
Connemara Ct 1 N10
Cooinda St 2 A7
Coombe St 4 F4
Coop St 2 C13
Cootharaba Rd
  Gympie 2 G16
  Victory Heights 2 L11
Copp Rd 3 J6
Corbet Rd 4 E15
Corella Ct 1 H4
Corella Rd
  Araluen 1 H2
  Gympie 1 H2
Correen St 2 H18
Counter St 4 G6
Coventry Ct 3 L14
Cox Rd 4 C11
Crawford St 4 D5
Crescent Rd
  Gympie 2 E16
  Gympie 2 F17
Crestwood Ct 1 K3
Cross St 1 K15
Crown Rd 2 D17
Crystal Ct 3 N8
Cullinane St 1 M11
Cummings St 2 B14
Currambine Av 2 H17
Daisy Ct 2 F13
Dalee St 4 C14
Danchia Ct 3 B6
Daphne St 3 C7
Darcy La 2 J11
Davey Rd 3 J7
David Ct 4 B12
David St
  Araluen 2 B5
  Gympie 2 B5
Davies La 2 C18
Dawn Rd 4 B18
Deakin Ct 3 H14
Decker Pl 3 E4
Denimar Pl 3 H9
Dennis Little Dr 4 P14
Dent La 4 B1
Derrilin Dr 2 H17
Diamond Ct 3 M8
Directors Cct 3 N15
Doak Rd 3 P17
Dominion Ri 3 M18
Dominique Ct 4 A12
Dons Ct 1 G3
Dornan Dr 1 N11
Dovetail Cl 1 J5
Dowdle Rd 2 J16
Dowling Rd 4 J12
Drummond Dr 4 N13
Dudley St 2 E16
Duffy Ct 3 H13
Duke St 1 K11
Durietz Ct 3 E5
Eagle St 2 C11
Eagle Hawk Dr 3 M14
Eagleview Cl 1 K5
Earl St
  Gympie 2 E18
  Gympie 2 E1
East Deep Creek Rd
  East Deep Creek 4 M4
  Monkland 4 J5
Eastview Ct 2 K14
Eaton Rd 4 F14
Edward St 2 D11
Edwin Campion Dr 4 K11
Eel Creek Rd
  Pie Creek 3 A18
  Southside 3 A18

Eldorado Rd
  Glanmire 4 L12
  Monkland 4 L12
Elgin La 2 A18
Elgin St 2 B18
Elizabeth St 2 E17
Elms Ct 3 M10
Elworthy St 1 J12
Emerald Dr 3 P7
Eminent Pl 3 L18
English Rd 3 K18
Ethan Cl 1 N9
Ettie Jane St 4 L11
Eucalyptus Av 3 D5
Eugene St 3 G1
Evelyn Rd 3 F6
Everson La 2 H14
Everson Rd 2 G14
Excalibur Cr
  Southside 3 P10
  Southside 4 A10
Excelsior Rd 4 B2
Exhibition Rd 3 G3
Fairview Rd
  Monkland 4 J7
  Monkland 4 M7
Fairway Dr
  Gympie 1 J5
  Gympie 1 K4
Faithdevere La 2 B16
Farleys La 2 J13
Farmborough Ct 3 H9
Fauna Rd
  Gympie 2 D6
  Gympie 2 D8
Federation Ct 3 L9
Ferguson St 2 B13
Fern St 2 B14
Fernvale Dr 3 A18
Firchester Ct 2 J13
Fisher La 2 F15
Fisher Rd 2 B4
Fitzpatrick Rd
  Jones Hill 4 D16
  Jones Hill 4 H18
  The Dawn 4 H18
Fleming Rd 1 B5
Flood Rd
  East Deep Creek 4 P3
  Monkland 4 P3
Florentine Ct 4 L7
Flynn Rd 2 H16
Fortune Ct 3 N11
Fossickers Ct 3 C2
Fox St 4 C2
Foxtail Ct 2 G10
Frangipani Rd 3 G12
Fraser Rd 1 E3
Friske Rd 2 J5
Furness Rd
  Southside 3 C3
  Southside 3 C4
Gallilee Rd 2 P11
Gambling Rd 2 P1
Gardenia Ct 3 J11
Garnet Ct 3 M8
Garrick St 2 B10
Gayle Ct 3 L7
Gebbutt St 3 F5
Gene Ct 2 H9
Geordie Rd 4 J10
George St 2 F17
Giles St 3 J4
Gladstone St 1 N17
Glanmire St 2 D14
Glasgow St 2 A8
Glastonbury Rd 3 A3
Glen Eden Dr 1 M8
Glynn Pl 2 F11
Goldstone Cr 3 N9

Golf Links Cir
  Gympie 1 H6
  Two Mile 1 G6
Goodwin Rd 1 B9
Grabbs La 2 E18
Graduate Cl 1 M9
Graham St 4 E4
Grammar Cl 1 N9
Grandis St 2 K8
Grandview Pl 2 G11
Grant St 3 H3
Granzien Rd 2 C1
Graystone Ct 1 K2
Greenmount La 1 P4
Greens Ct 3 E2
Green Trees Rd 3 A17
Grevillea Av 3 L8
Grice Cr 2 H15
Griffin Rd
  Gympie 2 J12
  Victory Heights 2 J12
Grosvenor St 3 E4
Groundwater Rd
  Jones Hill 3 E17
  Pie Creek 3 E17
  Southside 3 E17
  Southside 3 L13
  Southside 4 A12
  Southside 4 C8
Gully St 4 F7
Gumtree Rd 2 C4
Gympie Bps
  East Deep Creek 4 P3
  Monkland 2 N15
  Veteran 2 K3
  Victory Heights 2 N15
Gympie-Brooloo Rd
  Jones Hill 4 D13
  Southside 4 D13
Gympie Connection Rd
  Gympie 1 M14
  Gympie 2 G9
  Veteran 2 L7
  Victory Heights 2 G9
  Victory Heights 2 L7
Gympie View Dr 3 C2
Gympie-Woolooga Rd 3 H2
Haga La 4 H6
Hall La 2 A18
Hall Rd
  Glanmire 4 M13
  Monkland 4 M13
  Mothar Mountain 4 M13
Hall St 1 N17
Hambleton Rd
  Gympie 2 H18
  Gympie 4 H1
Hamilton Dr 2 G15
Hamilton Rd
  Araluen 1 J3
  Gympie 1 J3
Hampton Ct 4 B10
Harington Av 3 L9
Harkins St 4 D4
Haven St 3 J7
Heather St 3 G7
Heights Dr
  Gympie 2 C7
  Gympie 2 D7
Heilbronn Rd
  Jones Hill 4 B15
  Southside 4 B15
Helen St 3 J3
Helmsman Esp 2 E8
Henry St
  Gympie 1 K10
  Gympie 1 M13
Henry Parkes Dr 3 J13
Heritage La 3 N12
Hill St 4 F7
Hilltop Av 1 B18

Hillview Ct 1 L12
Hilton La 4 C2
Hilton Rd 2 B18
Horseshoe Bend Rd 2 B13
Horswood Rd 1 E2
Hughes Tce 4 D4
Hyne St 4 A2
Imperial Ri 3 M17
Inglewood Rd 4 E6
Inglewood Bridge 4 E5
Inverary Ct 3 E4
Inverness St 3 E4
Iris Ct 3 F14
Iron St 1 K12
Ironwood Cl 1 J5
Isabel Ct 2 J13
James St 3 H1
James Kidd Dr 4 K7
Jane St 1 J13
Jardine Cl 1 L4
Jaryd Pl 2 G10
Jasmine Av 3 J12
Jasper Ct 3 N8
Jaycee Wy 1 M16
Jeremy Rd 3 A2
John St 4 E2
Johns Rd 3 K8
Johnstone Rd 3 G5
Jones Hill Rd 4 D15
Jubilee St 4 G8
Judicial Cct
  Jones Hill 3 M15
  Jones Hill 3 M16
Julia St 2 B14
Julienne St 3 L7
Justin St 1 H18
Karibu La 2 B1
Katrina Ct 3 N5
Kelly Dr 4 K13
Kensington Dr
  Southside 3 P11
  Southside 4 A11
Kerr Pl 2 H15
Kesteven Dr 3 J3
Kestrel Cl 3 M14
Kidd Bridge 1 K16
Kidgell St
  Gympie 4 B4
  Gympie 4 C4
Killarney Ct 3 E4
Kimberley Av 3 H12
King Rd 2 K16
King St 1 K10
Kitts La 1 N17
Knightsbridge Dr 4 A10
Koala Ct 3 C9
Koumala Rd 3 H10
Kyla Ct 4 K7
Kyleigh Ct 3 D4
Lachlan Pl 2 F10
Lady Mary Tce 2 C15
Laing Cl 3 L12
Langara Dr 4 A11
Langton Rd 4 L12
Lapis Ct 3 M8
Lasiandra Dr 4 D10
Laurenceson Rd 4 L14
Laurie La 2 D17
Lawrence La 2 A12
Lawrence St 2 A14
Lawson Rd
  Jones Hill 3 D18
  Pie Creek 3 C15
  Pie Creek 3 D18
Leaders Ct 3 P16
Leavinia St 2 D10
Leeann Rd 2 M15
Lehn Ct 4 K8
Leonard St 3 G2
Liam La 4 C8

Lillis Rd
  Gympie 2 H13
  Victory Heights 2 H13
Lily St 3 D4
Lime St 4 E4
Lindsay St 3 F10
Lister Cl 2 F10
Little Channon St 1 L16
Lockhart Rd 2 N12
Loder St 3 J4
Louisa La
  Gympie 1 P12
  Gympie 2 A12
Louisa St
  Gympie 1 N13
  Gympie 2 A11
Lucknow St 2 D14
Luckona Ct 3 H8
Lyden Ct 2 C7
Mcauliffe Rd 4 K6
Mccullouch Rd
  Chatsworth 1 C2
  Two Mile 1 C2
Macdonnell Ct 3 G2
Mchugh Ct 1 G13
Mcintosh Creek Rd 4 A18
Mclellian Tce 2 J13
Mcleod La 4 E2
Mcleod St 2 B15
Mcmahon La 4 J10
Mcmahon Rd 4 J11
Mcphail St 3 E4
Mcvey Rd 4 K7
Maddonna Ct 2 C7
Magnolia St 3 E3
Mahogany Wy
  Gympie 2 G10
  Victory Heights 2 G10
Maiden St 3 L12
Maidment Ct 1 L4
Main St 2 C10
Majestic Pl 3 N16
Malabar Dr 1 K3
Malcolm Pl 2 E15
Managers Ct 3 P16
Maori La 2 D17
Mark La 4 D4
Marsh Rd 2 C2
Mary St 1 M15
Mary Valley Rd
  Jones Hill 4 C18
  Southside 4 D6
Mataranka Rd 2 M4
Matsen Ct 3 M9
Matthew La 4 B14
Mayfair St 2 K14
Megan Rd 3 A9
Melaleuca Ct 3 J12
Mellor St 2 B15
Melrose Ct 3 F7
Meridian Tce 2 C6
Mill St 2 D11
Miners Pl 3 C4
Ministerial Ct 3 N17
Moluccana Gr 3 H12
Monkland St 1 M16
Moreland Rd 1 B16
Moreton Ct 3 K10
Morris St 2 A6
Mt Pleasant Rd 4 D1
Mulcahy Tce 2 A11
Musgrave St 2 A11
Myall La 1 N14
Myall St
  Gympie 1 K9
  Gympie 1 M13
  Gympie 1 N14
Nahrunda La 2 B11
Nash Rd 1 N2
Nash St 1 M15
Navigator Cl 2 D7

Neil St
  Southside 1 G18
  Southside 3 G1
Nelson La 4 D3
Nelson Rd 2 C16
New Zealand La 2 C17
New Zealand St 2 B17
Neylan Rd 2 L17
Nicholas Christopher Dr 4 H9
Nicholls Rd 4 H8
Niven Rd 1 N4
Noosa Rd
  East Deep Creek 4 K6
  Monkland 4 H5
  Mothar Mountain 4 K6
Norman St 2 C12
Normanby Bridge 4 C6
Normanby Hill Rd 4 C7
Notley Rd 4 E15
Oak St 1 H11
Observer Ct 2 E8
O'connell St 1 N14
Old Imbil Rd
  Monkland 4 H10
  Monkland 4 H9
Old Maryborough Rd
  Araluen 1 K1
  Araluen 2 B5
  Gympie 1 K1
  Gympie 2 B5
Old Wolvi Rd 2 H8
Olive Tree Ch 2 G10
Opal St 3 N7
Organ Rd 4 P7
Outlook Cl 1 K5
Oxford Ct 3 K15
Oxley Ct 3 K10
Pacey St 2 E11
Palatine St
  Gympie 1 P15
  Gympie 2 A15
Palm Cr 2 C9
Pamela Rd 1 F3
Pan Pl 3 D4
Panda St 3 D4
Pandanus St
  Gympie 2 G11
  Victory Heights 2 G11
Paramount Ct 3 L11
Park La 1 N18
Park Tce 1 K15
Parkview Cl 3 C2
Parsons Rd 2 B10
Pedersen Rd 3 J15
Pengellys Bridge 4 G4
Penny Rd 4 P9
Peregrine Pl 3 M14
Perry La 4 C9
Perseverance St 4 B2
Petrie Ct 3 L10
Phoenix La 4 E2
Phoenix St 4 F3
Piccadilly Dr 3 K15
Pilcher La 2 E9
Pine St 1 G12
Pine Valley Dr 3 D18
Pinewood Av
  Gympie 1 F9
  Gympie 1 G10
Pinnacle Ct 4 B16
Pioneer Pde 2 J7
Poinciana La 2 G12
Pollock La 2 C15
Pollock St 2 B15
Popes Rd 1 M12
Potter St 4 H2
Power Rd
  Southside 3 H2
  Southside 4 A6
Power St 2 B13
Premier Av 3 N16

Presidential Av 3 N17
Primrose Ct 2 E13
Principal Pl 3 P15
Pring La 2 C16
Pringle Ct
  Gympie 1 P7
  Gympie 2 A7
Pritchard Rd 3 K6
Pronger Pde 4 P15
Quamby Ct 2 H17
Queen St 1 P13
Queens Park Dr 1 H14
Rafter Rd 4 P15
Railway Ct 4 N12
Ramsey Rd 3 H3
Randall St 1 P14
Randwick Rd
  East Deep Creek 4 M3
  Monkland 4 M3
Ranson Rd
  Gympie 2 E12
  Victory Heights 2 G11
Ray St 2 C12
Red Hill Rd 2 D17
Red Rover Cl 3 G12
Reef St
  Gympie 1 L14
  Gympie 1 M15
Regal Pl 3 M18
Regan Rd 3 A17
Revelation Rd 3 G11
Rice Flower Pl 3 G12
Ridgeview Dr 1 J5
Rifle Range Rd
  Gympie 2 E10
  Gympie 2 F11
River Rd
  Gympie 1 M16
  Gympie 1 N17
  Gympie 4 C3
River Tce 1 L16
Riverstone Cl 1 J4
Riverview Ct 4 G8
Rocklea Dr
  Southside 3 M9
  Southside 3 N7
Rocks Rd 3 A10
Rocky Ridge Rd 2 K3
Rodian Rd 3 H6
Rodney Rd 1 B11
Rogers Rd 4 K3
Roma St 4 G8
Rose Rd 3 H7
Rose St
  Gympie 3 P2
  Gympie 4 A2
Roselea Rd 3 A11

Rosella Cl 1 J5
Rosewood Ct 3 H12
Rosslyn Rd 3 M7
Rowe St 1 K14
Roy Rd 1 F5
Royal Ct 3 N18
Ruby Ct
  Southside 3 P6
  Southside 3 P6
Rudkin Ct 3 N12
St Andrews Cr 1 M9
Saleyard Rd
  Araluen 2 C3
  Gympie 2 C3
Sandy Creek Rd
  Veteran 2 H7
  Victory Heights 2 H7
Sapphire Ct 3 P7
Scarlet Moon Ct 3 G13
Scenic Dr 3 F13
Scholar Cl 1 M8
School St
  Gympie 1 P15
  Gympie 2 A15
Schumann La 2 B17
Scotia Pl 3 L12
Scott Rd 2 K17
Seafarer Cl 2 E8
Senators Ct 3 N17
Serena Ct 4 K7
Serenity Dr 3 K12
Settlers Cl 1 J5
Shanks St 2 C16
Shaw St 4 H5
Shayduk Cl 2 C8
Shields St 1 H10
Short St 2 B16
Silky Oak Dr 3 A2
Simone Ct 4 J11
Simpson Rd 4 N8
Skyline Tce 2 B7
Smalley Pl 2 E10
Smerdon Rd
  Southside 3 L6
  Southside 3 P5
Smith Rd 4 J7
Smith St 4 P14
Smithfield St 1 N16
Smyth St
  Gympie 2 E17
  Gympie 4 F1
Somerset St 2 D9
Sorensen Rd 3 K12
Sorrel St 2 F14
Spencer La 2 L2
Spicer St 1 N13
Spring La 4 H5

Spring Rd
  Gympie 2 H10
  Victory Heights 2 H10
Spring St 4 H5
Sproule Rd
  Gympie 2 F10
  Victory Heights 2 F10
Stanley La
  Gympie 2 D17
  Gympie 2 D18
  Gympie 4 D1
Stanley St 4 A1
Station Rd 2 D15
Steersman Ct 2 D8
Stephenson Pl 4 K8
Stewart Tce 2 E11
Stone St 1 N14
Struan Cr 1 L10
Stuart La 1 P16
Stuart St 1 N16
Stumm Rd 1 A17
Sullivan Rd
  Jones Hill 4 F16
  The Dawn 4 F16
Sunburst Pl 3 M12
Suncrest Ct 1 B17
Supremacy Pl 3 M16
Sweeney Ct 3 E17
Taylor Rd 2 L2
Teal Cl 1 K5
Teresa St 3 H1
Thomas St 2 B10
Timothy Ct 4 C14
Tin Can Bay Rd
  Gympie 2 J14
  Monkland 4 H7
  Victory Heights 2 J14
  Victory Heights 2 M11
Tobin St 4 C14
Topaz Cr 3 M7
Tozer La 2 D15
Tozer St
  Gympie 2 D14
  Gympie 2 E12
Tozer Park Rd 2 E14
Tracey La 1 G13
Trafalgar Ct 3 K14
Transport Ct 4 M12
Tucker St 2 C10
Tweed La 4 D3
Tyrrell Rd 4 H5
Union St 4 E6
Valentine St 3 G1
Van Doren Rd 3 B5
Vanessa Ct 1 F4
Venardos Av 4 N15
Venardos Dr 2 H16

Veronica Rd 4 C12
Victoria Rd 4 F4
Victory La 2 C11
Victory St 2 C11
Violet St
  Gympie 1 J11
  Gympie 1 K14
Vista Cl 1 C18
Voyager Pl 2 C7
Waddell Rd
  Araluen 1 F7
  Gympie 1 F7
  Two Mile 1 F7
Wagtail Cr 2 D6
Waldock Rd
  Jones Hill 4 A13
  Southside 4 A13
Walker St 2 B13
Walsh Ct 4 J6
Waratah Pl 3 F13
Waterworks Rd 4 E12
Watson Rd 3 F6
Watt La 4 C3
Watt St 4 C4
Wayfinder Pl 2 E7
Westphal Ct 3 D4
Whistlesong Ct 2 B6
Wickham St 1 K15
Widgee Crossing Rd
  Gympie 1 A12
  Two Mile 1 A12
  Widgee Crossing North 1 A12
Wilbraham Ct 2 G16
William St
  Gympie 2 F18
  Gympie 4 F1
Williams La 3 J2
Willow Grove Rd 3 L10
Winnington Rd 3 M11
Wises Rd 2 F18
Wisteria La 3 J11
Withey St 3 J4
Woodbine St
  Gympie 1 H11
  Gympie 1 J13
Woodland Dr 3 F14
Woolgar La 2 C16
Woolgar Rd 3 H3
Woolgar St 2 C16
Woonga Ct 3 C3
Wrangell Rd 4 B17
Yorkdale La 4 A14
Young St 1 N16
Zoe Cl 2 C7

MAP 1 GYMPIE

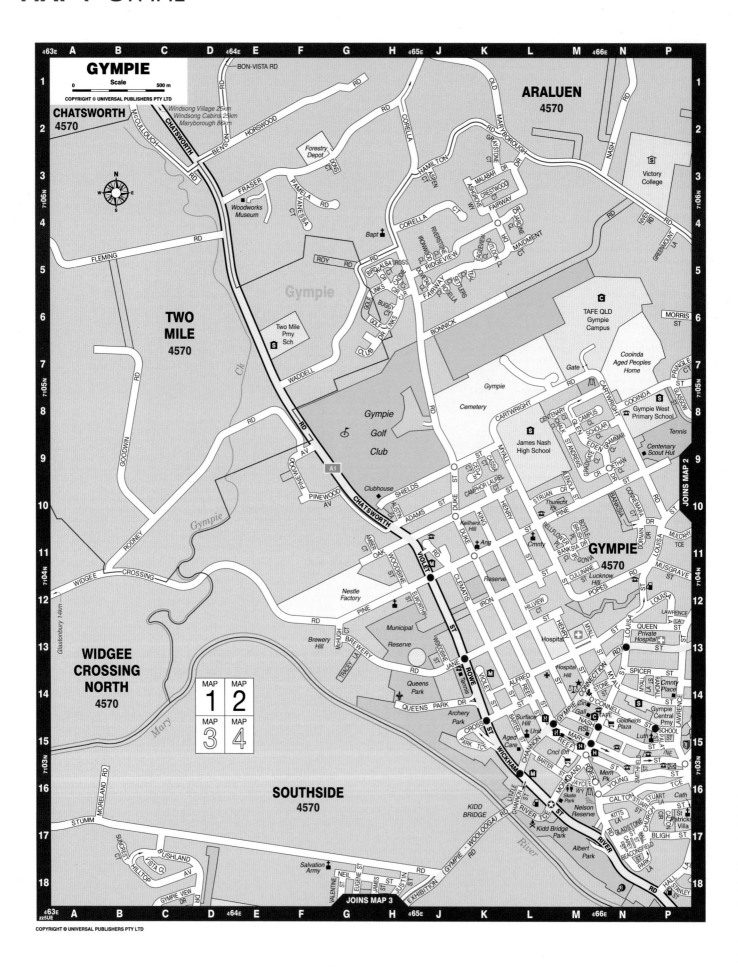

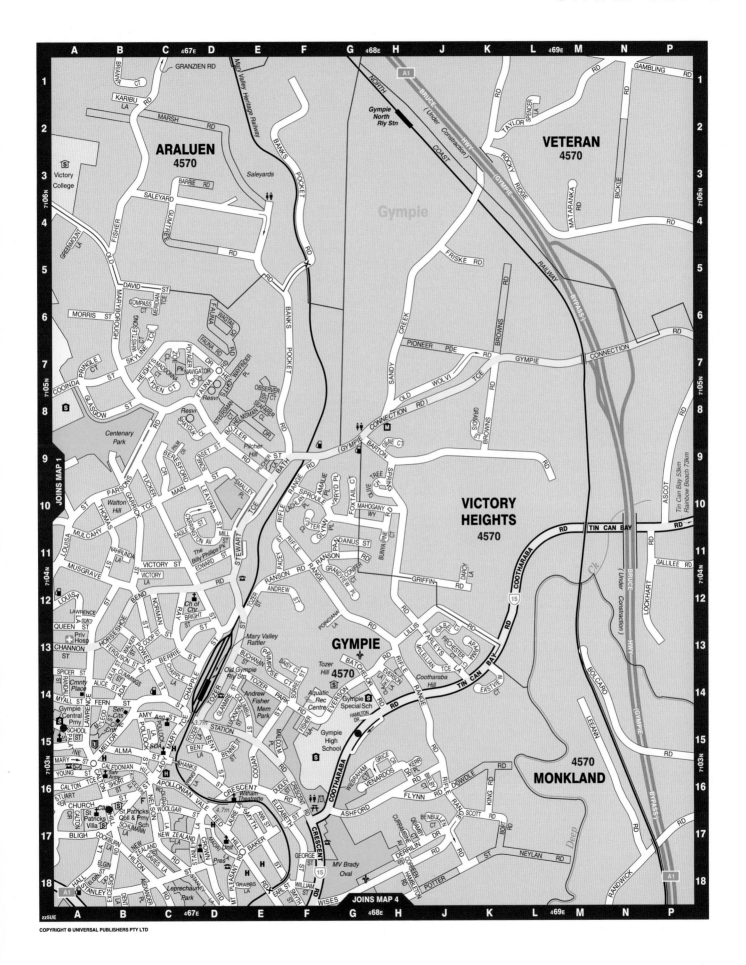

MAP 3 GYMPIE

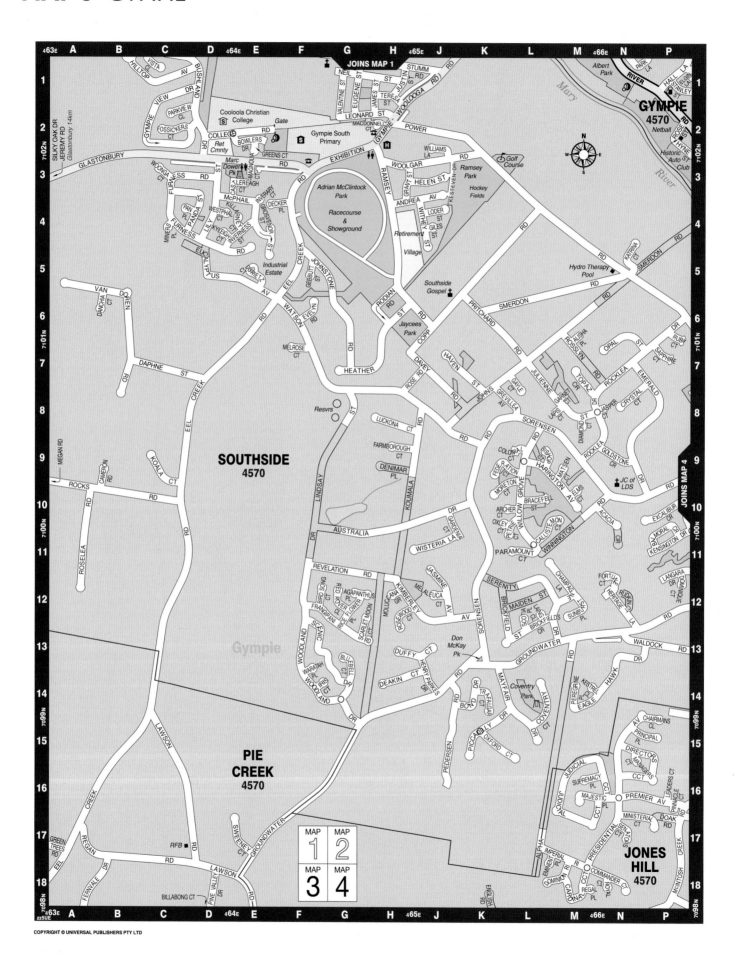

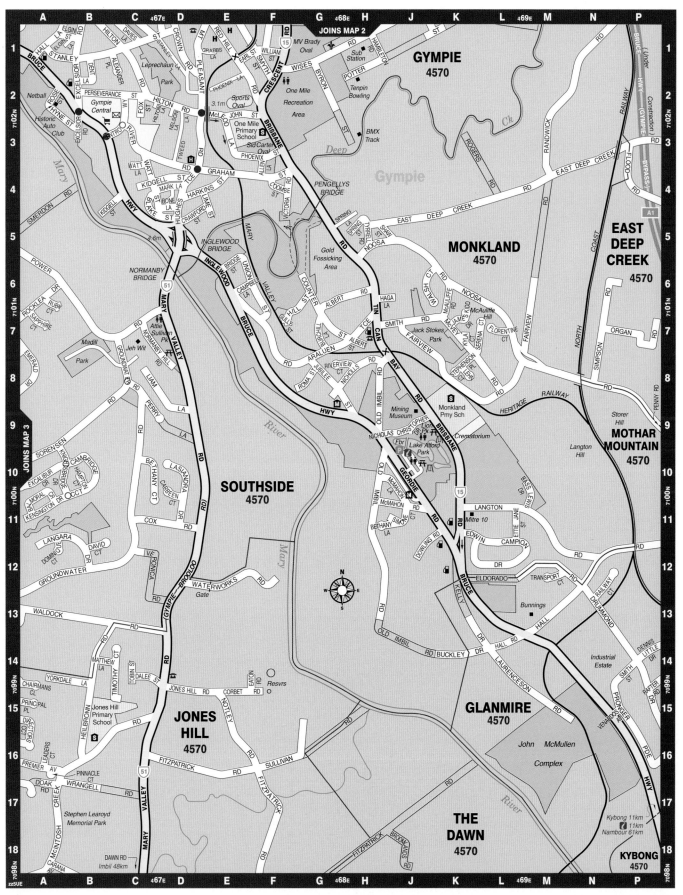